# Necessary Ports

Also by Roger Lee Kenvin

Trylons and Perispheres

After the Silver Age

The Cantabrigian Rowing Society's
Saturday Night Bash

Harpo's Garden

The Gaffer and Seven Fables

Krishnalight

# Necessary Ports

## A Travel Memoir

### Roger Lee Kenvin

### Verna Rudd Kenvin

July Blue Press

Published by July Blue Press, 126 Mt. Cardigan Road, Alexandria, New Hampshire 03222
jlybl@earthlink.net

First printing

Printed in the United States of America by Odyssey Press Inc., Dover, New Hampshire

**Library of Congress Control Number:** 00-091149

ISBN 0-9656635-6-6

## ACKNOWLEDGMENT

Parts of *VOYAGE TO BYZANTIUM* were published as "Turkish Delight" in *The Palo Alto Review*. The letters from Europe and India were collected by recipients Gladys Macdonald Kenvin, Rufus James Trimble, and Leigh Berrien Smith, and returned to their authors, thus making this book possible.

For our grandsons, Kyle and Dylan,
in partial explanation of all those
mysterious appearances and departures on
ships, trains, buses, planes, and
little red puddlejumpers

"Where one is born and dies are accidents of time and place.  The necessary ports are those one chooses that give shape, meaning, and  a particular singularity to the voyage."

Roger Lee Kenvin

# NECESSARY PORTS

# TABLE OF CONTENTS

## PARIS BOUND 135-225

## A VALENTINE FOR BROOKLYN 226-258

# VOYAGE TO BYZANTIUM

**Turkey, Greece, Ukraine 1992**

Roger Lee Kenvin

# VOYAGE TO BYZANTIUM

Sailing through the waters of Asia Minor gives one much the same sense of vision and discovery that the early Mediterranean navigators must have had. We sailed recently on a large ship from Piraeus, Greece on a voyage that took us across the Aegean Sea to Kusadasi and Dikili in Turkey, through the Dardanelles into the Sea of Marmara to Istanbul, and then through the Bosphorus to the Black Sea past Bulgaria and Romania to Odessa in the Ukraine and Yalta in the Crimea. On the return trip, we stopped at both the Dodecanese islands and the Cyclades in the Aegean, sailed into the Gulf of Argolis to Nauplia, around the Peloponnesus into the Gulf of Kaparissia where we stopped at Katakolo, and then sailed through the Strait of Otranto and up the Adriatic, carefully avoiding the Yugoslavian side, until we arrived at the Gulf of Venice where our voyage appropriately terminated in that fabled romantic city that blends so beautifully the East and West cultures we had just sailed through.

What is most memorable about any trip is the moment-by-moment discovery of things you never knew or thought you might find or of things that reinforce what you already know or have learned. You might, for instance, learn that the red-and-black sunset you cherish over Asia Minor is remarkably like the same one you have seen over Colorado, or the floodlit Gallipoli Monument you pass at night in the Dardanelles reminds you of a fleeting glance of a monument caught from a taxicab in New York City.

People, too, make significant impressions—whether they are friendly or discourteous, whether they are proud of their land or ashamed of it. And so often, our tour guides, those Charons of the modern world who lead us through and invite us to share their point of view, can make a big difference. Seeing a country through one individual's eyes is a way many of us first experience a new land.

Guides I have had in the past have been a mixed lot. Some have offered stale jokes and cynical comments about their own cities. Some have supplied too much detail, boring, memorized facts and statistics. Many have appeared to be in cahoots with local merchants and steer you to shopping places, working on the assumption that all tourists want to buy postcards and cheap souvenirs. But a good, informed, intelligent guide can make a big difference.

On our trip through Asia Minor, I felt the guides on land did an excellent job. Each person offered a different perspective and offered a point of view worth considering. Here they are, as I observed them:

## THE EASY ANN

He is a big man, pleasant-looking, with a face like a heavier Yul Brynner, warm brown eyes, olive complexion, even features, a constant smile starting at his lips. He is dressed casually, a faded blue shirt, dark trousers, the shirt sliding down to a belly beginning to protrude over his belt. His voice is a slow, rich baritone. He takes many pauses and looks far into the distance. He seems to reflect before he speaks, He repeats things twice. He has a poetry, a cadence of his own. He doesn't really want questions. His is a monologue, an ode to an ancient Byzantine, Greek, Roman, Turkish, Anatolian past.

"Look around," he says sweeping his arm in a slow semicircle. "Everybody here is crazy, crazy. They have built apartments, look at all those buildings, hundreds, thousands of them, on top of ruins. Nobody can get at them now. They are barbarians. Barbarians, that's what they were called by the Romans, and that's what they are. We are going to see Miletos, Didyma, Priene. You are going to see something. You will not be disappointed. Priene has been built so high up on a hill; that is what has saved it from the barbarians. The locals have not been able to climb up and cart away all the treasures. They are still there. Excavation has not yet begun. You will be there before the archaologists have dug it up. It is beautiful, beautiful. You will see."

We drive in silence to Miletos. It is early morning, sunny, hot. We are the first persons there. A few shops with boys and men selling onyx figures, ceramics, shirts, jewelry, and postcards are there, looking hopefully at us. Jihan ignores them. "What do you want to see?" he asks us. The answer is everything. "Everything in detail?" asks Jihan. Yes. "Then we shall see everything."

He takes us first to the big arch at the Bath of Faustina. We sit in the shade. Jihan looks long and hard at the arch. "Well, it is not Greek because it is an arch," he says. "The Greeks did not make arches. The Romans did, but there are no bricks, so maybe it is even earlier. You know, this bath was built by the Roman emperor Marcus Aurelius for his wife. Wasn't it a nice present?" He walks us through the baths, recreating vapors, oils, meeting rooms, and pools where no water flows today. A small, thin Turkish boy attaches himself to us. He speaks to Jihan. He wants to sell us sprigs of oregano he has plucked out of the walls of the ruins. Jihan cannot be bothered with this idle commerce. He is polite, but firm. The disappointed boy tags along anyway. He does not attempt to make a sale. He just looks hopeful if one should glance his way.

Jihan points out the low, large rectangular building which was the Caravanserai used by the Turks between 1071 and 1404 A.D. when they renamed the city Palatia.

"Once Miletos was a port," says Jihan, as we enter the theatre. "You see on top of this theatre they have built a fortress. You can tell who built it because you can see the bricks. When you see bricks, you know the Romans did it.

The Greeks didn't use bricks. This theatre was built in the Hellenistic Age, that is in 4th, 3rd, 2nd centuries B.C. The Romans enlarged it perhaps in 2nd century A.D. Originally it could seat 25,000 spectators. Think of it. People came from all over. How many do you see today?" In looking around, all one sees now are a few clumps of tourists risking a hot sun to step delicately over these relics of antiquity.

Jihan leads us next to the port gates and the toppled lion statues which once graced its pedestals. The lions now lie on the ground, all at odds with their surroundings. One appears to be emerging from the mud. In the rainy season, Jihan says, he appears to be swimming in a pond like a hippopotamus. Maybe that explains the slightly silly smile on his face.

Finding some shade on the steps of the Temple of Athena, Jihan wipes the sweat from his face and tells us this temple was probably built in the first part of the 5th century B.C., "the great period, the Golden Age," he says, "when you had Plato, Socrates, and Pericles, the statesman, and Aeschylus, Sophocles, and Euripides writing their tragedies. It was a great time, a beautiful period." Jihan's voice trails off sadly, as though recalling something from a great distance. He adds: "You know, I must say something, also. You hear a great deal in these parts about Artemis, whose Roman name is Diana, and you know she is associated with the hunt, the moon, and chastity. When you hear her name here in Turkey—no, not Turkey—we should not be called that—it is Turkiye, Turkiye—hear the difference?—we are thinking of Cybele, which is her ancient Anatolian name. She was the goddess of abundance and had a supernatural character and many names. So the Greek goddess Artemis is not exactly the same. Here, there are these layers of civilization. Can you feel them? It was a beautiful place, beautiful, but today, one doesn't know. One never knows."

We walk sadly through the fields of Miletos, Jihan telling us about the famous defeat at Miletos in 494 B.C. when Darius and the Persians overcame the Ionians and burned, looted and destroyed both Miletos and Didyma. Shortly thereafter, the Greek playwright Phyrnicus wrote a play called *The Capture of Miletos* which, when shown in Athens, caused the Greeks to weep openly, since they had tried to help the Miletians, with the result that, since the play was so overwhelmingly emotional to them, they passed a law that it should never be shown in Athens again, and it wasn't.

Jihan informs us that Miletos was the son of Apollo and that Miletos was exiled from Crete by King Minos, and so Miletos came to Anatolia and married the daughter of the God of Rivers. I note that the river that flows through the land here is the Maiandros. Is it related to our word "meander," I wonder?

Jihan speaks eloquently at times, most often in his silences. His accent is a little tricky, his pronunciations are his own. You have to come to them. He will not correct them to yours, and you would not be so rude as to offer to point out alternatives to him. His language is his pride, and a great strength. The Aegean Sea is quite simply the Easy Ann. Once you have heard it, it seems quite right, the Easy Ann Sea.

You do not have to ask Jihan questions. He will tell you everything in good time. He has said half his family is Muslim, half Christian. If you wonder which he is, he has already said, "I am Jihan, but I am not John the Baptist." He has taken us through a Muslim mosque in Miletos, but he has ignored the ancient muslim tombstones poking up at odd angles through the cemetery on both sides of the walkway leading up to the mosque's entrance.

Jihan disapproves of the new barbarians, but he doesn't even notice an old Turkish man with two oxen who lumber across our view with a strong lurch, like the past suddenly coming alive for a moment. Perhaps he takes these curious juxtapositions of time for granted.

"Now," he says. "We will go to Didyma. We shall have lunch first and then visit the Temple of Apollo, which is the largest one ever built to him. Would you like fish or meatballs for lunch? I must call ahead to order."

# DIDYMA

"Look how the barbarians have taken over," sighs Jihan looking at the coast where white two and three-storeyed buildings have sprung up along the Easy Ann. "People have built recreation homes to take advantage of the sea. So many of them!"

We pull into our restaurant, part of a small complex of shops and restaurants directly across from the Temple of Apollo in Didyma. For lunch, an open-air buffet is served, but it is so hot and humid all one really wants is something cold to drink. The different dishes on the buffet table look appealing—sliced aubergine in oil, dolmavas, yogurt, bean dishes, fresh fruit, good bread, but swarms of flies dart in and out, causing one to have less appetite than one thought. The fish served looks like a large trout complete with head and eyes. It is undercooked and not very attractive. I notice Jihan waves away the fish when it is offered to him. I fail to eat mine, although those around me bravely and delicately separate the bones and eat the fish.

Why does Jihan not eat at the same long table with us? There are many empty ones to choose from. He selects one all to himself right next to ours. Twelve people could have shared it with him. Does he prefer to be by himself? Does he think we should invite him to join us? Is he like a teacher, a guide, a god, who must have his own place, his own time, his own domain? I would like him to join us, there are many questions to ask, but one asks questions of him sparingly, he reveals everything in his own sweet time.

After lunch, we cross the street to where two enormous columns punctuate the blue sky marking the site of the Temple of Apollo. We see first a large Medusa head on a frieze, and then gryphons, tritons and sea-nymphs. Jihan tells us that the archaic portion of the temple was erected between 560-550 B.C. and that later, after it had been demolished, it was reconstructed by Alexander the Great, so that it has elements of both the Ionian and Doric styles

Jihan sits us down deep in the basement recesses of the temple to talk about the cult of the Pythian oracle and what rituals went on in this enormous temple. He speaks of drugs, trances, and tells a story about some tourists who argued with him once that orange poppies were the source of opium.

"But they do not know what real opium is," says Jihan. "In Constantinople, in Turkiye, we have always been in the center of the opium trade. It comes from the East to the West and we are the stopping-off place in between. Opium is made from the large pods in the white flower. It does not come from the small seeds in the orange poppy. Some people were with me once on a tour and they saw a whole field of these orange-red poppies and they said, 'opium.' I said no and thought to stop the bus so that we could get out and I could prove my case, but I did not, I did not. I hope by now they have learned their lesson." Jihan turns to look up at the pension-hotel overlooking the other side of the temple's excavations. It looms up almost as high as the columns. "My great wish," Jihan says, "my dream is to come back sometime with a beautiful woman and to stay in that pension on a moonlit night and discover the secrets of the Temple of Apollo. Could anything be better? Is it not beautiful, the most magnificent of temples? This is what Didyma is famous for, nothing more, this great Temple of Apollo. There was no commercial center here, just a place for Pythian worshippers to come."

# PRIENE

**W**e drive to a place where an enormous craggy mountain cuts high into the sky. "We shall climb," says Jihan cryptically. We all cringe, thinking of the impossibility of that task. Some refuse to leave the bus, announcing they will stay put. The rest of us follow Jihan, who says very little except, "You will see." Intrepid travelers are always held together by people who make promises.

One woman stumbles on the rocky path up and badly cuts her mouth. Jihan is sorry but stoic. The woman chooses to continue rather than go back to the bus. To Jihan, this appears to be the right decision. He does not think people on pilgrimages should allow personal inconveniences to interfere with what they came for. Jihan presses on, leading his smaller band of people to a very precipitous high place overlooking a fertile valley. He sits pensively looking out over a great distance. "The Easy Ann," he says sweeping his arm across. "Once all this was the Easy Ann. Now it is a plain." He turns back to the ruins, looking particularly at the five standing columns of the Temple of Athena.

"Priene is Hellenistic. They began their construction around 350 B.C. The architect was very famous, Hipapodamos." Jihan looks down into the valley again. "We are on a peninsula. There were actually two ports down there." He turns to look up at the high mountain behind the Temple of Athena. "Don't worry. We are not going to climb any more. That is Mount Samson. Up there is a Temple to Zeus (Jihan pronounces it "Zay-OOS.") Later, the Romans came and then the Byzantines, where in the 13th century A.D., Priene suffered earthquakes and people had to leave because of malaria. Why did they build so high up? Who knows, who knows? But isn't it peaceful here?" He pauses. I can feel the wind gently brushing my cheek. It is relaxing, soothing. "It is beautiful, beautiful," Jihan says. "Now we go to the theatre."

In the theatre, he sits for a while, talking about the differences among Greek theatres, Hellenistic theatres, and Roman theatres. He points out the five marble armchairs reserved for bigshots in the front row, the earthen floor, and how the Greek scene house was originally made of wood, but then gradually grew until the Romans erected an elaborate three-storey stage. He tells an anecdote about how the great American theatre designer and engineer, George Izenour, came to Turkey and Jihan drove him around while Izenour measured dimensions of many theatres in Asia Minor.

"There are so many ruins here," Jihan says. "Everywhere you go, but people don't care." A long pause, a long look. "Well, it is time to go, I suppose."

We walk back slowly, thoughtfully to the bus, back through the centuries, down from the tranquil high places, olive trees, and quiet white ruins of Priene to our modern minotaur, a shining Mercedes-Benz bus.

## PERGAMON

**T**oday, Jihan is taking us from the port city of Dikili to the ancient city of Pergamon, high on an acropolis overlooking the busy city of Bergama. He tells how in the 2nd century B.C. Eumenes II presided over the building of the Asclepion, a medical center supporting Asclepius, the Greek god of healing and the son of Apollo. Jihan tells us that at Pergamon one of the greatest libraries in the ancient world was located and that they invented parchment there for their books. "Another mystery," he says, smiling.

This time we do not have to walk. The bus drives us up a twisting mountain road around an acropolis overlooking Bergama, a town of olive trees and red-tiled roofs set in yellow earth resembling a town in Italy, Spain or Portugal. We pass an impressive mosque, a red basilica that Jihan says was originally built to worship the Egyptian deity Serapis, but later became the church of St. Paul, and finally a mosque, reminding us again of the Anatolian, Greek, Roman, Turkish, Christian layers we are constantly moving through.

Jihan seats us in a portion of the ruins, and when all is quiet, he says: "You are sitting now in one portion of the medical center that was reserved for talking things out. You know, people telling their troubles to one another. It was early psychoanalysis. People would tell their dreams and others would explain them. In the other part of the center, people would heal their bodies. There would be baths and springs, potions, medical treatments. Here it would be everything for the mind. Thus, the medical center healed the whole person. Isn't it something, long before Freud? And you know, the celebrated Greek physician, Galen, came here to practice medicine. It was a very famous center."

Jihan shows us the public toilets, very advanced for their time, which were available, and the small Roman theatre, as well as the impressive Temple to Trajan, built during the Roman period, and now being restored. We also see the large theatre built on the sloping hillside that slides down to Bergama, the most precipitous seating arrangement in any ancient theatre. "How would you like to see something there?" laughs Jihan. He points out, far in the distance, the Temple to Dionysos. "He was called Bacchus in Rome," says Jihan. "He started it all. You have seen the famous Theatre of Dionysos in Athens? It is where tragedy began; a spring ritual to Dionysos started it all."

We leave Jihan at harborside in Dikili. He has been a good Anatolian. He has given us a sense of the country's past, a respect for its traditions and richness, a sense of its importance, a concern for its future. He makes me suddenly believe in the Olympian gods, all of them, something for every element in nature, for he himself is like some important aspect of life in Asia Minor, something to be cherished and revered.

# BRIGHT STAR OF ISTANBUL

"That is no country for old men," wrote W. B. Yeats, "The young in one another's arms, birds in the trees—those dying generations." The words stick with me. They form my preconception of Byzantium, Constantinople, Istanbul. Will it be an old dying city, falling off the face of the earth with contemporary problems and populations, the way India's cities are doing? Will there be little trace of its ancient past, only the rubble and refuse of the impossible modern world?

Yeats, of course, was writing not about the real Byzantium, but about the artist's fictional city, and he probably had Dublin, London, and Paris more in mind, and maybe Europe in particular. For him, it was the condition of the artist and Byzantium he equated with Art and Beauty. I want to share that belief. I look for shards of these through my binoculars penetrating the morning haze as our ship sails into the harbor. I scan the dusty pink and blue horizon looking for signs.

Hills appear, a landscape of rolling hills forming a crescent like that on the Turkish flag 180 degrees from left to right, and now impressionistic minarets and domes are etched in, showing some of the over two-thousand mosques in Istanbul dotting the landscape. We pull into the harbor, perpendicular to a large rusty-red tanker from Teheran which stands as a final block to us from the land. On the tall buildings with shutters to the right, I can see office workers turning off night lights and preparing to open the building for the day workers. People are dressed as westerners, the buildings appear to be graceful and French, Mediterranean, at any rate. The air is hot, humid, close. Now I can see clearly the Mosque of Suleiman the Magnificent, large, sprawling, a huge beige mass, surely a central focal point above the harbor.

Our guide for the city tour is Kheliz. She is about 5'7" tall, tan, beautiful to behold with a stunning figure, well-dressed, silver-blue eyes, smart, sophisticated. Her black hair has been run through a copper rinse which is only apparent when she is back-lighted. She wears her hair pulled back, looking like film star Dorothy Lamour, she of the sarongs and South Pacific, in her prime. Kheliz speaks perfect English, moves and speaks at a fast clip, perfectly articulate, obviously conversant with and up-to-date on events in London, Paris, and the United States. She tells us she is Muslim, that she has traveled a lot, and lives out in the fashionable suburbs of Istanbul along the Bosphorus. "You may call me Star, if you wish," she says. "That is an approximation of Kheliz. Many of my friends call me Star."

"There are over ten million people in Istanbul," she reports. "You will notice that it is remarkably clean, which is amazing because we have just gotten over a garbage strike, and everyone was asked to clean up, which they did, so that is quite surprising. We have a big immigration problem here which is not helped by our governor who is responsible for many of the problems. He creates them. You cannot invite people to come here because there are no jobs and housing is expensive. But still they come. You know, there is a big difference in the East of Turkey and the West, so the people from the East want to come here, but it is ridiculous. It does not make sense."

Kheliz shows us the Golden Horn and says now it is not so important. It is this long estuary in the shape of a horn that flows into the Bosphorus. "Istanbul is very unusual because it is partly in Asia and partly in Europe. Two sides are in Europe, one only in Asia. We have three bridges across the Golden Horn, but the Galata Bridge has been blown up by Kurdish saboteurs from Iran, and so you will see this bridge lying on its side. I think it is too bad it could not be used again. It is so much better than the one they have had to put up to take its place, the New Galata Bridge. Today it is closed so we will be using the Ataturk Bridge and I think there will be very much traffic. I must confess that in Istanbul, red lights and stop signs are seen only as suggestions. Most people will just go through them. It is an accepted way, but you will see how congested the city is. It is quite impossible, and, of course, the Governor is not capable enough to do anything about it."

After talking about the movie *Topkapi,* Kheliz takes us to the palace itself. Cool, tall trees, long promenades, beautiful, formal gardens, pleasant, like being inside a cloistered monastery or a select university. We see the famous three emeralds set into the dagger, object of the theft by Melina Mercouri, Maximilian Schell, and Peter Ustinoff in the film, and the brilliant 86-carat diamond which is arranged so that it rocks from right to left to show off its dazzling facets. I notice that the dagger has been removed to a back wall display case instead of the center one where it was in the film. Why? Was the film too accurate in depicting how one might enter from the dome, hang down, and retrieve the dagger without setting off the alarm?

We view other precious jewels in the Treasury, see the outside of the famous harem, walk through the kitchen with its incredible store of Chinese, Japanese, and European porcelains and its enormous chimneys. This palace, called also the Seraglio, subject of an opera by Mozart, was built by Mehmet II in 1462. It still holds the aura of the ancient Ottoman empire, an unchanged place, where originally only the Sultan could pass on horseback through the courtyard we have just crossed. For just a moment, we pass out onto a terrace from which we look out the back of the palace over the Bosphorus and the Sea of Marmara. It is a beautiful view and one thinks of how the women locked up in the harem must have seen the same view and wondered at the world they would never know outside their privileged prison.

Kheliz takes us shopping on Istanbul's Fifth Avenue in the fashionable and impressively modern Lapis, a department store, where they give us the inevitable rug show and serve apple mint tea. The men cover the bare floors dramatically with carpet after carpet, piling them on thickly while one man talks about knots per square inch, districts like Kazak and Oushak, and the superiority of their work. Some people buy, others just watch and admire.  When it is finished, Kheliz points out the Covered Market, says we will be on our own there, and sets a time when we should meet her.  "If you are not here exactly at ten to the hour," she announces.  "We shall go without you. You can always take a taxi back to the ship if you miss us," she adds. Then Kheliz vanishes, but I discover later that she has had coffee with some executives in this smart department store. She is bright, chipper, efficient. She answers all questions expertly. She does not equivocate, invent stories, or offer apologies for anything in her country, except for the Governor of Istanbul whom she does not like. Kheliz is a modern, intelligent, sophisticated woman that any nation would be proud of.

## SECRET PRAYERS

"It is not important that you do not understand what the words are, what the prayers mean," says Selim whispering to our group clustered inside the dark, humid Mosque of Suleiman the Magnificent. "You pray for yourself, private prayers, whatever you want.  There is no special pattern."

Selim, like Kheliz, is an intelligent, modern woman of Turkey. "In fact, Star is my cousin," she announces. Selim tells us that she, Selim, is married, lives with her husband in the suburbs on the western shore of the Bosphorus, and, like Kheliz, she shares a dislike of the current Governor of Istanbul. A car with Turkish flags zooms ahead of us in traffic. "You see, that is the Governor's car," she announces. "I can tell by the number on the license plate. He does not do a good job.  He is different from the Mayor.  We like him, but we do not like the Governor."

You would not guess that Selim is a Turkish woman. Her British accent is flawless. She is attractive, very well-dressed, bobbed brown hair, some make-up, carefully chosen gold rings and jewelry, looking like a Londoner shopping on Bond Street. She even fools some Turks. They try to sell her postcards and souvenirs, thinking she is a foreigner.

But she knows her Istanbul, her history, her religion. She is a devout Muslim and is willing to talk Islam to anyone who is interested. She holds us a long time in this mosque. Like most mosques, the floor is covered with heavy red carpets, a large ring of lights is suspended over the center, there are some dimly illuminated stained-glass windows in the distance, and there are a few Muslims praying in the direction of the altar which means they are facing Mecca. We all wear special soft socks and carry our shoes.

"This mosque," Selim says, "was built by our great architect Sinan in the years 1550-1557. It stands on one of the seven hills of Istanbul and is near where Suleiman's palace was, which no longer exists. If you look up, you will see it is one central dome surrounded by two half-domes. Now where did this idea come from? You will see when we go to Hagia Sophia, built exactly one thousand years earlier. It was Sinan's idea that Hagia Sophia was so well-built that he wanted to copy the same idea. Sinan gained great fame in Turkey. He built over three hundred structures including other mosques, baths, hospitals, bridges. He is buried just outside this great mosque."

Selim takes us next to another area where we will visit Hagia Sophia, the Blue Mosque, and the Hippodrome area, all within easy walking distance of one another. Hagia Sophia is the most beautiful of Mosques, since it is an orange-red on the outside, and the interior gives the impression of being golden and black. It is not a mosque, nor a church anymore, but is operated as a museum. One sees the mixture of Byzantine, Christian, and Muslim elements in it. The name "Hagia Sophia" means "divine wisdom." For centuries it has been the symbol of this great city.

"Pay attention now," Selim says crisply to her charges. "You will notice the same structure as in the Suleiman mosque—a central dome with two half-domes. This was built by Justinian and dedicated by him December 26, 537 A.D., and it was built on the site where in 325 A.D. Constantine had built the first basilica. So it is very old. You will notice the dome, which seems to float because of all the windows around it, is built of very light bricks from Rhodes. It's the fourth largest basilica, after St Peter's in Rome, the Duomo in Milan, and St. Paul's in London."

We look at the large mosaics of the archangel Gabriel, Madonna and child, St. Ignatius, and St. John Chrysostom. We admire the enormous hanging green panels, resembling shields, containing the names of Allah, Mohammed, and his descendants, and the marble preacher's throne. "Is it not extraordinary," asks Selim, "to think that this great building took only five years to construct? Ten thousand workers did it under Justinian who gave bonuses to the fastest workers, maybe the first ever incentive plan."

We go out into the brilliant sunlight and see the Blue Mosque behind a huge fountain spraying up water in a garden of gorgeous flowers. Selim stops: "Here you will see the Blue Mosque. It was built by a student of Sinan, Mehmet Aga, and is called the Blue Mosque because of its blue tiles and because of some blue in its stained-glass windows, but I don't know why exactly. There is not that much blue. Anyway, you will notice it has six minarets, the only mosque in the world to have that many. It is built around a central dome with four half-domes. Inside, you will see many tiles with flowers and trees, but no human figures in them. You were lucky to have seen the fountain flowing today, because it is not on all the time, in order to save water."

Inside the mosque, Selim answers questions patiently about her religion. She points out that yes, one must pray five times a day and that the length of each prayer varies. "My mother, for instance, she takes longer, maybe thirty-five to forty-five minutes. For me I can do it in twenty-five minutes. No, it is not difficult if one is born into it. You can always make it up later if you have to miss it."

Outside again, she shows us the site of the ancient Hippodrome and tells us something about its history. It was originally built by the Roman emperor, Septimius Severus, but was enlarged by Constantine in 203 A.D. Today, it looks like a long public park with trees, flowers, esplanades through and around it. Few ruins from antiquity are left. At one time, there were columns with four bronze-gilt horses on them, but they were stolen away in 1204 A.D. and now stand on the Basilica of St. Mark's in Venice.

We also see the tall Egyptian obelisk that stands in the Hippodrome. This was brought to Istanbul by Theodosius I in 390 A.D. It sits on a marble base with reliefs that depict Theodosius with his sons, rewarding winners of the horse race, receiving tribute from his vanquished enemies, and watching the races in the Hippodrome.

Someone brings up the question of the sabotage of the Galata Bridge. Selim bristles. "Terrorists," she says. But when questioned about the Kurds, she resists the questioner's idea that the Kurds are being deprived of their land in both Turkey and Iran.

"That is not true," Selim asserts. "There was no territory called Turkistan. They do not have a right to land. I do not understand all this sudden dissatisfaction. There was no problem with them under the Ottomans."

That stops all conversation. One man mutters something about neither was there public dissension in the old Soviet Union, but Selim does not hear him and is marching on now toward the bus. We leave her, feeling saturated with the damp, claustrophobic atmosphere from the great mosques of Istanbul and the inflexibility of her religion. One wonders how an obviously smart, intelligent young woman like her can so agreeably cling to a religion which limits her role in the world. I wonder what her husband is like, what he thinks of her job as a tour guide. Or maybe I'm actually seeing and hearing changing views, changing attitudes that are part of the sweeping changes wrought by Kemal Ataturk in Turkey in the 1920s. After all, as Selim has indicated, nobody really knows what a Muslim is praying for.

## ON THE POTEMKIN STEPS

If you stand at the top of them and look down, all you will see are the terraces, several of them, sliding down to the sea. If you stand at the bottom and look up, you will see steps, one-hundred and ninety-two of them leading up to the sailors' monument in Odessa. There is a frightening scene in Eisenstein's film *Battle Ship Potemkin* where a baby carriage eerily bounces down nearly most of the steps to the sea.

The buildings are large, yellow, square, the port is a semi-circle, well-planned. You know instinctively that Catherine the Great commanded it to be built with a sweep of her hand. You know there will be an opera house, generous promenades, statues, schools, academies of art, and naval institutes. It is the third largest city in the Ukraine, about nine-hundred-thousand inhabitants today, and it appears to be a fairly conservative, middle-class city of hard-working, earnest citizens. One knows it from literature. Gogol wrote *Dead Souls* here, Alexander Pushkin spent one year here in 1823-24, Maxim Gorki worked in the port, Chekhov and others refer to Odessa in their works, Sergei Eisenstein's film *Battleship Potemkin* commemorates the mutiny in 1905 when sailors joined workers in Odessa in a revolution and were suppressed.

Our guide here is Lara. "You may call me Larissa, if you wish," she adds, smiling. She is about 5'4" tall, late thirties, dressed in a light tan business suit, high heels. She has her hair dyed light red and arranges it in a bouffant style. She wears no make-up which gives her a slightly plain look, at odds with her carefully coiffed hair. Her English is good, her pride in and knowledge of her city and her country exemplary. She is pleased when asked questions about authors and operas.

The first place she shows us is the elaborate opera house. She is proud that it was built in the Viennese baroque style (1884-87). She apologizes for the scaffolding around part of it where it is being repaired. She tells us it is beautiful inside, but we cannot go in at this moment. When we come back for a performance, then we shall see how grand it is, she promises.

"Changes," she says. "You ask me about changes. Well, frankly, it is puzzling. You can see we have many more cars here now. Yes, many more, but there is no petrol. Well, there is petrol, but there is trouble getting it here. Distribution problems. Also, we are the Ukraine, and they are trying to put in our own currency, so the Russian ruble is not really our currency. Isn't it confusing? To us, also. Many feel that we have been given our freedom, which is good, but the price is all the benefits go to Russia, to Yeltsin. We shall have to wait and see. I have hopes that things will work out all right."

I notice people walking dogs along the street. Many of the dogs have muzzles that look like perforated tin cans on their noses. "Dogs," I point out. I had never seen dogs in the old Soviet Union. "Oh, yes, more dogs too," Lara says. "Look at that? That man is walking three dogs."

Lara looks around. "You know, all these streets you see, they have gone back to the original names, but all my life I have known them as Karl Marx Avenue and Lenin Street, and now they are changed. Everything I learned I have to unlearn. It is not easy for the people, but they are doing quite well, I think."

"Now this building we are standing in front of is the Pushkin Museum, which contains items from his life, and then the Historical Museum with some Ukrainian art. We can now walk down the Primorsky Boulevard where you will see a monument to Richelieu who is dressed in a Roman toga and you will see Prince Vorontsov's palace and the Monument to Sailors. I cannot show you now, but underneath Odessa are many catacombs where people did hide out in World War II. We were beseiged by the Nazis for sixty-nine days in 1941 and many people had to hide and become, you know, resistance workers. In 1944 we were liberated and were officially called a Hero City."

Outside our bus, a little boy tries to sell us some souvenirs. We hear him arguing with Lara. She seems uncertain, but good-humoredly turns back to tell us, "This boy thinks I am a very unsympathetic person. He says I do not give you a chance to buy anything from him, so to be fair, I say do you want to buy something? If so, his price is a good one." She looks around expectantly. Nobody is interested. The little boy retreats. The bus of affluence moves away. Out the window I see the boy walking, temporarily defeated. It isn't easy moving into a free enterprise system and breaking away from a mother country.

## SEARCHING FOR CHEKHOV

Anton Pavlovich Chekhov, Russia's greatest playwright in my view, lived from 1899 to 1904 in Yalta, where he died of tuberculosis. During these final years, he wrote *The Three Sisters* and *The Cherry Orchard* there, as well as the story "The Lady with a Dog." His house has been preserved and a Chekhov Museum built next to it. It is the one thing I want to see in Yalta.

But other things come first—two huge palaces. The first, Livadia Palace, was, naturally, the Czar's summer palace, but it has gained greater fame as the site of the Yalta Conference in 1945 among Stalin, Churchill, and Roosevelt where the fate of post-war Europe was determined. Originally, Livadia Palace was built in 1910-11 by two-thousand, five-hundred persons who are alleged to have worked through the nights to complete it. The Russian architect, Krasnov, based it on Italian Renaissance designs. The main building is a large white palace and it is situated beautifully on a high point overlooking the Black Sea. The interior carefully preserves the atmosphere of the Yalta conferences. Here, one can see Roosevelt's private conference room, the room where the documents were signed, the reception rooms, dining room, and many original letters bringing up names from the past—Cordell Hull, Edward Stettinius, Sir Anthony Eden. among others. The place is immaculate, giving one the impression that Stalin, Churchill, and Roosevelt have just stepped out for a moment.

The Yalta Conference itself is still the subject of controversy, some people thinking it resulted in ruinous decisions for the world, others thinking a very ill Roosevelt gave away too much to the man of steel, Stalin, thus ushering in the Cold War. But Livadia Palace sits today just the way it was, serene, light, beautiful, remote—a place to concentrate, to think.

There is so much music in Yalta. Almost everyone who can sing or dance is out making money at it, now that the new freedom has come. Whole families play violins and sing folksongs. At every turn in Yalta, one is confronted by the sweet sounds of music out in the streets, in the gardens, in the parks. At Livadia, father, mother, sister, and son, dressed in colorful Ukrainian costumes, form a living singing, dancing band. A man with a reddish mutton-chops hairstyle and beard, right out of Chekhov, plays a large balalaika to the delight of tourists. Sturdy, blond-haired, blue-eyed boys, looking like future Olympics champions, hawk postcards and souvenirs, dependent on their persuasive personalities to make sales.

One sad note: A well-dressed older woman stands shyly to one side begging handouts from tourists, the only person I see who does this. She carries a pink silk parasol and wears white gloves. Everyone else offers something in return—a song, a dance, a souvenir. This poor soul makes me think of an aged Yelena in *Uncle Vanya*. Is this what happens to people who cannot do anything, who just fade into poverty? I should give her something, I suppose, but I don't. It shocks me too much. I didn't expect this sudden apparition. It doesn't seem correct, hardly the Ukrainian spirit, which appears to be one of succeeding through hard work.

Not only through music, but through art will they succeed. In Livadia Palace, the gift shop has been turned into several rooms full of art, all produced by local people. Many beautiful paintings here—oils, acrylics, watercolor—at reasonable prices. Everyone who can paint, does. These are unique souvenirs—art, music, dancing, a pulse of life. These are what we can bring back from Yalta, and these are why one will want to return in the future.

Aside from the people, who are quite splendid, so is the geography and the meterology. Yalta is a place of high hills, grand corniches, beautiful gardens, Mediterranean-type trees and climate. One thinks of Monte Carlo, Eze-sur-Mer, and Santa Barbara—the city has so many charming twists and turns to it and little villas perched precariously on hillsides and peninsulas.

One such villa is a fairytale castle called "Swallow's Nest" that clings like something out of a Disney movie to a cliff overlooking the sea below. Another is the bizarre Alupka Palace, built by Edward Blore, an English architect, between 1828-1848, for the flamboyant Vorontsov, who was the Mayor and Governor of Odessa. The style is a peculiar mix of English Tudor with Spanish Alhambra. The site, overlooking the Black

Sea, is, once again, spectacular, with lions decorating the staircase reminiscent of the lions we saw in Miletos, although these are said to be copies of the ones on Pope Clement XII's tomb in Rome. The gardens and the hillsides are punctuated with the dark cypresses that give the whole area an Italianate look.

Alupka Palace has extraordinary floors, a different parquet design for each room. Sometimes one thinks one is in a wood-paneled English drawing room, and then one passes by a window that looks out into a Moorish garden. In one room, a woman sits at a piano playing Chopin *études*—appropriate! The dining room is opulent, like something out of Kew Palace in England, suitable for George III or Prince Vorontsov, in this case, but the terrace overlooking the sea is light, lively, full of bubbling tourists in animated conversation, a very inviting, happy picture.

Our guide here is Olga. She is perfect, I think, petite, thin, pale, watery-blue wide-spaced eyes, light brown short hair worn in pageboy bangs. She reminds me strongly of a Ukrainian-American friend from Chicago, fragile-appearing, yet actually strong. Olga moves too fast. She darts. Older people have trouble keeping up with her. She speaks softly, too shyly for a guide. They cannot hear her. They misunderstand her. They feel she is running them ragged. Her bird-like hopping disturbs them. They complain. She is chagrined. She had no idea. She slows down. She tries to speak up.

"I want to go to Chekhov's house," I say to her. "You are Olga, one of the three sisters."

Her eyes brighten. "We will stop there on the way down," she says. "You can get off there. When you have finished, hail a taxi and give him one dollar to take you to the port."

When we arrive, she takes care to point out which is the house, which the museum. The bus glides off, disappears from sight. We are left alone. We enter a garden. There is a bust of Chekhov with afternoon light on it. A man sits on a bench nearby, thinking. We go into the Museum and find there a wealth of letters, memorabilia, and a marvelous docent who does not speak English but conducts us through, enthusiastically pointing out programs, Chekhov's medical implements, his gardening tools, letters, photographs, and telling us some new things, and other things we already know.

When we have finished with this museum which is more elaborate and contains more items than the Chekhov House in Moscow where he had lived earlier, we go next to the house where Chekhov lived out his last years. The garden is probably much fuller now. A gardener is hard at work clearing out weeds and watering plants. Three Ukrainian women in the house guide us, generously inviting us into each room, conjuring up through their reverent speech the very spirit of Chekhov himself, even in his bedroom where he died.

Chekhov's House is kept much the way it was in 1904. This is possible because Chekhov's sister, Maria, who was an artist, lived to be ninety-four and died in this house in 1956. The women in the family had greater longevity than the men, it seems. Chekhov's mother, who had her own room in this house, died at eighty-three. Chekhov's wife, Olga Knipper, the actress who created the role of Arkadina in *The Seagull*, died at ninety-one. But Anton, like his father and brother, had tuberculosis, and came to Yalta for his health, but, ironically, lost the battle here and died. Nicolai, one of his brothers, was an illustrator and wrote the first biography of Anton. Most of the paintings in the Yalta house were done by sister Maria. She also did a portrait of the mother which hangs in the mother's room. I think it is a fairly crude portrait and would say her other paintings are not particularly distinguished, but I like the idea that she did them and that Anton appreciated them.

Like the house in Moscow, the Yalta house is simple, functional, not designed to impress or fool anyone. There are no rugs on any of the floors. The furniture is fairly massive and not particularly comfortable looking. Chekhov's desk is a good size, but he has a more elegant one in the museum next door. There is a kind of cozy alcove with a couch behind his desk with a high window that gives a good light. His own room and bed are Spartan. There is a kind of amber light in his room. The woman lowers the velvet rope, ushering me into his room, urging me to take as many photos as I want. I take none. It seems a violation of an author whom I revere.

Before Chekhov built this house, he had lived in a pension in Yalta. After he built this house, he had some distinguished guests. They included Rachmaninoff, who played on Chekhov's upright piano, and Maxim Gorki who stayed in the guest room for a while.

Oddly, there are no books in the house, and nothing really theatrical, no posters or anything, which is curious, considering Anton was a playwright and Olga an actress. The largest room in the house is the dining room. Outside the front door, if you were calling on Chekhov, is a little brass plaque that says "A. Chekhov." There is a bell there, also, that when twisted, makes a little ring inside the house. I wonder if I ring it will it summon up Chekhov? He was only forty-four when he died.

Yalta sprawls for a considerable distance outside the port itself. It is a white city under a blue sky in a beautiful garden. There are still many sanatoriums there and summer homes for the wealthy. One of these is the dacha of Gorbachev where he was holed up during the changes that toppled him from power and wrought the revolution that freed the Ukraine and other areas from the communist yoke of the Soviet Union forever.

Only the sea disappoints here. The Black Sea, which apparently gets its name from the black fog which curls up on it sometimes, is a strange sea, with currents that run counter-clockwise, low salinity, gales which boil up suddenly, and no deep sea life in its stagnant lower reaches. Some people say it is polluted from the oil industry in Romania and possibly in Russia, or maybe from the clogging that occurs at the narrow Bosphorus. I don't think I'd want to swim in such a sea.

Still, when I think of Yalta, I hear music, I see water-colors, I feel the warmth of a gentle sun and a fair wind, and I see the opening scene of *The Cherry Orchard,* Lubov Ranevskaia returning from five years in Paris to her childhood, her youth, her happiness again, and I remember that the word "Lubov" means "Love." Yalta is one of the great romantic cities of the world.

## PATMOS

"I am Alpha and Omega, the beginning and the end," wrote St. John hearing the Lord speak in Revelations. This book by St. John the Divine is said to have been written on Patmos, a small, rocky island in the Dodecanese. We know St. John was banished there by Domitian in 95 A.D. He is said to have lived in a cave where these awesome revelations were visited upon him.

Today, the monastery at the top of the hill, named after St. John is the island's one attraction. This monastery dates back to 1088 A.D. and is still in excellent condition with little chapels, splendid arches, bells arranged artistically, and altars suitable for praying. Down the hill, the cave of St. John waits, set up as a shrine to the extraordinary vision that John experienced.

There is no one to guide us on this holy island. We walk alone through the ancient monastery, marveling at its nooks and crannies and its spectacular view of the sea, its picturesque arrangement of bells, and its inner courtyards with low-beamed doors. There is a very brisk breeze blowing in from the sea, almost an ominous one, which could be unsettling.

Later, down the hill, we walk down primitive steps leading into St. John's Cave, a small, fairly confined place, where a Greek orthodox priest is talking to a young man about religious matters, while tourists like us swarm through the place not really knowing, and some not even caring, what they are seeing. The place is decorated now with a lot of Greek icons, decoupage portraits of St. John, candles burning, whitewashed walls, a kind of golden patina filling the place. We move silently, tired now from climbing up the stairs in the monastery and down the steps to the Cave. We move back again to the port, the little town, where there is more life, more vivacity, more reality for us.

## SANTORINI

Once it was the round crater of a volcano. Now, parts are above water and some below. Two towns, Thira and Pirgos perch high up like white birds' nests on the chalky cliffs. A fine coat of pumice covers everything on the island. By rights, hawks or albatrosses should inhabit these rooks. The way up from the tiny port is either by foot (596 steps up), by donkey, or cable car. Santorini has enjoyed fame recently as a trendy tourist spot. A walk through Thira confirms this: shops selling jewelry and clothing, discos and bar-restaurants. Once in a while, a pleasing Greek church. Lots of flowers and cliff houses veering out over the edge. Picturesque cobbled streets, some Minoan ruins to the south, a museum which is closed, naturally, the day we visit.

A cobalt blue sky overhead, a bright sun, a gorgeous view of the sea below, an artist's paradise—but empty, empty, empty. Cold, white, chalky, no beach, no real people, only tourists, hundreds of donkeys to transport them, gold jewelry in shops, trendy people running things, waiting for the motion picture cameras to start turning.

# NAUPLIA AND EPIDAUROS

Aeschylus' trilogy the *Oresteia* opens with the watchman standing on the walls of Agamemnon's palace in Argos looking out over the harbor to see if he can sight torches lit from other promontories signaling that the Trojan War is over after seven years and the great general Agamemnon is coming home. As one sails into Nauplia, which is this ancient harbor, one passes through that same landscape immortalized by Aeschylus in his famous trilogy first put on in the Theatre of Dionysos in Athens in 458 B.C., ushering in the great age of Greek tragedy.

It is an expansive and impressive harbor, very large, very old, dating back to the Mycenean civilization which existed there from 1400-1100 B.C., coveted by the Romans, the Franks and the Venetians who seized Nauplia in 1388 A.D. and built a huge fortress, the Palamide Castle overlooking the harbor.

Today, the town is a quite charming port city of the Peloponnesus and Nauplia is known primarily as a resort.

Vana is our guide here. She wears a white shirt, voluminous white shorts, has dark, bobbed hair, beautiful dark eyes and Greek coloring, gold jewelry, very athletic, no-nonsense air about her, and she chain-smokes. Quick, alert, intelligent, she is extremely well organized. "We are going first to Epidauros," she says. "We will see the theatre which is very well-preserved. It was excavated by Greeks. The Germans have excavated Pergamon and Olympia," she announces.

We drive through very lush countryside. "There is a better climate here than in the islands," says Vana. "We get plentiful rain. They don't."

"Good," she says when we arrive at Epidauros. "We are here early. That will be an advantage. Come this way."

Vana seats us under ancient trees behind the scene house of the theatre. She draws diagrams in the earth with a long stick she has picked up. "This is the way the Greek orchestra looks," she says, drawing a circle. "Orchestra means 'the dancing place.' It is the place where the chorus, usually twelve or fifteen, entered." She points to the two side entrances from the stage. "These are the paradoi, the entrances. And, in the center, you will see a round stone in the earth. That was where the altar of Dionysos was, for, originally, tragedy was danced around the altar. *Tragos* is the Greek word for goat, and a goat was apparently originally sacrificed. This theatre is Hellenistic, which means probably 4th century B.C., and it has perfect acoustics. Why? One reason is the wind is at our backs so it would carry the actors' voices well. The other is the Greeks usually built on the side of a hill, and so the sound carries up well. In addition, the Greeks took care that the sun should be on the faces of the actors. In other words, they took care to take advantage of all the natural elements they could. Now, you go up into the seats if you want, and I will rustle some paper and drop a coin and you will hear everything."

We do this and are surprised at how excellent the sound is. Vana tells us the theatre at Epidauros is still used for special performances of classical plays at certain times.

I think the location at Epidauros is very quiet and serene, an ideal place for a theatre.

Vana also points out the ruins of the Temple of Asclepius and the medical center, but they are much less than the ruins at Pergamon, although Epidauros appears to be a natural place to have set up a hospital.

After driving back to town from the countryside, we climb up to Palamide Castle, a huge pile with an incredible view looking out over the bay to Mycenae and Argos. In the bay, there is a little island with a tiny battlemented fortress on it called "Bourdzi." This was another touch of the Venetians in their occupation in 1471. Very picturesque!

Back in the present in Nauplia, I walk along the port for a while photographing port scenes. I shoot some men drinking coffee and playing cards in a cafe with a marble terrace. Men in cafes are a staple in this part of Greece, as in Turkey. I see Vana walking along through the cafes to some destination in town after our trip. I wave to her. She smiles.

## KATAKOLO AND OLYMPIA

Giannis is our guide to Olympia. He is tall, good-looking, somewhat like the actor John Cassavetes, chain-smoking, fast-talking, even faster walking, but a little too soft-looking, not enough muscle. It shows in his arms and belly, too soon for such a young man.

My impression of Katakolo is that it is another small Greek port on the Ionian sea, a quiet town with many colorful fishing boats tied up and two big freighters, one of which is loading grain.

We drive from the little port town deep into the countryside, Giannis explaining to us what we are seeing. Why are the houses seemingly built on stilts?

"They build what they can afford first. Then, when they can manage it, they fill in the underneath part, when they are prosperous."

The fields and landscape are so lush and fertile.

"Yes, it is verdant here. The fields are full of tobacco, currants, and cotton. See, you can see some tobacco drying in that farmer's yard."

Why is this called the Peloponnesus?

"It means the island of Pelops. It was originally a peninsula, but since they have cut through the Corinth Canal, it is now an island."

We arrive, finally, at Olympia which lies in a valley where the Alpheios and Kladeos rivers meet. I am surprised to see that quite a modern town has grown up around the entrance to the ancient site of Olympia. Giannis speeds us through the entrance and into the setting which resembles a large park full of trees and ruins, very little of which remains upright.

"Hurry up," Giannis commands. "You will see the statues and friezes, the good things in the museum, but we will have trouble there because there are too many people."

One woman moves slightly to the right of Giannis to get away from the smoke of his cigarette. She amiably says, "You're an Olympian, Giannis, why do you smoke?"

"No, I am not Olympian," he replies quickly. "I am smoker."

"You are an Olympian smoker," I say to him. He likes that. He smiles and repeats it: "I am an Olympian smoker." I figure he will tell that one to his friends later.

He sits us down and explains the ancient Olympic Games to us:

"The Olympic Games began in 776 B.C. Only males could compete. They performed in the nude. Only males could watch them, naturally. The only woman permitted was the priestess of Demeter, for some reason. You will see they built a special throne for her halfway down the stadium. There was a story about a woman who was the trainer for her son, but she could not come to the games, so she disguised herself as a male in a robe, but when her son was winning his race, she became so excited, she threw up her arms which opened her robe and revealed her to be a woman. A woman could be put to death for defying the rules, but there are no records of any woman ever being put to death, so I think she was lucky that time."

Giannis moves us into the ruins of the Temple to Zeus where everything is on a colossal scale. Pieces of toppled pillars lie on the ground like enormous stone tires.

"Well," says Giannis. "Once there was a massive statue of Zay-OOS here. It was made of ivory and gold, but you won't see this statue in any museum or any others like it. Why not? Because they were stolen, broken up and used for other purposes. However, in the museum, I am going to show you the top pieces of the pillars which were on this temple. They are impressive. Now, we can go on to the stadium itself."

I observe the Olympic Stadium to be a long oval with green slopes on either side. "This is the way it was," says Giannis. "The spectators sat on the grass, not on seats. You see, halfway down on one side there are some steps. They are the only steps here. That leads to the section for the judges. Now, look across, on the other side, you see there the throne for the priestess of Demeter, the only woman allowed. Now, here at this end, is where the Olympic torch was lit. Today, they light it at another site. I will show you. They do it because there are some standing ruins nearby. It is only to make the photograph more pleasing, not for any real reason."

He leads us near some Roman ruins with standing pillars, which is where he says the torch is lighted now. "It makes a good picture," he claims.

"In 1896, the modern Olympic Games began again," he announces, "but do you know when began the custom of taking the torch from one country to another? No, you can't guess. The 1936 games in Germany," he says. "Hitler thought it would be a good idea to show his power going from one country to another, and so ever since, other countries have thought so too, so we keep it. It's odd that a good idea should have come from Hitler, isn't it?"

We go into the museum next, where all the artifacts have been arranged with exquisite care. Here, one can finally see  up close the incredible marble pediments from the Temple of Zeus. The west pediment shows Apollo in the middle with the centaurs at the time when they got drunk and tried to abduct the bride and other women at a wedding. The east pediment shows Zeus with Pelops and Oinomaos before their chariot race. The major prize in the museum, however, is Praxiteles' Hermes, (340 B.C.) in which a somewhat insolent Hermes is gracefully sculpted of marble. Yet Giannis insists that we walk around behind the statue to see that the back of it was merely roughed in and has two small holes in it, indicating it was intended to be attached to something.

One woman in our party strays too far into another room. Giannis calls out to her: "You, there, pay attention here. You cannot see everything. It will take you five days. I will show you the highlights. You must stick with me."

When we get back to Katakolo, I figure Giannis will slip away and join the men in a portside tavern for a beer and a smoke, boasting about his trying day shepherding wandering tourists through the ruins of Olympia.

---

Tomorrow we depart for Venice. We shall sail through the Strait of Otranto into the Adriatic Sea to all that magnificence at the northern end called Venice. We have been to Venice many times before. Now it seems like the appropriate end for this journey back through time in Asia Minor. To reenter the West through the beauty of Venice will set us in an artistic Byzantium and give us a new perspective on our time and culture, a better understanding of how it all came about, what it meant, and what it signifies to generations yet to come.

# SMALL WAR IN INDIA

## Letters 1965-1966

Roger Lee Kenvin

# PREFACE TO SMALL WAR IN INDIA

In the mid 1960s, a group of women's colleges in the United States, working under the Fulbright program, formed a consortium with some colleges for women in India to exchange professors. The Americans were paid entirely in rupees, frozen assets of the United States in India. Among American colleges participating were Sweet Briar, Mary Washington, Mt. Holyoke, Barnard, Bryn Mawr, Western, and Randolph-Macon Women's College.

I was the second professor participating from Mary Washington College and spent the academic year 1965-1966 teaching at Isabella Thoburn College in Lucknow, Uttar Pradesh, northern India. My wife, Rudd, and daughters Brooke (5) and Heather (4) accompanied me. On this trip, we went around the world, flying (and making appropriate stops) from Newark to Houston, San Francisco, Honolulu, Tokyo, Hong Kong, Bangkok, New Delhi, to Lucknow. On the return, we went to Moscow, Helsinki, Berlin, Paris, Holland, London, and New York.

These letters recount my impressions and adventures in India. It was a remarkable time, and the whole experience influenced me in many ways. In addition to these letters, I also wrote a play based on the Radha-Krishna myths, several short stories, gave slide-lectures on India, and presented a paper on "The Traditional in Modern Indian Theatre" at a meeting of the Asia-America Association in Toronto, Canada.

R. L. K.

198 Faizabad Road
Lucknow, India
July 26, 1965

Dear Friends,

If you were to come to Isabella Thoburn College, you would enter through an iron gate and see directly in front of you a yellow sandstone building with Roman columns in front and two long wings on either side. It might remind you vaguely of some rural W.P.A. post office somewhere or another Washington, D.C. clone. You would then cross a brick-lined courtyard to the building and go up the steps, maybe three or four of them. Once inside, you would enter a hall with a single portrait on the wall. The portrait is of Isabella Thoburn, American founder of the college. Underneath the painting, the decor is carefully arranged, as around a shrine. There is a little low table with a cloth draped upon it, and on that a potted palm. To the left and right of the table are larger potted fern-like plants.

In the portrait, Isabella sits in a stiff-backed chair, whale-boned and well-corseted, with a little ribbon at her throat. Her hair is parted in the middle, pulled back, and arranged in a small bun on the back of her head. Over one arm a shawl is draped, providing a softening touch to the *Major Barbara* grey of her dress. In one hand she holds a book (a Gideon *Bible*, I should say). You would recognize her the minute you saw her. She is Clara Barton, Lydia Pinkham, and Susan B. Anthony. She is Chickering pianos, Henry James' *Washington Square*, and Edward McDowell's "To a Water Lily." 1870 was her big year. With six girls as her first students, she founded Isabella Thoburn College in the exotic Aminabad Bazaar of Lucknow, Uttar Pradesh, India. Today her formidable spirit marches on, aided by the Woman's Division of Christian Service of the Methodist Church in America with the cooperation of the United Presbyterian Mission Board.

Am I painting too austere an opening picture of the college? What else does one see? On an outside wall, surrounding the college, there is written in large painted letters:

GET YOUR MALARIA SHOTS.
REPORT ALL FEVER CASES AT ONCE

On several trees lining the road there are affixed metal signs proclaiming in red letters:

DR. S. CHOUDYN, SEXOLOGIST
28 FAIZABAD ROAD

Sometimes one sees monkeys swinging in the trees or running along the roofs of college buildings. Occasionally, peacocks strut on the front lawn or water buffalos help themselves to petunias. Around the main gate, there is always a covey of dark, gypsy-like rickshaw drivers and their brilliantly decorated rickshaws. At one corner, under an ancient tamarind tree, an old man sits, reading palms, dispensing fortunes in Hindi. I am tempted to stop, but am fearful he will echo T. S. Eliot's *The Wasteland* and tell me something like, "Fear death by water."

If you, like me, think of a library as the heart of any college, you would be wrong here. This library has only 28,000 volumes, although it was described to me as one of the best college libraries in India. Usually the library is quite empty. Sometimes it closes down for whole periods during the day. It stays open only until 9:00 p.m. Its strongest collection is that housed under the classification "Religious Literature." It boasts many books of the inspirational Fulton Oursler type, mostly lives of Christ, or other books of a starchy, moralistic, uplifting nature.

The real heart of this college is its chapel, quite a handsome building with modest, sapphire-blue stained glass windows, functional cane-chair pews, kneeling cushions, and a good organ. The Methodist-Episcopal hymnals are all dated 1938, Nashville, Tennessee. Every morning compulsory chapel is held here, led by the faculty, and every evening, compulsory vespers, led by the students. In fact, the evening dinner hour is divided in half—half of it spent in the dining hall eating, and the other half in the chapel praying.

My introduction to life at the college began one morning at 8:00 a.m. when there was a loud banging at my bedroom door. Mrs. Jordan (Indian Christians have intriguing names like Mrs. Paul, Miss John, Mr. Michael, and Mr. Philip) came, she announced, to take me to "retreat." At first, I thought perhaps the Red Chinese had come swarming over the Himalayas or the Pakistanis had struck, or the dacoits, who often strike terror hereabouts—but no. Off we went to a communion breakfast, followed by a hymn-singing faculty meeting in the auditorium, complete with  sermon by an English minister. Then we progressed to a series of seminar discussions on how we could infuse spirituality into our daily lives, and, finally, four hours later, we wound things up with holy communion in the chapel, where we gave thanks (excessively, it seemed to me) for all the suffering we'd been undergoing.

By the time of our next faculty meeting, I was not at all surprised to find the *Methodist Hymnal* there in front of each of our places. However, this time, after opening prayer, we had to sing *a capella*, without benefit of organ. This proved a little embarrassing to me, since I can sing only four notes, b, c, d, and e in the lower register, and I sat next to the Geography teacher, male (there are only four men on the faculty), who has an abnormally high falsetto. I had to settle for making vague, droning sounds. You might have thought I was a plane in the distance, had you sat next to me, or something faulty in the overhead ceiling fan. Surrounded by those shrill female voices, all singing with missionary fervor, every verse of every hymn, I had to sit, lumpish and ill-at-ease, certain that I was letting down my country, not to mention the Good Lord, in ambassadorial singing goodwill.

The acting principal of the college is a rather extraordinary woman. Dr. Marie Sommerville is an African-Indian and looks very wise, often with soulful or merry eyes (depending on her whim), a little pug nose, and a pert mouth.She has a good, deep theatrical voice and speaks wonderful stage British. She has remonstrated with me good-humoredly about my American accent and told me to broaden my "a's.""No, no, Dr. Kenvin, not Pakistan. It's PAH-ki-stahn."

She is a Christian, and, in her speeches to both faculty and students, is much given to using cliched religious parallels. For instance, we, the faculty, are the sowers, ideas are the seeds, and the students are the fields. In her opening lecture she urged the students "to grow. G-R-O-W." She spelled it out for them and then had them spell it back to her. When she discussed the faculty's role, she told the students, "You see, we are here to provide the manure." Nobody laughed!

I've told you that there are only four men on the faculty. Are you aware what this means? Men are clearly the inferior, second sex. You know Isabella Thoburn is a women's college, run by spinsters for spinsters. Men are actually restricted in their movements to certain areas of the campus. We cannot go behind the lines of the administration building and must stay on the covered verandah, going at right angles when it does so. Should we go to the library or chapel, we must walk in a straight line. The hostel area is absolutely forbidden to us. Sometimes Rudd brings over the children to play in the college yard, and then she and the children part company with me. I am an untouchable, an unwantable, it seems.

The subordinate position of men is made evident in faculty processions. All the spinsters show up wearing white saris. They come floating in like vestal virgins lining up at their shrine. The other three men are all dressed in white, also, like votaries of some strange religious order. They wear white shirts and white pants, and look to me like Good Humor men or bakers. I wear a white shirt, but I don't have white pants. When I walk in this white parade, I am aware that everyone except me conveys an aura of purity and virginity. I, in my white shirt and blue pants, can only hope to convey a dubious kind of semi-virginity. They will have to take me as I am, damaged goods. I am simply not pure and holy enough for them.

As for my classes, I have one with seniors and another with sophomores. Both classes meet four times a week, on a floating schedule, sometimes at 7:00 a.m., other times at 8:40 a.m., etc. I have about fifty students in all. For most of them, English is a second language, and all of them are being prepared for the standard bachelor of arts examination, administered externally by Lucknow University. I have to follow a prescribed syllabus for this, and so have no control at all over the content.

The level of English is very low, equivalent, I would say, to high school or junior high school work. For instance, in my senior class (I have the bright section), they have to read *Macbeth* and *Candida* and a few awful nineteenth-century poems like "The Lotus Eaters" and "Choruses from *Atalanta in Calydon*." My sophomores have a book called *Noble Men and Manners*. Talk about being trapped in the nineteenth century!

In addition to teaching, I am also directing the annual play, to which three thousand people are invited to two successive performances. The college also chose the play for me. They want *A Majority of One*, so I am currently involved in a talent hunt for a Jewish Indian Gertrude Berg type among the students, may the Good Lord help me!

Would you like to know what a typical day is like here? First of all, it begins at night. I am lying in bed tossing fitfully. I cannot sleep, partly because we don't have mattresses or inner springs. We sleep on webbing on top of which is placed a thin cotton pad. One's bones ache all the time.

I try to sleep, but the whirring from the great helicopter of a ceiling fan keeps me awake. Then I start sweating. I am already sleeping without a top.

Soon a little breeze ruffles the pull-curtain that covers the screen door leading to the verandah. We are on the ground floor, off the verandah that looks out into the rose garden. I remember an old Paramount movie in which a curtain once rustled and behind it was a cobra. I wonder if a cobra will slither out now and float over to my bed to kill me noiselessly. I remember my landlady poohpooing the idea when I questioned her about snakes. "No, we have only a few poisonous kinds." I think of the mongoose I saw sprinting through the rose garden a few days ago. I think of the snake charmer in front of the Lal Bagh Methodist Church. Wasn't that a cobra he was charming?

It is easing into the early morning hours now. I decide the cobra won't get me, after all, and, even if he does, I don't care. I am troubled with a mosquito now. Has he come bringing malaria? Shall I huddle up under the sheet and roast to death, or shall I expose my chest and arms, and face malaria like a man? I decide to chance it and confront disease, trusting that the chloroquin pill I took last Wednesday will do its job.

Sometimes in the night, too, there are the sounds of exploding fireworks, near and far, like so many hand grenades. I no longer fear them. They are standard sounds at late-evening wedding celebrations. But, other times, I hear weird barking noises in the distance. I think of the time five years ago when jackals came out of the forests and stole away thirty children from Lucknow—"Jackal, jackal, burning bright, in the forests of the night," I chant to myself.

Then, suddenly, the whirring from the fan stops, the light from the street lamp goes dark, the curtain rustles. I hear a scraping noise. What is coming now? I listen for drums. If I hear them, it will mean the dacoits are coming. Has the word gone out in the half-world that a rich American lies waiting to be plucked in his verandah hideaway? I decide that, yes, the dacoits are indeed advancing, and I try to think of the word for "poor" in Hindi. Is it *"gureed"* or *"gurdeep?"* I can't remember. I will try out both words on the dacoits. Maybe they will only steal my rupees and not cut my throat or those of Rudd and the children. The children! I sit up, horrified. If anything should happen to them . . . . I decide that I will offer up my puny life to the dacoits if only they will spare Rudd and the children. Then I worry that Heather's red hair may magnetize them and unsettle them completely. I wonder what red hair fetches on the black market these days. Perhaps I'd better go in and stash Heather away under her bed, while she is still sleeping soundly.

Then, just as suddenly, the lights go on again. Later they will go off once more, but now I realize it is one hour before dawn when all street lights are regularly turned off. I drift off for a few minutes, awaiting the arrival of either dacoits or cobra, whichever comes first.

6:00 a.m. There is a loud banging at the back bathroom door. I stumble out of bed to receive from Rahat my morning allotment of a shaving mug full of hot water, there being no hot water in our house. After breakfast, I go to the college for my two classes, then return home for lunch, usually around 1:00 p.m.

What do I eat? Rahat can cook almost anything. He makes his own potato chips. He cooks the best omelets I've ever eaten. He knows I love mangos, and, since we've been here, I have always had a mango for dessert at both lunch and dinner. He makes hamburgers when we want them. He makes delicious beef curry, hot or mild, according to one's taste. He cooks excellent chicken and pot roast, and knows just how to prepare my coffee. He is spoiling us. I wish we could bring him back with us. He has a grand sene of humor and clowns around with the children. He has a little pixie of a son himself, and, very often, one gets a kind of Indian *Our Gang* picture with Brooke walking along the verandah, followed by Heather, then Rahat's tiny son, like Dopey in *Snow White and the Seven Dwarfs*, followed by at least two of the Shuklas' three dachshunds.

We enrolled the children in La Martiniere Girls School, (the male part of which was immortalized by Rudyard Kipling in *Kim*), but the first day in school, Heather's teacher said, "All right, class. Let's do our ABCs." Then she belted out "A," to which the class responded "A." Next "B" to which the class responded "B." When she got to "D", there was a loud wail from Heather, "I want to go back to Virginia." This was not her idea of kindergarten, nor ours. So we withdrew her, and the next day Brooke wanted to withdraw also. Why force them into an Oliver Twist-like existence in a nineteenth-century British institution?

After lunch in this northern part of India, everyone naps from 1:30 p.m. to 3:00 p.m. Then, I often take a rickshaw and go into town to shop in the Hazrat Gunj or the Aminabad Bazaar. The Hazrat Gunj is familiarly called "The Gunch." It represents the Anglo-Indian side of Lucknow and is patronized only by the wealthy class. The Aminabad Bazaar is built around Aminabad Park. All four classes meet here—rich, middle, lower, and poor. Old Lucknow melts into new Lucknow here. It is a wonderfully fascinating bazaar, with sections for silk saris, copper and brass, books, toys, etc. There is also the Fugi Bazaar (for fugitives), people who have fled from Punjab and other states.

It took me three weeks to get up enough courage to go back to the Aminabad after I had been there once. Rudd is more squeamish than I. She does not like to bargain, and she has to pretend not to notice the extreme poverty and filth. I look at all these things steadily. I just have had to adjust to things as they are, and they are, frankly, often ugly and upsetting.

After I return from the bazaars, Rudd and I often play cards with the children. We have four games—Authors, Animal Rummy, Gold Fish, and Old Maid. Every time the old maid comes up, I can't help thinking of Isabella Thoburn. Did she know she was immortalized in a card game?

Dinner for the children comes at 5:30 p.m. For Rudd and me around 7:00 p.m. One goes to bed around 10:00 p.m. We have no television or radio. We subscribe to the local paper, The Lucknow *Pioneer*, for which Kipling once was editor and Churchill, a correspondent. Rudd and I often discuss Lucknow in the evening, or the college, or we read, or I prepare lessons, grade papers, or talk about our return trip home. We are hopeful of coming by way of Moscow.

Our love to all of you. Think of Rudd and me, like Bea Lillie and Noel Coward, riding to town in our rickshaw with pith helmets and umbrellas to the tune of "Mad dogs and Englishmen go out in the noonday sun."

Roger

Lucknow, India
August 20, 1965

Dear Friends,

I think I've discovered what happened to Kay Francis. Remember her in those 1934 movies, shuttling back and forth between George Brent and William Powell, wearing her silver lamé gown with leg of mutton sleeves and plunging neckline, her black hair neatly parted in the middle to form two giant sophisticated waves on either side? Well, she has been metamorphosed into an Indian woman and is now teaching at Isabella Thoburn College. I see her sitting across from me at faculty meetings, gazing out from under those great black silver screen brows. There is no mistaking her. Only I know who she really is. She goes by the name of Miss Gilead here. I am thinking of dropping her a note reading, "Kay Francis, you gorgeous movie star, you, your secret is safe with me. Shall we say cocktails at five? Love, Roger."

These are heretical thoughts, I know, when everyone else is piously singing hymns or listening to biblical explications of St. Paul's letters to the Corinthians, but such is the low state into which my Christianity has fallen since I've been over here. Instead of fanning it, I'm afraid these missionaries are extinguishing it altogether. I've even toyed with the idea of becoming a Sikh, Jain, or Parsi.

The Sikhs seem to me to have the most dash. They wear bright red turbans, dark beards, and open-chested Harry Belafonte shirts. Sometimes they sport pointed slippers with curled-up toes, like Ali Baba's. They look as though they zap around on magic carpets. I am told they all have the same last name—Singh. Roger Singh. How does that sound? Could Kay Francis and I escape together to my palace in Udaipur or my summer one in Kashmir?

---

Now Playing:

KAY FRANCIS and ROGER SINGH
in
**KASHMIR KAPRICE**
With George Brent

"Their love transcended even the Khyber Pass"

---

How does that sound?

But, in actuality, there is no escape. I confess I've joined the students' Christian Association. Margaret Nacqvi, one of my students, asked me to be a "senior friend" at a cost of two rupees. I told her I was a senior friend, if anyone was, she could count on that. The next thing I knew, I was sitting in the chapel taking part in an ethereal ceremony of light, with vestal virgins all dressed in white once more, holding lighted white candles, and singing unto the congregation with a glad voice, "Follow, follow the gleam!" One virgin, apparently the leader, came down the center aisle, bearing what looked like the Olympic torch itself. Then they formed two long lines outside the chapel, and I had to pass down this mystical corridor of angels and archangels before I could get to the outside world again. I was the only male present. It was like the entrance into Shangri-La in *Lost Horizon*. The other cowards must have chickened out.

Only 25% of the I.T. students are Christians. They are generally day students and often so poor they cannot afford textbooks or lunch. The Jains, Parsis, Muslims, and Sikhs are the brightest. The Hindus are the biggest problem. They apparently operate under an ethical system all their own. We have a whole committee, the Ideals Committee, of which I am a member, that exists primarily for the Hindus alone. They literally have to be taught such concepts as honesty, dependability, broad-mindedness. For some of the teachers here, the greatest reward comes in watching a Hindu transformed into a responsible human being over four years.

Expand this thought a little. Realize that 85% of Indians are Hindus, and you have a good idea of what one is up against in India. Just to mention a few manifestations of popular Hinduism, there are animals everywhere in the streets, newspapers regularly carry accounts of mothers who murder their female babies in the hope of propitiating the Hindu gods who will then reward them with males. In Benares on the burning ghats, cremated corpses are then pushed into the Ganges River, and it is from this river that the city gets its drinking water supply.

The situation is not at all helped by the fact that the great Indian leaders, Gandhi and Nehru, were both Hindus. Gandhi maintained that the culture of India rested in the "deep reservoir of spirituality" to be found in the Indian peasant living in the villages. But this "spirituality" could also be interpreted as a resignation, more of a consenting to one's destiny, an idea easily acceptable if one is born into Indian village society. Then, too, Hindus believe in the transmigration of the soul. One can always come back as an Irish rat or an enchanted prince. Maybe this explains the reluctance to change the present life, the triumph of superstition over practicality. Since 75% of Indians are illiterate, it is hard to lead them out of acceptance of the status quo.

I bring up this subject probably because all four of us have just come through periods of ill health, thanks to contaminated water or food, we don't know which. I have had a severe intestinal illness for over three weeks, and Heather is suffering from what the doctor claims is an enlarged liver, the result of vitamin D deficiency. There is a milk famine now in Lucknow, and what milk one does get is adulterated and has to be boiled. My ration is 7/8 of a glass a day. I put chocolate in it and bolt it down. It tastes like terrible milk of magnesia. They say no one can get pure milk anywhere in Lucknow. Sugar is also rationed. We have had nothing but cube sugar since we've been here.

On the brighter side, though, we have gotten Rudd into saris, and she looks lovely in them. Mrs. Indira Gandhi-Kenvin, I call her, although she finds them hot and has the constant feeling of being about to come apart. . . .

Two odd facts about our household: Did you know that we have no bathtubs? A shower sprays out onto the bathroom floor. The children have to sit in large metal pails to take their baths, great fun for them. The second oddity is that all our windows have steel bars on them, as in a jail. I couldn't figure out why until one day a mother monkey and her baby jumped into our yard and began hopping all over our various roofs and banging against the window bars.

Our three servants have now mushroomed into five at this writing. We now have an *ayah* (maid-governess), who makes the beds and horses around with Brooke and Heather, and the *mali* (gardener) has been supplying us with fresh flowers daily and has been added to our payroll.

Indians are very frank in asking you what you make and how much anything costs. One asked me the other day what my salary was in the states, so I gave him my annual average. Without batting an eye, he asked, "A month?" Several have inquired if I brought over my car with me. Even before I arrived, my landlords sent me an airmail letter requesting that I also bring a stove with me. Images of America!

Of course, many of the Indians with whom I work at the college are very fine people—keen, delightful, with good senses of humor. Some have sharp, analytical minds and are highly critical of their own country. Still, some very funny exchanges occur when cultures clash, such as the following:
This is a common scenario between me and my banker. First of all, purge the image of the American banker and his bank—that marble halled, Beethoven's *Fifth*-like pomposity. Imagine, instead, a den of thieves, somewhere in a burning desert, housed in an old, crumbling hacienda, paint peeling, dingy walls, one naked lightbulb overhead. There is a plain, wooden table, behind which a gang of thugs sits. The customers enter and leave, dressed in what appear to be their pajamas, clutching in their paws grimy, rupee bills. You might think you've made a mistake, but no, this is the place you're looking for—the bank.

My particular banker in Lucknow is a tall man with soft, patrician features, who smiles a lot, chews pan, offers it to me politely, although I always refuse it. (Don't ask me what pan is: It comes rolled up in a little leaf, that's all I know.) He invites me into his office, and our set routine goes something like this:

BANKER: Dr. Kenwin is it? Or Dr. Kenvin?
KENVIN: Kenvin.
BANKER: With a "v?"
KENVIN: Yes.
BANKER: Kenwin?
KENVIN: No.
BANKER: Kenwin? With a "v?" Have I got it now?
KENVIN: Yes, now you've got it.
BANKER: (smiling) "V." Kenwin.
KENVIN: (smiling with pain) Yes.
BANKER: So you teach at the I.T?
KENVIN: Yes.
BANKER: What do you teach?
KENVIN: I teach English. I teach English literature.

BANKER: You teach English?

KENVIN: Yes.

BANKER: You teach English literature?

KENVIN: Yes.

BANKER: I, too, would have liked to teach English literature, but fate would have me here. (looking around)

KENVIN: (looking around also) Oh.

BANKER: (smile of deep understanding) It is true. (Pause) Do you also teach American literature?

KENVIN: No.

BANKER: No?

KENVIN: No. I teach English literature.

BANKER: You teach English literature, but you don't teach American literature?

KENVIN: That is correct.

BANKER: That is too bad. I am very fond of your American writers.

KENVIN: (warming up) Oh? What writers do you especially like?

BANKER: (thinking) O. Henry. I am very fond of him. Do you know him?

KENVIN: (disappointed) Yes.

BANKER: He is quite good. Pearl Buck? She is quite good, too.

KENVIN: Uh-huh.

BANKER: Also James Michener. I am reading *Sayonara*.

KENVIN: Oh.

BANKER: You have been to Japan?

KENVIN: Yes.

BANKER: Is it a gay country?

KENVIN: (brief pause) Ye-e-s-s.

BANKER: Is it the gayest country you've been to?

KENVIN: I guess so.

BANKER: What?

KENVIN: (speaking up). Yes. It is quite gay. Bangkok is gay, also.

BANKER:  Bangkok is gay, also. (pause) I believe Michener
               also wrote a book called *Hawaii*.
KENVIN:  I believe so.
BANKER:  You have been to Hawaii?
KENVIN:  Yes, I have been to Hawaii.
BANKER:  And do you know what the name of Hawaii, your
               newest state, means?
KENVIN:  No.
BANKER:  It means "airy."
KENVIN:  What?
BANKER:  Airy.
KENVIN:  Airy?
BANKER:  Yes. I read this in *The Reader's Digest*. It is quite
               good, *The Reader's Digest*. Do you know it?

And so this strange effort at communication goes every time I go to the bank to cash a check. One has to devote an entire morning to the whole procedure. It is not one simple, boring exercise in patience, as it is in an American bank. Here, one signs many odd pieces of paper and is reviewed by many people before one gets any money.

    The first time I cashed a check, it was for 3000 rupees. The teller asked me in what denominations I wanted the rupees, and I blandly requested ones, fives, and tens. He seemed surprised, but I stuck to what I had said, remembering that perhaps it was better to save face, then to admit to a mistake. With that, the teller starts the flow of reams of bills in my direction. For about three minutes, they came flying through the window, enough to fill a small satchel. I was equipped with nothing but a little envelope and didn't know what to do. So I lined up the bills on the counter in several enormous piles and began counting them, as I might have done back home. I thought to myself, "Cash a check, and the pot starts boiling. Stop, pot, stop."

    By this time, a crowd has been collecting behind me, forming a little semicircle, watching curiously. Apparently they had never seen an American break the bank before.

Slightly embarrassed now, but determined to act cool, I stopped counting after 250 rupees, pretending that everything looked just fine and dandy, and then I began stashing away the bills in whatever pockets I had available in my pants and shirt. When there were no more pockets, I scooped open the front tail of my shirt, as I sometimes do on the beach when gathering shells, and shoveled the rest of the bills in there.

Walking in a concave, stiff manner, for fear of spilling bills, I emerged into the sunlight, fearful now that I'd be set upon by a whole cordon of pickpockets. I tried to act as nonchalant as possible and hailed a rickshaw. The driver looked startled, as though had I just robbed the bank, but I got in with great dignity, clutching at my cache, and rode away, leaving astonished bystanders behind me. Now, Rudd has equipped me with one of those reddish accordion folders that says "Speedwriting" on the side, and I use this folder exclusively for bank purposes. . . .

We are supposed to go to New Delhi for the big Fulbright meeting from September 5th to September 17th. After that, in October, we had thought to go to Kashmir for the Dasehra holidays (October 1-10), but, what with our health problems, the expense, and the border fighting up there, I don't know if we will make it. All our Indian friends here complain that the Kashmiris are personally so dirty. Should we wish anything further on ourselves?

In the meantime, the social whirl continues here in Lucknow. The invitations pour in. Let's see: "The Lucknow Y.W.C.A. cordially invites you to a Members-Get-Together." Well, that sounds like fun, doesn't it? . . .

Love from us all,

Roger

Lucknow, India
August 27, 1965

Dear Friends,

It is one thing to be a damn fool in one's own country; it is quite another to be one in a distant land. Consider the following, for example. I had written to my father-in-law, asking him to send me his hat size so that I could buy him a *topee* (pith helmet) with which he could Rudyard Kipling it on his farm in New Hampshire. He responded with a 7 3/8." Armed with this information, off I go to the Aminabad to a shop resplendent with *topees*, shooting sticks, canes, and umbrellas, but, unknown to me, a mathematical metaphasis, or power failure, has taken place inside my brain, so that the following exchange takes place:

KENVIN:  Good morning. I want one of those pith helmets.
          Those over there.
MERCHANT: (indicating *topees*) These?
KENVIN: That's right.
MERCHANT:  Size?
KENVIN: 4 3/8."
MERCHANT:  (eyes widening) Hunh?
KENVIN:  Size 4 3/8."
MERCHANT:  No.

KENVIN:  What do you mean, "No?"

MERCHANT:  Too small. No have size like that.

KENVIN:  Of course you do.  That's a standard size. Just look in that batch over there.

MERCHANT:  (handing out a *topee*) This smallest I got.

KENVIN:  (looking at it) But that's size 6. That's far too big.

MERCHANT:  (incredulous) Too big?

KENVIN:  Yes. That would never fit my father-in-law. He'd drown in it.

MERCHANT:  Smallest size there is. Don't have 4 3/8."

KENVIN:  Well, you must have. Or perhaps you don't use the same measurements that we use in England and America. Are you on some sort of different standard here in India?

MERCHANT:  No. Is same.

KENVIN:  Well, look here, I'll show you this helmet is too big. Here, let me put it on. (tries it on, finds it's too small) What the . . ! Oh, . . . 7 3/8."

MERCHANT:  (smiling) Yes, sahib.

KENVIN:  7 3/8." Of course. That's my father-in-law's size.

Or should I have saved face by telling him that my father-in-law really was a pygmy actively engaged in the head-shrinking business?

If you'd like to transform yourself into an Indian for a moment, first shake your head "no."  You have just said "yes." Indians bob their heads from side to side to indicate "yes." Try this on some unsuspecting friend and, in a minute or two, watch the reaction. Whenever you want to agree with your friend, bob your head "no" and say "yes." Then, the second thing you must do in conversation is mutter "*ah-cha*" every few minutes. This means "You don't say?" or "Is that so?" I can carry on whole conversations in Hindi just by bobbing my head "no" and saying "*ah-cha*." It's a good word. It rhymes with "hotcha." If you want to express surprise, accent the second part of the word, like this, "*ah-CHA?*"

If you wish to be a Hindu for a moment, the next time you meet someone, clap your hands together in front of your chest, as though in prayer, and say *"namaste"* (Nah-mah-stay). If you prefer to be a Muslim, give a sloppy salute with your right hand touching your brow and say *"salaam"* (sah-LAHM). Want to know how to pronounce the name of your country Indian style? It is not the United States. Instead, it is Ah-mer-REEK-ah. I like the sound of it. "Yes, I live in Ah-mer-REEK-ah." Nice cadence to it. Sounds Italian, doesn't it? "Io sono Americano from Ah-mer-REEK-ah."

One of you has asked if I've seen any Gunga Dins or cashiered English army officers. The answer is yes. Lucknow is, after all, Rudyard Kipling's old stomping ground. We even have authentic peons (That's what they are called), message carriers, dressed in what appear to be leftover World War I khakis, several sizes too large, many of them sporting walrus-like handlebar mustaches.

We are very nineteenth century here. In fact, Rudd and I determined that our actual time here (as opposed to calendar time) is 1890. This doesn't bother us particularly because, sometimes out in King George, Virginia, we had the feeling that the actual time was 1865. (We were all engaged in Reconstruction of one sort or the other, as I remember.) When we visited Yugoslavia in 1955, we were certain that it was 1912. And Vienna has always seemed to me to be 1922. So, taken all in all, 1890 is not too bad. We've just gotten through the gaslight stage, motor cars are about to come in, and, any day now, we have the feeling the Empire may start its decline. But God save her majesty anyway, and, thank heaven all our Anglo-Saxon values haven't quite perished yet!

I'm wrong. We're not quite in the motor car stage yet in Lucknow. Only the very rich have them—Indian-made cars called "Ambassadors," which they drive on the left hand side, honking their horns angrily as they go. Our principal means of transportation is still the rickshaw. Lucknow has 10,000 of them, and, interestingly enough, 30 of the drivers have B.A.

degrees and 5 of them have M.A.'s. The rickshaws are decorated with shiny tin, etched in unusual designs, and the hood, interior, and cloth pieces of the rickshaw feature bright colors and interesting patterns. They are quite striking looking. We also have a lot of tongas here—horse-drawn carts—with the horses sometimes decorated, and always with ringing sleigh bells and a cart full of people. The bells give out a nice sound in the streets. The other day, I saw a proud-looking camel gliding down the street, and our first day in Lucknow an elephant lumbered by right at the corner by Isabella Thoburn College.

I especially enjoy riding in a rickshaw at dusk. Lucknow fills up with thousands of people then because it is cooler and shopping is possible. Typically, stores open at 10:00 a.m., close because of the heat from 1:00 p.m. to 4:30 p.m. when the stores re-open until 9:00 p.m. As twilight falls, the sunset is very beautiful over the Gomati River, which now takes on a jade-like color. One sees Moghul-style buildings with their onion-shaped domes etched in black silhouette against the amber sky, little lights beginning to flicker on in the distance, a boat or two drifting down the river. All the unpleasantness of the day begins to disappear, so that one can give oneself over completely to night sounds—high-pitched voices intoning strange nasal tunes, the scratching of matches at little fires in charcoal burners along the side of the road, the staccato commands of goatherders driving their flocks home. Everything is close by you at night as you drive home from town in a rickshaw. You can just hear them—even the fortune-tellers prophesying to the hushed, listening, invisible people around them.

At night, this isolated, insulated quality is a pleasant feeling. So close to people, yet protected from them. One of the saddest lessons I had to learn about India is that you cannot give yourself over completely to this country as you can, for instance, to Italy or England. There is just too much raw disease, poverty, and filth. You will be hurt if you try to do it. Part of you must hold back. Cynthia Bowles, daughter of

U.S. Ambassador Chester Bowles, in her book *At Home in India* tells how she tried to lose herself to India through her nursing work, but even she contracted trachoma. Isn't this what the British always did in India—held themselves aloof? This is a distasteful idea, perhaps, following Colonel Blimp's prescription, but it does make sense.

India is so complex that there are many circles here, many worlds that people draw around themselves. Because of my position at this Methodist missionary school and because of my Christian landlords, the world I mostly exist in here is the Indian Christian world. This, again, is a special world, a minority world here. The Indian Christians hold themselves aloof from the Hindus and Muslims. My landlord, for instance, wrote to me before we came that he preferred Christians to stay in his house.

One of the salient characteristics of the Indian Christians we know is their Americanophilia (Does this word exist?). Many of them have been educated partly in the United States, or traveled there, or model themselves on Americans, or prize U.S. products, such as toasters, refrigerators, automobiles, or even subscribe to publications like *Ladies Home Journal.* They differ from us mostly in their over-developed sense of what constitutes Christian worship. At the college, for instance, in addition to daily chapel, daily vespers, a sung grace before meals, hymns and scripture readings at faculty meetings, invocations are also offered even before small committee meetings. At the last meeting of the Ideals Committee, it went something like this: "Oh, God, our Father, who so wisely watches over us, help us on the Ideals Committee, who have entrusted into our hands so much responsibility for the ideals of these young students, to perform our duties rightly and to instil in their hearts a proper sense of thy guiding spirit."

Not that there's anything wrong with this, but it appeals to my sense of comic incongruity to notice the humble Indian Christian who offered this prayer suddenly transformed into an enraged Saracen on the loose once the actual work of the Committee was before us. Miss Jonathan is a type of Indian woman I've met frequently here—the born bull-dozers, I call them.

Miss Jonathan was one of the guests at a dinner party given recently by our landlord and his wife. They invited about sixteen Indian Methodists and very kindly included Rudd and me (quite rightly, I think, since I was baptized and confirmed in the Methodist-Episcopal Church). The whole evening was rather elaborately planned. Tables, chairs, even oriental rugs (one a Bokhara) were brought out from the house by the servants and re-arranged on the lawn. Then floor lamps were brought out, plugged in, as well as a battery of electric fans.

The guests assembled around 8:00 p.m. and we had about forty-five minutes of talk and lemonade. Finally, the hostess annnounced that dinner was ready and would we all please stand and sing the doxology. There we were on the front lawn, in an outdoor living room, as though it were a Hollywood movie set, singing "Praise God from whom all blessings flow" in loud, strong voices.

After that, we repaired to the table for food, one side of which featured Indian food and the other western food (chicken, which is very expensive over here). I wish you could have seen the Indian guests bypass the Indian food and dive into the chicken! Such finger-licking and chomping of jaws from such good Christians! I took Indian food, hot and spicy, ideal for me, and both Rudd and I finally tried pan, offered to us at the end of the meal. Pan is made from betel leaves filled with nuts, lime, spices, and sometimes tobacco. It's supposed to be a digestive. It stains the teeth red. Neither of us liked it. Rahat, our cook, was part of the *corps des servants* that night, and he was greatly amused watching Milord and Lady Disdain chewing pan.

In conversations that night with my Indian friends, I listened to stories of daughters in Baltimore, sons and grandsons in Brooklyn and Forest Hills, reminiscences of old days at Northwestern and Union Theological Seminary, life in

Kansas in 1948, old classmates now in Portland, Oregon—all of it quite familiar to an American ear. One of the sad things for many Indian parents is that sons and daughters, once they get out of India, never return to it. Everyone well understands why, but they don't like to discuss this painful subject, and some of them feel the younger generation is a little traitorous to India.

Fortunately, Rudd and I have been able to break through the Christian mold occasionally. We have Hindu friends next door, the Barghavas, high caste Brahmins from Kashmir. She's a Barghava. He's a Barghava. (Roosevelts marrying Roosevelts?) Then we also have Muslim friends in Lucknow. Some of you know our good friend, Mustafa Kamil, now at Harvard University. His nieces and nephew called on us, and we have returned their visit several times. We have seen something outside our own little I.T. circle. But the Christians are reluctant to let us escape. They hold fast to us, even though we've told them we're Unitarians, in the hope this might ward them off. (I always remember the Episcopal minister in King George who said to me, "To what have you fallen?" "To Unitarianism," I replied. "My God," he said, "You have fallen!"

Since I'm talking about our little world of Christianity here in Lucknow, another topic suggests itself. A perpetual annoyance to me is missionaries. They dart into one's life with such alacrity, popping out from behind rickshaws, store counters, and stamp windows, confronting one with their vigorous presences. Every fifth American in India seems to be a missionary. Many of them exude an offensive inner-strength superiority and give one the impression that Jesus Christ is their next door neighbor back home in Wheaton, Illinois. They say things like "Before I came to Christ" and "Well, we do want to bring them to God, don't we?" or "Before I let Christ into my life . . ." (as though Christ were a cat one let out the night before). They make it seem that coming to God is a kind of palship—Buddies in Christ, or something.

But English missionaries are the ones I seem to attract. They are stringier than Americans, all elbows, index fingers, and bony forearms. They don't really speak to one; they jaw-bone their way into one's face, working that lower jaw like Margaret Rutherford or Joyce Grenfell, dropping their voices in cascading private asides, delivered so *sotto voce* that one has to bend an ear to hear them.

One such missionary attacked all four of us in Kwality (so help me!), the local tea-room, the other day. She detached herself from the table—a long, lean hank of hair with steel spectacles and a yellow pigskin satchel of a face, the lower jaw thrust forward with that fixed "Abide with Me" smile on it. She aimed first at Rudd:

"Oh, hello there. Lovely to see you. I thought I recognized you. Saw you at the "Y" the other evening, didn't I? Yes. Lovely party, wasn't it? Yes. Great fun. (To me, accusingly) So soddy you weren't there, Doctor Kenvin. Yes, of course you were. Of course you were—sick. Oh, yes, I guite understand. Quite."

Then, at the Dinner party the other night, another one leaped (leapt for Britishers) into my presence:

"Oh, so there you are, Doctor Kenvin. Caught up with you at lahst, didn't I? (Here a merry peal of laughter) We missed you the other evening at the "Y." Yes, of course you were. Of course you were. I do understand. Yes, truly. Did you get the message I sent you by way of Joan? Oh, good. Good. You did try it, didn't you? Just ten drops of essential oil in water. Yes, it is nahsty-tasting stuff, isn't it? But it does do the trick, doesn't it? What? Your doctor was veddy angry? Ray-ally? Ray-ally? 'Symptomatic, not curative?' Oh, my. Well, look here. Don't tell him when you use it, d'ye hear? Oh, my, yes. We use it all the time. Just heaps and heaps of times. I give it to all the Peace Corps people. They pop right back to work the veddy next day. Lovely seeing you. Lovely. We will see you a-gain, won't we? Oh, goo-oo-d. Yes, great fun. Goo'bye then."

The best thing to be said about these English missionaries is that they are eaten with regularity by tribesmen in Ecuador and New Guinea.

Newsflashes from the Lucknow newspapers, *The Pioneer* and *The National Herald*:

### *Headline*: "BOOKS, BABY FOOD, CONTRACEPTIVES EXEMPT FROM IMPORT DUTY"

*News item*: "Bristol, England, August 22—a 24-year old Indian, Jaspal Singh, escaped from a blazing house by climbing down his turban.

Jaspal and two other Indians were asleep upstairs when fire broke out in the basement on Friday. One leapt to a garage roof, spraining an ankle. Another scrambled down a wall.

But Jaspal quickly unwound his turban, tied it to a bed, and climbed down it from the window."

*From an ad*: "IPCO DENTAL CREAMY SNUFF is the first toothpaste of the world manufactured from tobacco. Regular use of this IPCO paste not only cleans the mouth but also prevents the dental troubles such as Toothache, swelling and decay of Gums, Bleeding from Gums. It definitely strengthens weak and spany Gums, stops bad breath, destroys the harmful bacteria and prevents Pyrrhea and stimulates the mind and gives a spur to the action."

### *Headline*: "DACOITS ACTIVE AGAIN: 2 SHOT"

### *Headline*: "NOTORIOUS DACOITS ARRESTED"

*News item*: "August 23—A batch of 11 naked women yesterday started ploughing their fields offering prayers to God and singing kirtan "Hare Ram, Barso Bhagwan" in the village of Kisen Niwada.

"A similar report has been received from two villages, Dhanni Niwada and Uchhaan, in which young girls and ladies offered prayers to the Rain God singing devotional songs.

"Fourteen earthen chulahs were broken with the pledge that they would not cook food till it rained.

"Recourse to this extreme step has been felt necessary to avert a serious drought which is threatening to engulf, very soon, the entire district of Kanpur, in some parts of which near drought conditions are already obtaining."

Who says we lead a dull life here? Oh, no! Rudd just handed me a note which reads, "Dear Dr. and Mrs. Kenwin (Note that ubiquitous "w") The Lucknow Y.W.C.A. Membership Committee would like to entertain you very informally on Saturday, August 28th . . ." Here we go again. Back to the missionary circuit! *Ah-cha*.!

Love to all,

Roger

198 Faizabad Road
Lucknow, U.P., India
September 20, 1965

Dear Friends,

We returned to Lucknow this morning from New Delhi where we have been since September 4th. We went ostensibly for the big Fulbright orientation program, but found ourselves, instead, plunged into the middle of the present emergency between India and Pakistan. Now, tonight, there is rumbling on the Sikkim-Tibet border, and we will probably know by tomorrow if China intends to come in on Pakistan's side. If so, I should imagine that all Americans would be evacuated from India in short order.

Our conference in New Delhi began in routine fashion. We were housed at the India International Centre, about one-hundred and thirty of us, men, women, and children, Fulbright professors and students, stationed in all parts of India. Three of them were not to return to their posts in the Punjab and are now officially refugees living at the American Embassy in New Delhi, along with other American refugees from Rajasthan and Kashmir.

U.S.E.F.I. had lined up about thirty important people from all walks of life in India to speak to us. One of the first was Chester Bowles, U.S. Ambassador to India, who was to speak to us on the morning of Tuesday, September 7th, and then, that evening, he and Mrs. Bowles were throwing a cocktail party for us at his residence. On September 5th India had crossed the cease-fire line in Kashmir, on the 6th it had invaded Pakistan, and, on the morning of the 7th, General Ayhub Khan was announcing that Pakistan was at war with India.

We crowded into the meeting that morning to hear Bowles speak. He seemed outwardly calm, told us not to worry, and to sleep easily. All that day bulletins came pouring in to Delhi from the front in Kashmir. Suddenly, a blackout for that night was called, and a curfew began at 7:00 p.m. The Bowles' reception was hastily called off, and we all went to dinner that night at the Centre by flashlight. Our food from the Bowles' reception went instead to the American refugees now arriving from Kashmir and the Punjab.

In the middle of the night, I was awakened by the scream of sirens over Delhi. Air raid. I went up on the roof, scanning the skies with other watchers, but could see nothing. Back to try to get some more sleep. In the early hours, another siren. Still, I could see nothing. The papers the next day told of aircraft approaching Delhi and of a new front being opened in the Punjab, of air raids on Jodphur and Jaipur, and, worst of all, in the east, of an air raid on an air field near Calcutta.

For three nights, none of us had much sleep. On the fourth night we had one raid shortly after midnight, for which I got up, but, then at 4:45 a.m., the sirens went off again. I rolled over, exhausted, and told Rudd I wouldn't get up for this one. But now we heard the poom-poom of anti-aircraft guns. Suddenly, the telephone rang beside my bed. A voice said, "Bring your family downstairs immediately. There is danger." We gathered up Brooke and Heather from our third storey room down to the ground floor, where we lined up deep in one corridor with other members of our group, dazed, sleepy, uncertain. That night a Pakistani plane, one out of four, was shot down as it attempted to approach Delhi.

It readily became apparent to me that the modern glass and concrete India International Centre was no place to be in an air raid. One entire wall of every bedroom is all glass. There is no basement, and the Centre is located less than a mile away from the air base where Indian Air Force planes are housed.

At night we would gather in groups in the lounge to listen to news broadcasts in English on the radio. We would first hear Radio Pakistan, then Radio Peking, then Radio India. Pakistan and India would contradict each other almost completely. Radio Peking harped on what it called "Indian aggression backed by U.S. imperialism." Indian newscasts gave us the impression that India was pushing back the Pakistanis and defeating them soundly. Still, it was difficult to sift out the truth. All of us Americans, used to instant communication via television, felt as though we were trapped in a frustrating news vacuum.

Poor little Heather, like some of the other young children, was terribly frightened by the sudden presence of war, and cried and trembled for the first three or four nights. She would run in great fear the minute she heard a siren, or thought she heard a siren, even if it were only a car horn. Every night she would ask, "Are we going to be killed tonight?" The idea of men flying over in airplanes dropping bombs on other people terrified her. We kept her in little pools of light in the room as much as we could, until, slowly, she got over her fear.

We were not allowed on the streets of Delhi after 7:00 p.m. During the day we went about our business quite normally, but at night everything was dark and an ominous stillness hung over the city. Those three nights that I spent on the roof were under a sky illuminated by a bomber's moon. I often thought back to World War II. I guess I expected to see wave upon wave of airplanes zooming in on Delhi in one great blitzkrieg.

(The air raid siren just sounded here in Lucknow. Lights all turned off for a few minutes. Now we have draped the windows and closed the doors, so I am back at the typewriter. Rahat told us that this was the second one; last night was the first—an unidentified aircraft circled around Lucknow. There is an army cantonment at the other end of town.)

Anyway, to get back to the pattern of bombing, it soon became evident that the Pakistanis were bombing in little groups of three and four planes, and that the mass attack I feared would not materialize. It was crushing to read that all the Pakistani equipment, planes, and tanks, were American made. Initially, the Indians were highly indignant about this. I had taxi cab drivers and shopkeepers alike ask me sharply what I thought about American military aid to Pakistan being used on India.

The first few days in Delhi the air was electric with war fever. There was, at first, almost jubilation, a sense of joy on everybody's part. One of our speakers explained to us that the Pakistanis had pushed India around long enough, that India was tired of being called soft and weak, of hearing the jibes that one Pakistani could lick five Indians. So the mood was a joyous one, and then it soon gave way to an inordinate fear of saboteurs. Suddenly everyone was being suspected of operating as a Pakistani spy. The Pakistanis had, by this time, been dropping paratroops wearing Indian uniforms into Indian territory, particularly in the Punjab, and one Pakistani plane bearing Indian Air Force insignia was shot down.

The panic spread. A member of our group, Douglas Davis, was surrounded by a group of people who thought he was a Pakistani agent because he was photographing the action from a bridge. He was saved by the intervention of Judy Gotsch, who, luckily, had her passport with her. Davis could not produce his when the police asked him to.

Another time, I happened to be in the heart of Delhi, on the Janpath near Connaught Circus, when, suddenly, I saw a great crowd collecting. My taxi driver pulled up short and jumped out to see what it was. He and another man came running back to the cab in great excitement to tell me, "Pakistani spies. One with diagrams and photographs of bridges. Other man working as *mali* in Parliament gardens." Then the police burst through the thirsting crowd, leading two tired-looking men tied together at their wrists. The enormous crowd followed with satisfied smiles on their faces. I got out of there quickly.

Wherever one went in Delhi, the war fever reached. It seemed a curiously unifying force in a country that needed something to unite it. Now, Indians of all kinds could at last stand together against a common enemy. I remember, especially, at our conference, the brilliant, moody Nath Pai, M.P. of the Praja Socialist Party, looking like an angry Yul Brynner, telling all of us emotionally that India would not desist until Pakistan retreated completely from Kashmir.

Motivated now, Indians wanted to help in the war effort. Some government official hit on the idea that they all dig trenches, so, like a gross caricature of a W.P.A. project, trenches were dug all over Delhi. You have never seen anything like it. In the most unlikely places trenches appeared, zig-zagging their way across the corners of parks or gardens. Inspecting the Moghul ruins of Humayan's tomb in a remote corner of Delhi, I was astonished to find a freshly-dug trench, waiting, no doubt, for any armed Moghul ghost that happened to be caught in an air raid. Other Indians occupied themselves by pasting paper all over windows. (You can imagine the immensity of the task in a place like the India International Centre. They were still working on it as we left.) And signs mushroomed all over town, reading "HOARDING IS UNPATRIOTIC" and "DON'T WASTE PETROL."

Troops are on the move all over northern India. Last night we took the sleeper from Delhi to Lucknow, passing through the eerie darkness of the railroad station on the way to our sleeping car. Everywhere there were clumps of Indian soldiers sitting patiently in the dark on their piled up gear, waiting for their trains. Our train was full of Indian troops going to the eastern front. Signs had quickly been plastered up all over the station, "FREE CANTEEN FOR INDIAN TROOPS."

We were lucky to have our Fulbright program going
on because almost every speaker touched on the present
"emergency," which is the word we are officially using at the
moment in India. The prevailing position taken by most
Indians is as follows: Kashmir belongs to India legally because,
at the time of partition back in 1947, it was given to the
Maharajah in each state contiguous to India and Pakistan to
decide what country his state would join. The Maharajah of
Kashmir hemmed and hawed, but, when Pakistan began
agitating, decided to throw his lot in with India. So, legally,
Kashmir belongs to India, and India is no more obligated to
hold a plebescite there than, say, the United States is in Texas.

The Indians further explain that Ayub Khan wants to
make Pakistan a theocracy with an official Muslim religion.
The majority of people in Kashmir are Muslims, and this is
why Ayub Khan wants to annex it, which he thinks he could
do if the Kashmiris were allowed a vote on the issue. India
explains that it is a democracy, not a theocracy, and that India
has sixty million Muslims who live at peace with Hindus,
Christians, Jains, Sikhs, etc. Here the matter rests. India has
had to put up with the incursions and internal agitation from
Pakistan since 1947. In addition, it had China at its borders in
1962 and now again in 1965.

I don't know what will happen as a result of this. It
seems to me that both Pakistan and India are weak militarily
and cannot afford a full-scale war. If reports are true, then
Pakistan has already been thoroughly drubbed by the Indians.
But the Indian temper is running high. They have been stung
and are not going to give up without getting exactly what they
want, which is Kashmir intact and Pakistan out of it. What
China will do, however, is anybody's guess.

Americans have been evacuated from Pakistan to
Teheran and Manila, at Pakistan's request. India has not asked
us to leave, and the American Embassy is adopting a wait-and-
see attitude. We have all gone back to our posts now, except
those few I mentioned who cannot return to the Punjab.

One of the highlights of the conference was a visit to the presidential palace, Rashtrapati Bhavan, to meet President Radhakrishnan of India. Photographs were taken there, and I am sending home to our families copies of the ones showing Rudd and me shaking hands with the President. We also went to visit Parliament at the height of the crisis, when U Thant was in Delhi. We visited both the Lok Sabha (Lower House) and the Raja Sabha (Upper House). Prime Minister Shastri was in his seat in the Lok Sabha at the time we were there. The Congress Party, which is the ruling party, occupies over half the seats, and the other parties are ranged out in a semi-circle, the Communists occupying the far right as you look at the house. We had the odd experience of hearing a Communist in the Raja Sabha argue in favor of fewer restrictions on business in India. He said a visit to Hong Kong had changed his mind.

Another highlight of our program was a visit to villages under the community development plan. Rudd went on one trip, and I on another. Rudd's bus went into the Punjab and had to pass through a barbed wire barricade complete with armed soldiers. She said that the people in her village turned out with a brass band that accompanied all the Americans as they walked through the streets looking at tractors, seeing how material is block-printed, how the potter works, and how the new plough, of which the people were very proud, works.

My bus went to a village in Uttar Pradesh near the Punjab border. You cannot imagine how warm the reception was that we received. The whole village (2,800 people) turned out to meet us and gave many of us garlands of flowers. We toured the village, seeing their prize cattle, visiting the women's club (which boasts two sewing machines), the home of the president of the farm cooperative, and then to a school where a group of girls loudly sang a song about Indian-American friendship and kept on singing until some official shut them up. Then to the boys' section, where we passed through an honor guard of boy scouts, who held up long bamboo poles for us to pass under. More loud songs here.

More speeches. Hundreds of curious faces staring at us. Good people, all of them, many women with veils on their faces, hanging back a little shyly, some of them peering down at us from rooftop refuges. Of course the people had prepared a feast for us—coca-cola, melons, bananas, and nuts. I was happy to visit this village. This showed a touch of the hopeful India. If they can do this, they can succeed. But the problems are gigantic, and now are complicated by the drain of war.

One of the Fulbright students, Reid Gilbert, is studying at the National School of Drama in New Delhi. I went over and visited the school on two separate occasions. The students were pleased to see an alumnus of the Yale School of Drama, and we had long discussions, which were refreshing to me, and I hope to them. Brecht and Strindberg are their passions at the moment. Their school is new, government-sponsored, the first of its kind in India. It is housed in a smart, modern building, and I was very impressed with its director, E. Alkazi, a dynamic, progressive man of the theatre and the forty students of the school. I also attended a class in mime which Reid is teaching, and that, again, was interesting to see. The students are talented and hard-working. They (the students) took Reid and me, and another friend of ours, Ralph Sisson, to a Rajasthani puppet troupe in Delhi which makes its own puppets out of wood, and performs. We arranged for a performance back at the India International Centre for the children, and it was a fascinating show, rather primitive, with a woman in a bright yellow sari beating a drum and chanting the whole time. I bought some puppets from this workshop and had two puppets sent to Al Klein at Mary Washington College. I also had two Ramayana masks sent to Al, one of Hanumon, the monkey god, and the other of Sita.

During the conference, people spoke to us on economics, politics, family planning, music, dance, art, and literature. The man on literature was Dr. Prabhakar Machwe, who is a Special Officer (Hindi) in the Union Public Service Commission. For those of you, like M. J. Woodward, interested in Indian literature, Dr. Machwe discussed, first of all, the Indian writers who write in English. Obviously, he disapproved of any Indian's writing in English.

About R. K. Narayan, he said that he was clever, facile, but lacked depth. He said he thought *The Guide* was good, but he kept using the Dostoyevskian and Tolstoyan canon and kept wishing Narayan would strike deeper metaphysical notes. He also said that Narayan's books do not translate into Hindi or Tamil at all. Dr. Machwe made much of this business of translation. For him, a book, to be good, has to be able to be translated into all languages.

The major part of Dr. Machwe's attention was given to those Indian writers who do write in Hindi, Tamil, or Bengali, most of whom were totally unknown to us. Bengali literature, apparently, is the richest, from his point of view. Machwe seemed to want a strongly realistic or naturalistic novel with a universal religious or philosophical theme. He pointed out that the Rabindranath Tagore, or diaphanous Tennysonian school had so nauseated the Indian literati that nowadays they were looking for something more basic, earthier in novels.

About Ved Mehta, Aubrey Menen, Santha Rama Rau, and others, Dr. Machwe had great scorn. Naurally, these were the writers all of us knew best, so we asked him about them. He said that, having deserted India and expatriated themselves, they were Indian writers no longer. He stated that most of them expressed a nostalgia in their writing which he supposed had a certain value, but "it is almost as bad as E. M. Forster, that outsider's way of looking at India." He said some of these writers stressed unduly the exotic in India. We couldn't shake him on this point. He simply ruled these writers out of serious consideration, rather unreasonably, we all thought.

I also enjoyed the lectures we had on Indian music. I have become very fond of this kind of music, although many Americans at the conference couldn't take it because of its lack of harmony. It is different, but I respond to the odd, twanging sounds instruments like the sitar and veena make, with their sympathetic overtones. I could listen to intricate ragas for hours, which is precisely what one has to do if one goes to an Indian concert.

Curiously enough, returning to Delhi this time was rather pleasant. Back in June, Delhi had been just a yellow and red blur in the howling, dusty heat of the hot, dry season. Now, everything is lush and green; things look much better. To us, from our big country-town, Lucknow, Delhi seemed, this time, as elegant as London or Paris. Or do you suppose that Rudd and I have simply lost all sense of perspective now that the intital cultural shock has passed?

At any rate, our stay during the daytime, at least, was enjoyable. Ambassador and Mrs. Bowles threw open their private swimming pool at the residence, Roosevelt House, to all of us. I took the children there several times for swimming. Then Rudd and I decided that, we would investigate the top restaurants of Delhi. We went to the brand-new Intercontinental Hotel, full of blonde American women wearing jade earrings . . . to the Imperial and the posh Ashoka, run by the government, the only five-star deluxe hotel in all India. Here, everything is finished, the swimming pool in order, the pastries superb, everything clicking. We decided that if we came back to Delhi in the future, we would stay here, since it costs about the same as our glass-and-concrete India International Centre, which we do not really like. We took the children to tea at both places. This was a satisfactory arrangement. They had a good time, and so did we.

The Fulbright conference was designed to bring all of us Americans together so that we could compare experiences. I found that many people had had the same problems I had. One seventeen-year old boy had nearly died of bacillary dysentery in the south of India. Others had had malarial problems. One family, in an isolated location, had had a cobra problem. But none of these experiences was more binding than the one we had shared together, of suddenly becoming aliens in a country at war. We made several good friends at the conference—the Paul Prices (He is a physicist with General Electric) who have a daughter named Heather, the same age as ours; the Ralph Sissons (He is studying linguistics here in Lucknow); our dear friend, Sarah Nooe, now in Madras (She is the original "African Queen," a bird watcher, non-smoker, with a glorious North Carolina mountain accent, to boot).

The day we left Delhi, the Chinese news was all the talk. Two taxi drivers that I had that day (both Sikhs) asked if I were quitting India. "No," I said. "I'm not leaving India. I'm not afraid of the Chinese. I'm just going back to Lucknow." This seemed to please them. I think many of the Indians feel a little left out in the cold right now. The United States has supplied tanks and airplanes to Pakistan. Harold Wilson is making equivocal statements in London, instead of coming to India's aid. Russia remains inscrutable. Indonesia is threatening on the east. China in the north. If ever a country deserves the backing of friends, it is India now.

Love to all,

Roger

Lucknow, U.P., India
October 1, 1965

Dear Friends,

Surely God does move in mysterious ways his wonders to perform! I have just made my debut in the pulpit. I led the worship service in the Isabella Thoburn Chapel this morning, complete with hymns, prayers, organ music, and a magical waving of my arms which commanded the congregation to rise or be seated at my wish. I did the whole thing myself, composed my own sermon, chose the hymns, chucked out the responsive reading as being too slavish, and wrote my own final benediction.

It was quite an occasion. You can imagine the preparation that went into it. First of all, there was the question of my costume. Would I appear in a cassock or not? (How I longed for a Bishop's mitre and cap.) Should I bless the congregation before or after? Should I hire a few acolytes to precede me down the aisle? Would my service be high church or low church?

Then there was the determining of my voice style. Should I use my Richard Burton Shakespearean voice that went over so well when I discussed *Richard II* and *Hamlet* with my students last year? Or should I aim for a modest, Jimmy Stewart approach—clean-cut, hesitant, the all-American stuttering boy? Perhaps, if I thundered from the pulpit, like Father Coughlin in the days of old . . . ? Or would I just be plain scared to death and use my natural, nervous, scared rabbit, strangulated voice?

The thought of myself in the pulpit gave rise to other speculations. What if I should succeed? Would I receive a message from Rome, perhaps offering me a small bishopric down in Kerala to begin with? Or would the National Council of Churches prefer my services, I being ostensibly a Protestant? But no, I held out for Rome. Suddenly, I had an intense desire for all that color, pageantry, and splendor. The question naturally occurred as to what name I should choose. I told Rudd I thought "Innocent" would be suitable, but she replied—a shade too sarcastically, I think—that "Urban" would be more appropriate. Anyway, I definitely decided it would have to be something with XXVI, or other similar glittering long Roman numeral after it.

Next, the subject matter of my sermon had to be considered. I felt that, in these difficult times, I should offer some comfort to the students. But who am I to offer anyone comfort? I would try to offer them some American truth. I chose, at Rudd's suggestion, as the heart of my sermon, Robert Frost's poem "Mending Wall." But my sermon soon began getting political. I found myself enamored of my image as another John F. Kennedy. My phrases began to ring out in New Frontier style. Sample:

"Or does uneasy lie the land that builds a wall around itself? I do not know; I have not been to China. I do not know; I have not been to Berlin. I do not know; I have not been to Pakistan. I have not seen those places for myself."

Since I now thought of myself as President Kennedy, I wanted, as one of my hymns, the Navy hymn, "Eternal Father," which, you remember, was played at Kennedy's funeral. Then I began to brood deeply once again over the loss of Kennedy and wanted to do a sermon on him instead. I checked with the calendar. There was no significant Kennedy date at hand. Out went "Eternal Father." Gone was the Kennedy image.

Now, I began to get quite militant. I thought, well, what the hell, let's have a couple of rousing choruses of "Onward, Christian Soldiers" or "The Battle Hymn of the Republic." Then we'll march right out of the chapel down to the Gunch and incite an anti-Pakistan riot in the streets. But reason dictated otherwise, of course, in its sensible way, and that revolutionary image vanished also.

I had other worries, also. Especially about any mention of the Holy Ghost, out of consideration to my newly-found Unitarianism. So there were to be no references to the Holy Ghost, and God and Christ were to be considered as two separate persons, or things, or forces, or what you will.

The one frill I insisted on was a brilliant fanfare to herald my arrival, something worthy of the Pope or Queen of England, preferably played upon a sextet of French horns. But, failing that, I chose a hymn, "God of our Fathers, Whose Almighty Hand," where each chorus is introduced by a little fanfare—"Dum duma-dum-dum-dum, ta tata-ta-ta-ta." It sounded quite grand on the organ. We sang all the choruses of this hymn, as we do of every hymn at I.T. College.

At the appointed hour, I delivered my sermon to a packed house. I had a microphone on my pulpit, and it carried my words nicely. I loved hearing the soothing sound of my own voice. I worked on shading and nuances. I aped Robert Frost's dry Yankee voice. I made bold literary leaps, from Robert Frost to John Donne, from Shakespeare to Ecclesaiastes. (I refrained from quoting Omar Khayyam. Everyone uses him in I.T. College sermons.) There were significant pauses in my speech. I fixed my eyes on students in various parts of the congregation, looking them straight in the eye. I bowed my head ever so professionally when I said, "Let us pray."

Apparently it went over quite well. Miss Qamber, who booked my performance, told me it was "most inspiring, beautifully appropriate." But I don't want you to think that this minor success has gone to my head. I am no cock-sure Billy Graham, bent on converting millions of Hindus in mass demonstrations. I am more a slightly quizzical, ironical, urbane Fulton J. Sheen, one who might do well in more intimate sesssions, such as on television programs. From another point of view, doesn't this prove that even an ordinary garden-variety kind of Protestant can succeed, as Norman Vincent Peale suggests, if only he has the Power of Positive Thinking and Believes in What He is Doing?

Frankly, I think Rudd is a little envious of my success. But you mustn't pay too much attention to her. She told me that she was once asked to deliver a sermon in the Vassar College Chapel, and so she did, taking as her text, "Why an Anthropomorphic View of God?" She had the temerity to demand of her congregation, "Why do you always refer to God as "he?" She was never asked to speak in that chapel again.

I, on the other hand, look to be asked back. I am working on a thundering Jeremiah voice now, which will be reinforced by El Greco's great portrait of him. There will be a loud noise heard throughout the land when I start rattling about the *Book of Revelations* over here.

In line with this, I have vowed never to malign innocent missionaries again, as I have so egregiously done in other letters. All this, I hereby abjure as Chaucer did his *Canterbury Tales* and Prospero his magic art. You may treat this as my official recantation. I have completely stricken from this letter my latest satirical lampoon against these dear, conscientious missionaries, as well as my mock alma mater for Isabella Thoburn College. Sample:

> "All hail to thee, Isabella,
> Never touched a drink or fella.
> But what the hella, Isabella,
> Salvation, to thee, was swella."

That was the old Roger—insensitive, Rabelaisian, jejune. The new man has now taken over. I have arrived at my Eliotean

"Ash Wednesday." No more these foolish diatribes against "the innocent, the lost, or the unsure"—a quote from my sermon. Do you like it?

Aside from my sermon, the other important news from us is that we were robbed (literally) last night. Somebody broke into our kitchen and stole two loaves of bread, a big can of cooking oil, a smaller container of fish oil, and one broken thermos bottle. (Is it just me, or is there something vaguely Biblical about this theft?) The thief broke a lock on the door to gain entry, and took a wicker chair and put it up near the back fence. He, or she, ransacked the kitchen, but ignored other, more valuable items, in favor of these few things.

Before I tell you about the investigation, let me review the lay of the land for you. Our house, like all those around, is entirely surrounded by a brick and sandstone wall, six—and in some places, seven—feet high. There is an iron gate in the front which is locked at night, and we have a night watchman who sleeps out in the front yard, a mali who sleeps there also, and three dachshunds to keep guard. Our apartment is on the ground floor, in the rear of this large house. A wide verandah winds its way around two sides of the house. Our kitchen is a detached summer kitchen, like Mary Washington's in Fredericksburg, and about as well equipped. Our bedroom window is the closest to our kitchen. We sleep under swooping mosquito nets in our beds and keep the ceiling fan on at night, which is why we heard no suspicious noise.

Rahat discovered the burglary this morning, and Mrs. Shukla immediately called the police. About eight policemen responded. We were all interrogated, whereupon the head policeman gave his diagnosis: It was an inside job, pulled off by somebody living close to us because he or she stole only items that could not be easily identified. (The loss of the thermos bottle had not yet been discovered.) The chair put up by the back wall leading into our neighbor's yard was a decoy. The dogs did not bark because they knew the perpetrator. The person was self-assured, went up on the verandah, right near our bedroom door, and boldly took one of the wicker chairs. Had I sat up in bed, I would have been able to see the culprit.

Mrs. Shukla, Rudd, and I found it hard to believe that it could have been one of our servants. Between us and the Shuklas, we have eleven servants, some of whom live in the house with us—including our cook, Rahat, his wife and three children; the mali, his wife and two children; Saina, our ayah; and the night watchman. The other servants, including Mrs. Shukla's cook, live out.

The police brought in the fingerprints experts, who began taking prints, and, then, men from the Central Intelligence Agency arrived with a police dog on a leash. They let the dog smell the lock and follow the scent. We all watched eagerly. Quite a spectacular performance. The dog took the scent from the lock, rushed out of our kitchen, went directly to the wicker chair by the fence, then behind the house, past our bathroom, to the courtyard behind Brooke and Heather's room, where the sweepers keep their brushes. Then, the dog came around the side once more, jumped up on the verandah, ignored the main entrance to our apartment, as well as our bedroom door, went around the corner, right through the Shuklas' main entrance into their living room, and began sniffing down low around the furniture, rugs, table legs. Next, he went into their dining room and repeated the performance. After that, the policeman brought him down along the verandah to where I stood with our main door open. The dog entered, sniffed around the furniture and rugs, sniffed in the bedroom under Brooke's bed, went into our bedroom, poked around under Rudd's bed, went to the place where we put up our laundry, and then left.

The inspector said to our astonished group: "You see, it is a common house servant."

Here, the investigation rests at the moment. The dog's behavior would lead one to suspect the sweepers. There are four of them, all Hindus, a father, mother, and two daughters.

But they sweep for about ten or twelve families around, and Rahat thinks they are of good character.

What do you think, those of you who read Agatha Christie? You have a wide choice. Could it be the dhobi, whose salary we just raised? He has a large family, and was overjoyed at his raise. He was late one day in coming this week. Could it be Saina, converted Christian, personal lady-in-waiting to our Queen, Mrs. Shukla? Mrs. Shukla swears by Saina, claims "there isn't anything she wouldn't do for you." Is it the mali, sullen, dark, inscrutable, out there among his roses in the garden? Could it be our fun-loving Rahat, whom we all adore? Or could it be the father of the sweeper team? Mrs. Shukla told Rudd he drinks, and you know what that can do to a person. Or could it be one of the sweeping daughters, who appear sometimes in rose-colored saris, with many bangles on their arms, and are the ones most intimately familiar with all the rooms here? Or, as I said to Rudd, could it be the German shepherd itself, a clever dog who has seized on this gimmick as a way of making his living? The police are still working on the case. We will let you know the outcome. In the meantime, I've asked Rahat for extra locks on the bathroom door and the inside bathroom, because both places have doors leading to the outside.

Here is a little exercise in communication for the English Department at Mary Washington College. The library at Isabella Thoburn College does not have E. M. Forster's *A Passage to India* or Henry James' *Daisy Miller*, both of which were on a reading list I posted for my students. I decided to buy copies of each book in town and present them as gifts to the library. I had no trouble finding *A Passage to India*, but I walked into a bookstore and asked for the other book. Here is what happened:

KENVIN: Good morning.
CLERK:  May I help you, sir?
KENVIN: Yes. I'd like a copy of *Daisy Miller* by Henry
         James.

CLERK : (Drawing himself up straight) I'm sorry. We
don't have it.
KENVIN: Are you sure? You have lots of fiction here . . . .
CLERK:   You won't find *that* book in *this* bookstore.
KENVIN: But it's published even in the Penguin editions.
CLERK:    We have nothing by him.
KENVIN: Not even *The Ambassadors, Portrait of a Lady?*
CLERK:    (Looking straight in my eye) We do *not* carry books
by Henry Miller here.
KENVIN: I said Henry James, not Henry Miller! They are two
totally different authors!
CLERK:    (determined not to acknowledge his mistake) No.
I'm sorry. We have nothing by him.

Surely, it's an absurd world that confuses Henry James with
Henry Miller, isn't it? I felt for a moment like leaning over
confidentially and saying to the clerk, "Come on, I know ya
got Hank James' books under the counter—*Tropic of Kama
Sutra, Memoirs of Fanny Hurst,* and *Portrait of a Lady* (with
anatomical illustrations.)

Thanks, all of you, who have asked about our health.
My problems seem to have been the most serious. I had a
painful and debilitating bacillary dysentery for about a month.
It was not helped by Dr. A. C. Das in Lucknow, who gave me
massive doses of potent medicines, three at once, one of
which was a drug that affected my eyesight, making me
suddenly far-sighted, reversing my normal near-sightedness. I
have lost a great deal of weight during my various illnesses,
but have managed to gain some back now, and so am only 18
pounds below my usual 165 pounds—but, still, I can't afford
to lose weight at all. In Delhi, I was fine, but the day after I
returned to Lucknow, I was hit with dysentery again, which I
now have, and am trying to cure it with a diet of toast and tea,
entero-vioform tablets and sulfa guanidine. It is distressing,
but apparently quite common in India. Rahat thinks the
extreme heat is causing it. In New Delhi, we existed in air

conditioning, but here it still hits 97 degrees during the day. If I can shake this, I will be all right. If the water is the cause, all I can say is that the water in Lucknow tastes much better than the water in Delhi. It's hard to know what's causing it. Why haven't Rudd and the children been hit with dysentery as often as I have?

As for Heather's enlarged liver condition (Dr. Das' diagnosis), we took her to the best Indian pediatrician in Delhi. He had studied at Harvard and done work at Children's Hospital in Boston. He examined both children thoroughly and said that Heather does not have an enlarged liver or vitamin D deficiency. He thinks the pains in her left leg and arm are growing pains.

Rudd looks fine. She hasn't lost a pound, much to her annoyance. I might add that I noticed in Delhi that out of our group on the Women's College Program, three out of four men have lost a great deal of weight, like me, but only one of the women has.

We are still concerned about the emergency in India. It looks as though Pakistan has no intention of keeping the cease-fire. They have already violated it forty-two times. The blackouts have been lifted, but we feel now, that, if they resume, Rudd and the children will have to fly home ahead of schedule. Heather has had some bad dreams about war, and Rudd is apprehensive about having to go through a last-minute evacuation. Even the best attempt just gets you out of the country in the nick of time. We understand that the American evacuees from East Pakistan arrived in Manila with just the clothes on their backs.

Christmas is coming, and so we are sending off packages to relatives in the United States. It takes a little over two months for packages normally to get there.

In addition, we have sent gifts to the following people in Fredericksburg, all of whom were helpful to us in some way in getting us here, either by getting us into the program itself, or by taking care of our luggage, or of us, as Sidney Mitchell so kindly did when we were stranded at the railroad station in Fredericksburg with the Volkswagen: The Simpsons, Croushores, Michael Houstons, and Sidney Mitchells.

But, remember, no gifts *at all* for us this year. Duty has to be paid on everything coming into India, except, as I indicated in an earlier letter, on "books, baby food, and contraceptives," none of which I think we need at the moment.

Will some of you in Fredericksburg manage to get yourself invited to or drop in at 1225 Parcell Street, which is where most of our furniture is at the moment, being used by Liz Clark, Cecille Pelovitz, and Emily Haynes. Remind Liz to get the grey wool rug from Nu Way Cleaners, if she hasn't already. We will be moving into 1225 when we return to Fredericksburg, but check to see if the furniture looks all right there first, and send me a report. Remind Liz—no wild parties!

We have had several letters from Keith and Marjorie Britton who bought our house "Celtwood" in Dogue. They had a wonderful summer there with the ten kids, except that most of them came down with poison ivy. They are going to use it as their country house, holding on to their other house in Washington. How we miss that beautiful place and everything we had in our rich life there. One of my last memories of it was of Rudd's mother standing in the upstairs hall last Christmas, telling me a little tearfully how sad she was to think that she would never come to "Celtwood" again. We lost her and the house forever, almost on the same day. We turned a very sharp corner in our lives then.

That is about all the news from here for now. Hope you are enjoying a cool, crisp autumn. Our autumn here is reminiscent of Virginia in July!

Roger (The *Very* Reverend)

198 Faizabad Road
Lucknow, U.P., India
November 1, 1965

Dear Friends,

Do you know Thornton Wilder's play *The Skin of Our Teeth,* that "cosmic fantasy" in which he shows how Mr. and Mrs. Antrobus (symbolizing humankind in general) have survived ice age, flood, famine, and war by the skin of their teeth? Well, you might say that October was our *Skin of Our Teeth* over here, because, having survived an undeclared war with Pakistan, milk famine in Lucknow, monsoon winds and rain, near disaster when a firecracker blew up in Rahat's hand, robbery, and illness, we were hit again by another more serious illness—amoebic dysentery which led to chronic amoebiasis, and, in my case, became so resistant to cure that we were almost forced to return to the United States.

The danger with amoebiasis is that the amoebae can invade the liver, lungs, or central nervous system. I had had two courses of treatment altogether and responded to neither of them. Each day I kept sinking lower. The dysentery aspects are not what bothers one; it is the pain, the nervousness around the heart, the dizziness, and the inability to keep anything down. I had three doctors and two nurses prescribing for me, all of them offering contradictory dietary restrictions, which didn't matter much anyway, since my appetite was shot. At the crucial point, an American missionary doctor, Dr. J. H. Schoonmaker, who just happened to be visiting in Lucknow, came to see me, and immediately put me on a three-week course of four medicines prescribed by the Calcutta School of Tropical Medicine. He had seen his own brother-in-law eaten out by amoebae and forced to return home from India. At last I began coming around and now am hopefully on the road back to good health. I won't tell you how much weight I've lost now, but I looked a little like General Wainright when he was released from the Japanese concentration camp. My 29" waist is the envy of Rudd.

Lucky me to have had both types of dysentery over here—bacillary back in July-August, and amoebic in September-October. Neither was the result of carelessness. I've been extremely careful. Dr. Dahwan, my Hindu doctor, quite brilliant, said that almost everyone in Lucknow has amoebiasis at some time or other. He said the micro-organisms are on all fruits and vegetables, on people's hands, etc. He said that one out of three cases he treats everyday is for amoebiasis. Our friend, Harriet Sisson, puts it succinctly: "There isn't a proper movement in all India!" So it seems it is a matter of chance whether one gets it or not. Rudd, Brooke, and Heather all contracted it too, but were cured by the second course which failed with me.

I said to Rudd, "Maybe it's not India's fault at all. Maybe it's mine, because I am an ectomorph, and ectomorphs, who are all spinal columns and nerve ends, in addition to their low pain barrier, catch all kinds of things, especially skin and nerve diseases." Then, too, I must have a peculiar constitution. I am one of those persons who is allergic to penicillin. And, even odder, is that when I was in the U.S. Navy, my blood type was "O," but when I married Rudd in Montclair, my blood type became "A." I asked somebody once how this could be. He said it couldn't, not unless you died.

At any rate, the one positive thing I've gotten out of all this has been a thorough course in pharmacology. My bedroom looks like a druggist's shop (chemist's over here). I know all about sulfa drugs and anything that begins with chlor. You name it; I've had it. I have had opium, belladonna, and codein. You can buy any drug you want over the counter in Lucknow, and very inexpensively, too, which is a good thing. Isn't there some second-rate college of pharmacology in, say Kansas City somewhere, that would be willing to award me a degree in pharmacology for what I know?

However, I know now that, once I leave India I shall never set foot in a tropical country again, not because I won't, but because I can't. Do not look for me along the banks of the Amazon or in Bechuanaland. I won't be there. Look for me in Biarritz, Juan Les Pins, or Gstaad, among the fashionable idlers in paradise, sipping vermouth cassis, discussing the latest Chagall *vernissage* or last season in Sardinia.

---

I hope you have gotten the general impression from my letters that I am enjoying myself in India. If I seem too critical or satirical at times, just remember that I am only hard on those things I care about; if I weren't finding the whole thing an enormously absorbing and rich cultural experience, I wouldn't bother to write about it at all. I write half the time tongue-in-cheek, seeing humor in almost everything human, including myself in my own ridiculous postures. I suppose this makes me an anti-romantic, really. Actually, I romanticize very few things in life: the world of the theatre, Italy, Gstaad, John F. Kennedy, Katharine Hepburn, King Henry V of England, winter sports, sailing, the coast of Maine, the south shore of Long Island, and two Claudes—Monet and Debussy—but little else. In class, I am just as hard on Shakespeare and Donne, as I am on India, but that doesn't mean I don't love them all.

It is difficult for me to give you the feel of my emotional attachment to India, but it is a strong one, so strong that sometimes I think I should join the *jawans* at the front in Kashmir. I am very partisan in India's favor in this conflict. Despite all the terrible problems of India—the brutal climate, poverty, diseases—I feel very warm toward its people, most of whom are delightful, friendly people, sadly underfed, easily misunderstood. Often, when I go downtown, Indians, as they ride by on bicycles, turn around and stare openly at me. One rode up to me once and said, "I have been hoping to meet you. I wanted to talk about India and Pakistan." So we chatted as we rode along. Some Americans don't understand the stares we all receive, and resent them. Harriet Sisson stuck out her tongue at an Indian who stared at her. Ralph Sisson said to one, riding his bicycle alongside him, "Why are you staring at me?" The reply? "Because you are my brother."

Then, too, the texture of India is rich and fascinating. Those of you who like William Faulkner's novels probably respond to the dense layers of cultural heritage he writes about—native Americans, Spaniards, French, Creoles, Octoroons, Anglo-Saxons. That same kind of texture, only deeper in its hues, is found in India. In the North, we have Aryans; in the South, Dravidians. Cultures are widely different in diverse regions—the Punjab, Rajasthan, Orissa, Kerala, Kashmir. We have many tongues—Hindi, English, Tamil, Bengali, Marathi, Telugi. There is color and excitement everywhere. Think of Hinduism alone! It has over 30,000 gods in its pantheon. How can simple western Christianity hope to compete with that? The Hindus can put on shows that Rome never dreamed about. India may be many things, but it is never dull. That is one of its prime attractions.

I had no illusions about India before I came here. Chancellor Simpson at Mary Washington gave me all of Ruby Turner Morris' letters. She was on the program last year and had been Rudd's economics professor at Vassar. Ruby looked at India always through very observant, realistic eyes. I wrote to her on my own, also, and she laid India right on the line for me. Two other people on the program to whom I wrote and said, "What's it like? Tell me all about it," only wrote equivocal, pleasant letters in reply. I can't believe that, even with all the health problems I've had, these non-commital  people profited more from the experience than I have. In my own way, I love the country and I love the people.

One has to be careful about making generalizations about India or life in India. One person's experience is not necessarily another's. Fred Rowe, from Randolph-Macon College, and now at Indraprastha College in Delhi, teaching psychology, said that his students compare favorably with the best at Randolph-Macon. That is not my experience at Isabella Thoburn College. But we are at two different colleges, teaching two different subjects. The Reusses down in Bangalore are having a ball, living it up with the maharajahs, and so forth. The Scherers in Hyderabad find it confusing and rather impossible. I, in Lucknow, have had the worst health problems. But if any of you were to come to India, your experiences and reactions would be totally different.

So, please make this basic assumption—that I am enjoying this time in India. So is Rudd, although she does not have the naturalistic eye that I have and cannot look on poverty or filth as calmly as I can, nor as dispassionately. The children are having a better time than either of us, primarily because they are protected from these larger problems, although Heather was frightened by the onset of the war. The children laugh, play, and adore their Rahat, and are squeezed, pinched, and hugged by college girls and other Indian children alike. A rickshaw-wallah even lifted Heather down from the rickshaw tonight and gave her a great big kiss because she looked so cute in her Kashmiri outfit.

As a matter of fact, all four of us are taking Hindi lessons three times a week. A college girl is teaching us, and we are making good progress, Rudd especially. I can see the roots of the Indo-European languages exposed: The word for "tooth" in Hindi is "dant"; in French it is "dent." The Hindi word for shirt is "kamiz"; In French, "chemise"; in Spanish, "camisa"; Italian, "camicia." The children, of course, know more Hindi than I. "What did he say, Heather?" I had to ask her when someone spoke to me in Hindi the other day. Imagine having a four-year old translate for you, big college professor that you are!

I've just sent out a letter to a young Muslim student from Lucknow University who lives in the Aminabad, and, who, on my first visit there, said to me on the street, "May I help you? You look as though you are in some confusion." And then, for three hours, Qamar Husain Hyderi took me on a thorough tour of the Aminabad, as only one who lives there can know it. He stopped by the college the other day to see me, but I was ill and at home. I've just written to him, telling him to come and visit us at home anytime.

When I was sick in bed, almost my entire senior class came over to visit, bringing a bouquet of hand-picked flowers and a hand-decorated card which read, "Get well soon." These are kind, intelligent people, and I think, if it weren't for the searing poverty, most Indians would naturally be that way also. They are handsome people here in the north, worn lean by climate and deprivation, with teeth stained red and rutted out from their addiction to pan, but they are resolutely good-natured, even the merchants with whom one has to haggle over prices sometimes. If I sense that it is fun for them, a game, I haggle. Yankee against Indian. Each gives a little; each gains a little. A tug of war, but a friendly one—the way it is in Italy too.

Ruby Turner Morris said that people who like to camp out would enjoy living in India. That's pretty much the way it is for an American who comes over here. And when you camp out, you run some risks, don't you?

Professor Reuss, who is Roman Catholic, said that what he found so interesting about India was that Hinduism was so close to Roman Catholicism in its ritualism that he could see the ancient roots of his own religion deep in Hinduism. He also told me about the Parsis in Bangalore who have a "tower of silence," which is their way of burying their dead. The tower is a tall, brick one, and, when, a Parsi dies, no part of him is supposed to defile the elements. They don't cremate, bury, or submerge their dead. Instead, they tie the corpse on ropes and suspend it at the top of this tower of silence which is open to the sky. Then the vultures come and eat away the flesh, and the bones dry out. Then the corpse has been arranged so that the bones fall into a pan down below, and so none of the elements are defiled. The Parsis are one of the religions imported into India—from Persia originally, I believe—and related to Zoroastrianism in that they revere fire. The Parsis have done a great deal of improvement in education in India. Some of them are also big businessmen down in Bombay.

Of the three religious offshoots of Hinduism in India, you probably know the story of Prince Siddhartha, who sat under a peepul tree one day in the sixth century and got "enlightenment," then turned his back on his wife and child and went out into the world to become Buddha—the Enlightened One. Buddhism spread from India to Ceylon, China, and Japan.

But two other Hindu offshoots, Sikhism and Jainism, are even more interesting. The Jains revere all life, as Albert Schweitzer did. Jain monks and nuns actually wear cloths over their noses, not to protect them from the flu, but so that they won't inadvertently inhale any bugs and kill them. The Jains are mostly hard-working, middle-class shopkeepers who do not take intoxicating drinks. From the Jains' reverence for life comes the doctrine of non-violence, which Gandhi got from them.

Just as the Jains are peaceful, so the Sikhs are warlike. They weren't always so. They began as an offshoot of Hinduism that believed in only one god (30,000 were too many for them) and were opposed to the Hindu caste divisions. They did not relish ritualistic or image worship. But their last Guru formed them into a military community in the seventeenth-century, and they have been warlike ever since. Their particular enemy is the Muslim. During partition, Sikhs migrated from Pakistan back into India, and Muslims went from India into Pakistan, and they met each other on the way and indulged in wholesale slaughter. Mrs. Jordan said it was horrible how trains would arrive in Lucknow with the throats of the passengers all cut, and blood all over the place. Many of the war heroes in the current conflict have been Sikhs. They all have the same last name, "Singh," which means "lion."

The Sikhs are the most colorful people to look at. They wear turbans over long hair, which is rolled up into a bun on top of their heads. They all wear beards, and, around one arm is a steel bracelet to remind them when they lift their hand against another man they should not kill unjustly. The Sikhs are a virile lot and great drinkers—sort of Marlon Brandos in turbans, I suppose. For some strange reason, most of the taxicab drivers in New Delhi are Sikhs, as are most of the Indian airline pilots. In Lucknow, we have very few Sikhs, mostly Muslims.

Hinduism, as you know, has its own trinity at the top—the three gods, Brahma, the creator; Vishnu, the preserver; and Shiva, the destroyer. Brahma is worshipped hardly at all in India. In north India, Vishnu is generally worshipped, and in the south, Shiva. Shiva is the one you see in the *nataraj,* the dancing figure in a circle of fire. I call Shiva the "sex god," because, in his cult, the lingam (or phallus) is worshipped. Much of the temple architecture takes this shape. There is even a giant lingam in ice deep in a cavern in the Himalayas that the Shivites make a pilgrimage to every year to worship.

The caste system in Hinduism goes as follows: At the top are the Brahmins, the priestly or ruling class; then the Kshatriyas (pronounced Shot-TREE-yaz) who are the warriors; the Vaishyas are next, mostly merchants; then the Sudras, generally clerical workers; and finally , the untouchables, who just don't belong—sweepers, menial laborers. Actually, there are not supposed to be any untouchables in this new India. They are called "Scheduled Castes" now. Pronounce that "SHED-uled" over here, please.

My favorite god in the Hindu pantheon is Krishna, the cowherd-god. He is almost always depicted with his beloved, Radha, and her companions, the *gopis,* or milkmaids. Krishna represents the supreme soul, while Radha and the *gopis* represent the souls of men, perenially in dalliance in the forests of Brindaban on the banks of the Jumma River. Their illicit love is supposed to show the desire of all human beings to be one with the Supreme, kind of an early D. H. Lawrence cult, I would call it. In the doctrine of *sahaja,* which is a kind of free love, the adoration of beautiful young girls was thought to be a way to salvation.

On some of the Christmas cards we sent out this year, there are representations of the Krishna story in varying forms. On a rug that I bought (made by a prisoner in the jail at Agra), Krishna and Radha are shown under a tall tree, swinging high in the air on a swing. They are standing up on the swing and gazing straight into each other's eyes. The ladies are gathered into two groups in the foreground. One has a mandolin, another has a drum, and three ladies are beckoning to the others to come and eat what look like apples or tomatoes. A line of purple appears on the horizon in the distance over the hill. This is the *bursaat,* the monsoon, and Krishna and Radha are out relaxing in the coolness that comes after the rains.

Enough of Hinduism for the time being. We are looking forward to November, which will be a busy month for us. We will be entertaining, at the college and at lunch at our house, the Dean of Barnard College and the President of

Connecticut College, from the 7th to the 10th. The play I am directing, *A Majority of One*, goes on the boards on the 13th and 14th. And Rudd is delivering an address to the entire college on the 18th. Her topic will be "Some Problems in American Education Today." And, at long last, the weather in Lucknow is getting cooler!

Love from all of us,

Roger

P.S.
      Latest count of servants on our payroll—six. Rahat's uncle, an old, bent-over sickle of a man, is our personal night watchman and sleeps outside our kitchen door. When I saw this frail creature, I said to Rudd, "Give that beard and bones my bed, and I'll sleep outside and guard him."

198 Faizabad Road
Lucknow, U.P., India
January 10, 1966


Dear Friends,

In December I went to Jaipur. On a Tuesday evening, just after dark on that day of the week holiest to the Hindus, I went out in an open rickshaw in search of Krishna idols in the bazaar. It was chilly, and so I buttoned up my wool jacket and turned up the collar against the cold. Fires from little coal pots and oil lamps flickered all along the road where men in great turbans huddled close together, blankets wrapped around their hunched-over bodies. Thick smoke lay like an undulant fog over everything. One saw the world, as it were, as in a very dark chiaroscuro oil painting.

Up ahead some bright shafts of rectangular light criss-crossed one another over the heads of the people. This was a *sadhee*, a wedding, in which the *duhla*, the bridegroom, dressed in an elegant silk suit and wearing a jeweled turban, rides on a splendid horse trimmed with silk, brocade, and gold tassels, and is followed by a procession of friends, all carrying over their heads great crystal chandelier-lanterns, lit with oil, which shine and tinkle brightly in the night air. As we passed along through the darkness, we came into four or five pools of light from these *sadhees*. This holy night in December seemed to be the night to be married in Jaipur.

Nearing the red sandstone Ajmeri Gate at the very entrance to the inner pink city itself, the press of humanity thickened around us, and we moved along in a swelling tide toward the narrow gate. Suddenly, we were caught up in another wedding procession. I could hear the chants of the joyful marchers now and see their uplifted faces. The bridegroom, a young boy of about sixteen, sat, faintly smiling, high up on his daintily stepping horse. On another horse nearby rode his younger brother, self-consciously proud, dressed in shining white, embroidered silk.

Just before we came alongside the bridegroom himself, I felt a great surge of humanity against us on the right. There were more flashing lights over our heads, more clinking of chandelier-lanterns. I heard the low tones of the marchers' chants, announcing a different rhythm this time.

In the instant in which we were squeezed next to the flank of the bridegroom's horse, with light from his splendor spilling down brilliantly on our heads, the central object in the other procession passed by on my right, so close that I could almost touch it.

I held my breath.

High above the shoulders of the marchers, on wooden boards, and wrapped in white linen, was a corpse being borne in quick-step toward a burning ghat for cremation. Thinly wrapped, it looked like a mummy; one could see the impression of the features through the cloth and the hands gently folded on its stomach.

Just one instant of life and death passing so close that they almost touched each other, except for me, the idol seeker, in the middle.

A confusing flash of lights, a move forward, and, suddenly, we were pushed through the narrow Ajmeri Gate and propelled into birth in the larger color and life of the Johri Bazaar itself.

I had the rickshaw driver pull over to the side of the road for a moment. We were in front of a small Hindu shrine where a crowd of people stood, clapping their hands and chanting, *"Ram, ram, hare, hare,"* and making offerings of flowers, money, and other gifts to the illuminated idol inside. The smoky air was rose-colored and heavy now. One's lungs were filled with it; one's being became part of the mystery of the Jaipur night itself.

"Will you have this Krishna for decorative purposes, or do you wish it to worship?" the shopkeeper asked, smiling darkly at me.

I hesitated, and then withdrew.

I did not buy the marble Krishna that night.

I had gone to Jaipur at the invitation of the United States Information Service, which asked me to take part in a week-long program at the University of Rajasthan. I was to be a guest lecturer and expert on American drama. I was treated like a V.I.P., with an airplane to transport me from Lucknow to Delhi to Jaipur, and a car with chauffeur to meet me and whisk me anywhere I wanted to go. I led a three-hour seminar on "Major American Playwrights" and delivered a lecture on "New Directions in the Theatre Arts." The participants in the conference were teachers or graduate students from the University or nearby universities. It was intellectually very stimulating, and, coupled with the Fulbright conference in Delhi last September, has been the most rewarding part of my academic experience in India.

Jaipur is a beautiful city, lying on the vast Rajasthan desert, surrounded by mountains reminiscent of the Apennines in Italy. Many of the buildings in the old quarter of Jaipur are made of red sandstone which has faded until it has become a pleasant pink color. The whole city is quite graceful, with a light, airy feeling about it—different from Lucknow's slightly heavy Moghul flavor.

And the Rajputs themselves are warm, fascinating people. They have a tradition of being great warriors, and are tall, proud, handsome people, rather unspoiled since British rule never really took hold here as it did in Lucknow.

The men wear orange, yellow, red, or pink turbans with the tail flaring out in back on their shoulders. Sometimes they wear a small, gold earring in one ear, like pirates. White teeth, flashing smiles.

The women wear cheap, bright, yellow and red cotton peasanty prints, much tinsel and glitter, and cover themselves up most of the time. It is hard to photograph them. Sometimes, you will get a shy smile, but, more often, there will be a sudden pulling of the veil across the face, leaving just an amorphous blur of yellow and red in front of one, making one wonder about what one has just seen and sad that it has so quickly vanished.

As the time draws near for our departure from India, I find myself thinking about the Indian friendships I have made. We have many good friends among the faculty at Isabella Thoburn College—Shanti Manuel from Trichinopoly, whose father was an Anglican priest; Joan Humby, a brilliant Englishwoman (M.A. from Oxford) who is far above the level of I.T. College and who will be leaving soon to join an Indian university; Leila Advani, a Sindhi Hindu from Pakistan who fled to Lucknow after partition in 1947; Mrs. Farr, a North Carolinian, who is the librarian here and who smokes cigarettes on the sly in her room (Dr. Sommerville, the Acting Principal, actually forced her to consult a psychiatrist); Mary Abraham (good Indian Christian name), a giantess of a woman from Madras, who comes on strong like a major-general and who ordered me out on the field to play first base for the I.T. College baseball team and got away with it; Kathleen Misra, a warm, motherly Economics teacher (The rumor is that I appeal to the maternal instinct in her); and Mrs. Jordan, a hard-driving Punjabi, daughter of a Methodist minister, great friend of America, who powders her face white, and, during conversations, metamorphoses herself into a Barry Goldwater type American. But it is none of these fascinating women whose friendships have been most meaningful to me. I think that, long after I have left India, I shall remember best three people, all of whom, coincidentally, happen to be Muslims.

I

The first of these is Rahat Ali, our grand *khansaman,* our cook-bearer. I have written about him before. How much a part of our household he has become!—so much so that Brooke and Heather will not go to sleep at night until he pokes his head into their room and exchanges *salaams* with them. Rahat (the very name means "pleasure") is about forty, I would judge, thin, but strong, with a face that can look as inscrutable as a Tibetan hill-dweller's or as wide-eyed and delighted as a child's on Christmas morning. He usually wears a little black velvet orthodox Muslim hat. When he takes it off and we see his shining black hair, we do not recognize him. Lately, in this cold weather, he has been wearing a brown Persian lamb Kashmiri hat—like Ayub Khan's, I tell him. His wife is in *purdah* and almost always hides behind her *burka.* She does lift it to say hello to us, though, so that we have seen her face.

Rahat and his wife have four children. The oldest is a girl of eighteen who did very well in school and has moved away to Kanpur and gotten a good job for herself. But she has caused Rahat great sadness because she has fallen in love with a Christian boy and it is rumored that she has been living with him. We do not discuss this problem with Rahat, but we gave him the day off one time in tacit agreement that he should go to Kanpur to see her. In the Muslim household, the father is the sole authority. He picks out the mates for his children and they must be Muslim. The Shuklas, Rudd, and I have all indirectly tried to persuade Rahat to let the couple marry. The boy has said he will become Muslim. We fear the daughter may be pregnant. But we do not know Rahat's decision. He has to wrestle with this dark problem himself.

His other three children live here with him and his wife. They are Imtiaz, a boy of ten, who was sickly as a baby, but who resembles his mother with big brown popping eyes and a smile that lights up his whole face. He helps Rahat sometimes and is being groomed, I suppose, to become a cook-bearer himself someday. Roshan Jehan, a girl of seven, is next. She is pretty, neat, and loves to pinch Heather's cheek in a friendly Indian way which Heather does not understand or like.

Last of all, there is Muntiaz, a tiny drop of a boy, aged three, who is all eyes and mysterious smiles and who fears nothing on earth except his own father. He has the same effect on one as Dopey in *Snow White and the Seven Dwarfs*. He, rather than Imtiaz or Roshan Jehan, is the playmate of Brooke and Heather. Sometimes they pick him up like a big doll and deposit him in a heap in a chair. He, in turn, chases them, calling, "baby, baby." Often, I might be sitting in the living room late in the afternoon when, suddenly, the door will open quietly. I turn to look and there, well beneath my gaze, is Muntiaz oozing into the room. Without a word, he comes and sits in a chair, his expressive eyes glancing around the room, looking awed at the ferocious Ravanna mask on the wall or amused at the Ganesh (elephant god) mask. Then his eyes go to where candy is usually kept. A long look there. Finally, I offer him some candy, and then he executes a smart salute, gives a husky *salaam* and oozes out the door. He is full of the old Nick, though, and once caused Heather great anguish when his attempted abduction of her beloved "Raggy" almost succeeded.

Rahat is an excellent cook. I have already written about his versatility in preparing Indian or Western dishes. But where he triumphs especially is in handling the highly individualistic tastes of all four of us. Sometimes one meal will consist of three or four different orders, all of which he manages with skill and good humor. Children are notoriously hard on cooks, but Rahat is a wonder with ours, and never does his patience seem strained. There are times when, as I told Rudd, I would have taken a bowl of food and dashed it over Brooke or Heather's heads for their sheer arrogance, but not Rahat. He particularly adores Heather and she him. Heather has already told Rahat that when she is married and has a baby, she is coming back to India to see him. She was saddened when he reminded her that he would be an old man then.

We pay Rahat now twice the going rate for cooks here. Many Americans follow the stingy rich Indian rationalization that you must never pay any servant more than the going rate "because you will spoil them for other employers" or "because they will only spend it on liquor and cigarettes," but this philosophy is just what it sounds like—a vicious lie where people like Rahat are concerned. He is probably the best paid private cook now in all Lucknow, but, to us, he is still underpaid.

He keeps most recipes in his head and measures things by "hands." Rudd has shown him how to make brownies, fudge, and Parker House rolls, and, believe me, he cooks them beautifully. When Dr. Charles Shain, President of Connecticut College, and Dr. Boorse, Dean of Barnard College, were here, they came over to our house for an impromptu lunch, and Rahat prepared pancakes with his special syrup for them—which delighted them, since (unknown to them) they had been eating only goat meat and water buffalo at Isabella Thoburn College where they had been staying. The food there is very poor in quality.

Rahat's English is weak, and so Rudd has been giving him nightly lessons after work in reading English. He won't sit in a chair, but insists on sitting on the floor Indian style for his lessons, so Rudd has to come down to his level. I walk into the living room and see the two of them squatting on the floor with a blackboard and chalk in their hands.

The main thing that gives balance to Rahat's personality is his grand sense of humor. Rudd and I often notice the suppressed mirth in his eyes as he observes us or the children. We have said, "Rahat, what tales will you tell of us after we've gone?" And he laughs because he knows he will have many good stories. Rudd and I often get Rahat to tell us about the old days. He has been working here now at the Shuklas for about fifteen years. Once he was their cook but they went to England for two years, leaving him behind to cook for the Americans who rented the house, and then, when the Shuklas came back, she decided that she would do the cooking, and so they assigned Rahat to whoever was renting the apartment in their house. Later, they decided that cooking was too much for her and so had to hire another cook, an older man, who has just moved into the house with all of us here.

Rahat often tells us of our American predecessors—of Dr. and Mrs. Crawford who gave splendid parties for sixty or eighty people at a clip. (How Rahat loves the big parties—a holdover from his race memory of the Moghul past, I tell him), of the Sunandas (He would eat only Indian food, she only Western food), but the best stories of all come from the days before Independence, in what Rahat calls "Inglis-time." Then Rahat was younger and just a bearer (waiter). He served an Englishmen who, as Rahat puts it, "Six courses had every night dinner, seven when company." Rahat tells how first came cocktails, gin or whiskey, then sherry came with the soup, white wine with the fish, then red wine, and so on through to the brandy and after-dinner drinks. His eyes widen as he recreates this past epoch. "Rahat, no!" Rudd and I cry out in mock horror. "Not more wine, not three cocktails gin!" "Yes, three cocktails gin," Rahat replies.

When I was seriously ill and it appeared as though someone in the house were acting as a carrier for amoebiasis, many people said summarily, "Fire Rahat." I told them I would not, for it would be like asking a member of my own family to get out. All of us are going to miss this wonderful human being when we come home.

## II

Qamar Husain Hyderi comes from a different level of society than Rahat. Hyderi (He uses that as his first name) is the son of a Lucknow doctor and descended from a long line of Lucknow nabobs. The nabobs were, at one time, the rich landlords who rented out their lands to tenants. Hyderi's father has two wives and two sets of children, all of whom live in the same house. Hyderi says they all get along just fine. The grandfather has seven wives. He is sixty-seven years old, and Hyderi says the grandfather is about to take an eighth wife because one of his wives just died. I said to Hyderi, "And you? How many wives will you have?" "Just one," he replied.

Hyderi is twenty and will receive his B.A. degree in Economics from Lucknow University this June. I met him first a long time ago in the Aminabad where he lives. He came up to me and took me on a long tour of the Aminabad. He has since taken me all over Lucknow, showing me the city through his eyes. He has taken me to the oldest Urdu bookstore in Lucknow and to the very newest. He has shown me places where he stood as a little boy and watched Mahatma Gandhi pass by and where Jawaharlal Nehru patted him on the head. He has taken me by night to Hindu temples (where non-Hindus are not admitted) and we have stood outside up close and watched the rituals—especially at the temples of Krishna and Hanumon in the Aminabad. He has told me horrendous tales of dacoits and cobras on Faizaibad Road, of savage hidden rivalries between Muslims and Hindus in Lucknow, shown me places where Urdu poets died of drink in the gutters of Ganna Wali Gali (Sugar Cane Lane) where Hyderi's house is. He has acted as interpreter, advance man, bargainer, guide, and explainer for me. He has done some leg-work research for me, since I am trying to do a paper on Wajid Ali Shah and his contributions to drama in Lucknow. Hyderi, who knows Urdu, has dug out lots of records for me and interviewed people.

When I told him that Lew Fickett at Mary Washington was interested in the Praja Socialist Party, out went Hyderi to interview P.S.P. leaders in Uttar Pradesh and wrote Lew a mammoth tour de force of a handwritten letter, revealing his findings.

Hyderi is a short, wiry individual with a kind of pushed-in face, accented sometimes by a squint in his eyes. There is no stopping him when he starts speaking. He inclines toward the dogmatic and has a rather acerbic wit. He is one of the more intellectual students at Lucknow and expresses a constant dissatisfaction with the quality of the education there. He especially deplores the emphasis on Hindi, his own tongue being Urdu (which was the language of the court in India), and he delights in writing his name in Urdu, defying the government's wishes.

He is known and liked by practically everybody at the University. He has taken me over there and introduced me to both students and professors. As a matter of fact, Hyderi insisted that I become an honorary member of the Lucknow University Political Science Club. I told him I knew nothing about political science. "That does not matter," he said. "Do not talk about political science or philosophy with the members. They will only say, 'Stop boring me.' Talk about gunching, or motor cars, or music." (Gunching means going down to the Gunch to watch the girls pass by!) And so, to please him, I am now a dues-paying member of the Political Science Club. Our first meeting was a three-hour musical program!

Rudd, as you know, is ardently pro-India in the Pakistan-India conflict. She and Hyderi sometimes reach the boiling point in arguments over the war because of Hyderi's marked pro-Pakistani point of view. We now find out that he has a brother in the Pakistan army. Many of our Christian friends here believe that if Pakistan successfully invades India all sixty million Indian Muslims will immediately join up with Pakistan. Hyderi, as a Muslim, is very bitter about the Hindu control of India. I expect the police will arrive any day now to arrest all of us as Pakistani inflitrators, charging Rudd and me with having personally supplied Patton tanks to Ayub Khan!

With Hyderi, also, I have gone to bazaars, museums, and art exhibitions. He reminds me so much of another Lucknow friend of ours from the European days, Mustafa Kamil (now in Cambridge, Massachusetts). Kamil, too, had a thorny personality with a very odd, sardonic sense of humor.

One time, a few weeks ago, I asked Hyderi to go to an exhibit of a modern Indian artist's paintings at the Lal Baradari. We went. Hyderi did not like the abstract expressionism of the man's works or his concern with burlap-like textures. As we left, we were asked to sign the guest register. I wrote my name, but did not write any comment under the "Comments" column because I did not feel like saying anything.

Hyderi then wrote his name rather defiantly in Urdu (which, incidentally, is a beautiful looking script), with a comment in Urdu after it. Next, I saw him reach up to my name and add a comment in English after it. I peered over his shoulder to see what he had written. "This exhibit really touched my heart!" was what he had written. Yet, you wouldn't guess to look at this great stone face that it masks a waspish sense of humor.


III


The third member of my Muslim triumverate is Mahmood Hassim, who, at nineteen, is one year younger than Hyderi. Mahmood Hassim is a rickshaw driver from Sultanpur. He is married, but childless, and is the sole support of twelve people. His father is blind, which handicaps him in work. His brother, Mahmood Ayub, suffers from periodic bouts of tuberculosis. Mahmood Hassim used to station his rickshaw by I. T. College and sometimes would drive me to and from my house or down to the Gunch or over to the

Aminabad. At this time, I began taking Hindi lessons, and I soon found that Mahmood Hassim was willing to let me converse with him, and so I did, un-self-consciously. Gradually, I learned something about him and his life. He seemed to me such a bright, happy soul, singing away in Urdu at the top of his lungs as we rode along. I wondered how one could find anything to be joyful about in this miserably wretched profession.

I have written before about rickshaw drivers. There are 10,000 of them in Lucknow. The rickshaw itself is a three-wheeled bicycle-like contraption, with a brightly decorated hood and a leather or plastic seat in which three people at the most can ride. There is no fixed price, but one pays whatever one agrees upon with the rickshaw driver. Many of the rickshaw drivers are homeless men or boys. They often live right in their rickshaws. One sees them curling up under blankets at night in their rickshaws, or washing themselves by fire-hydrant-like water taps early in the morning. Many of these unfortunates are racked with tuberculosis or other diseases. Many have taken to drink or drugs. Many find solace only in gambling. Sometimes in the winter, during cold spells such as we are having now, rickshaw drivers are found dead of exposure in their rickshaws in the morning.

In Lucknow, they earn between 5 and 10 rupees a day (that is, between $1.05 and $2.10), but the vicious thing is that most of the rickshaws are not owned by the rickshaw-wallahs, but by rickshaw landlords who require the drivers to pay between 45 and 60 rupees a month to them in rent. How, then, can a rickshaw driver ever get ahead? He can't. He must just keep on going, until one day he dies an early death of tuberculosis, exposure, or is brutally beaten by robbers or the police. (The police are notoriously corrupt here, often ride in rickshaws and pay nothing at all, and often extort money from rickshaw drivers.)

It was in this light then that I first saw Mahmood Hassim. As time went on, he appointed himself more and more the personal driver for Rudd, me, and the children. He was wonderful with the children, taking care of them, treating them well, protecting them from lepers and beggers in the Gunch (Heather is terrified of them). You could see that he was a boy from a good family background. He was clean and neat, with a boyish, cherubic face and an infectious smile. When the cold weather suddenly came upon us, I realized that he had no warm clothes at all, and I bought him a sweater, cap, gloves, socks, and shoes, then gave him some of my own clothing to keep him warm. One day Hyderi laughed when he saw him and said, "Mahmood Hassim, you are looking very American today!"

At that time, also, I decided that I would go alone to Benares for a week end visit to that city, Rudd having no desire to go to that holiest of all cities for the Hindus. But, then it occurred to me that my money might be better spent if I could release Mahmood Hassim from the grip of the rickshaw landlord by buying his own rickshaw for him. That would make me feel better, too, since I didn't enjoy knowing that anyone who worked for me, or with whom I was friendly, was, in effect, existing in servitude.

I consulted with Hyderi about this, and we told Mahmood Hassim what I intended to do. Rudd and I agreed that we would tell Mahmood Hassim that he would have to pay back some of the money at first, say 20 rupees a month to us, so that he wouldn't feel he was getting it absolutely for nothing. Mahmood Hassim's reaction was not one I was prepared for. He, like Rahat, is a Sunni Muslim. (Hyderi is a Shia Muslim.) Mahmood Hassim told Hyderi that it was *kismet,* that I was an apostle sent down by God who had looked down on Mahmood Hassim and knew that he was the breadwinner in the family.

Hyderi said "nonsense," that it was not fate at all, but one human being doing something for another. At any rate, I bought the rickshaw for him (It cost just under $100) and he sings happily as he drives along now, ringing both bells imperiously as he flies by in the multitudinous Indian traffic. He brought his brother, Mahmood Ayub, down from

Sultanpur, also, and, since his health at the moment is all right, Mahmood Ayub is driving a rickshaw on hire.

But how long will this period of relative prosperity last? Originally, Rudd and I had thought we would take the money Mahmood Hassim turned back and put it in the bank for him and show him how little deposits could accrue interest. But the family is desperately poor and banking now seems out of the question. When the time came for Mahmood Hassim to make his first payment to me, I told him to keep the money, that it was Christmas and that he had earned the rickshaw. But, again, how long? Ten years? And what kind of a future for this bright, happy spirit?

---

November and December were very busy months for both Rudd and me. We have been having a fifth season that we never knew existed. We have blue skies, brilliant sunshine, cold nights, and the most beautiful flowers—poinsettias, bougainvillea, cannas, gladiolus, chrysanthemums, roses—all in bloom at once. We have taken the children often to Banarsi Bagh, our favorite place in Lucknow. Banarsi Bagh is the zoo, and it is one of the most relaxing, pleasant zoos I have ever seen. It is beautifully landscaped for one thing, and the animals are splendidly displayed in natural settings. There is a lion there that is amazing. He has the most impressive roar. It reverberates for miles around. And he sits up, proudly and regally, like the MGM lion himself. He is most obliging. When one approaches him with a camera, he opens his mouth magnificently and shows his teeth, but roars silently, thus not offending the ears. There is also a great elephant there, on whose back the children, Rudd, and I have all ridden in true Indian style.

We visited Literacy House in Lucknow also. Literacy House was founded by an American woman, Mrs. Welthy Fisher, to try to help eradicate illiteracy in the villages of India. This was Gandhi's advice: "Go to the villages of India. And there begin your work." And so Literacy House invites all the leaders from villages to come in, and it holds lectures for them, discussions, and teaches them to read and write Hindi, how to take home to their villages what they have learned, and how to use what they have learned.

Literacy House sends out mobile libraries to the villages. It has its own printing press. It provides classrooms and runs a writers' workshop to train writers to write for its students. It uses puppets as a medium of education sometimes, and makes its own puppets, four of which we bought. The motto of Literacy House is, "It is better to light one candle than to curse the darkness." Rudd and I thought of this when we bought Mahmood Hassim his rickshaw.

Stephen Blickenstaff, the director of Literacy House, took us on a thorough tour. He said that when you educate people, you never know in what direction they will move, but that is a risk you must be willing to take. He said many people are afraid that newly-literate Indians will turn to communism first as a solution to their vast problems. He says so they might, but he cites the example of Soviet Russia, which now has modified its brand of communism. He thinks eventually the same kind of softening of communism will take place in China when they reach a certain level. Both Rudd and I were impressed with the valuable work Literacy House is doing here. (If any of you are interested, send your contributions to Literacy House, Lucknow, c/o World Education, Inc., 667 Madison Avenue, New York, N.Y., 10021.

At the College, Rudd lectured to the entire student body on "Some Problems in American Education," led a class in Adolescent Psychology, and is slated to speak in Education classes. I also addressed the students on "Major American Writers" and did a chapel stint at Christmas time (Read T. S. Eliot's "Journey of the Magi," Thomas Hardy's "The Oxen," had them sing "What Child is This?" and "We Three Kings" and called it a day.

The play I directed for I.T. College, *A Majority of One,* was presented for three performances back in November, and it was a great success, much to my happiness, since I used experimental techniques in directing it—a student carrying great program cards, no curtain, actors entering and exiting down the auditorium aisles, Japanese off-stage noises, music under the scenes, pantomime, and the notion that the audience were residents of Brooklyn. Many people at the College apparently felt the whole thing would be a disaster. But I wanted to show them that one could work against a large auditorium with bad acoustics and still make a play intimate and charming to an audience. I proved my point.

Our landlords, the Shuklas, during November and December (the high season over here) took us to a number of events. With them, we always sit in the front row seats marked "donors" or "guests." One night we saw a performance of Kathak dancing, for which Lucknow is famous. Another night we went to a celebration for the leading guru of the Sikh religion. ("Once a guru, always a guru," said Governor Biswanath Das in his speech that night.)

But the classiest event of all was the Beating of the Retreat and horse show, put on by the Police Reserve Unit on their handsome parade ground.

We sat in armchairs and couches in the front row and were served tea and mixed nuts. Carpets were placed on the grass in front of us, and magnificent potted chrysanthemums banked the field.

Bagpipers played, men in brilliant uniforms marched smartly, the governor spoke, and then the horse show itself was spectacular, with Bengal lancers on horses flying down the field, cutting down trees, and picking up pieces of ribbon—real Gary Cooper stuff—and jumping over hurdles in a steeplechase, four at a time.

The show was an all-day affair. One went to a morning performance, and then to a late afternoon performance.

Ladies wore their best silk saris, and men favored blue blazers with brass buttons and old school badges.

Some of you have wondered what kind of Christmas we could possibly be having over here. Have you forgotten that we are living in an Indian Christian community and that we enjoy an intenser kind of Christianity, as a result?

The Christmas music program at the Lal Bagh Church was twice as long as usual, with practically every known Western Christmas hymn crammed into it. We had not one, but three groups of carolers come by our house, one group at quarter to midnight, another group at 5:00 a.m. holding candles in their hands, and another little group of poor Indian Christians on Christmas morning, singing carols in Hindi, while one man played the harmonium in tinny, Charlie Chaplin style. Rather charming and wistful, all of it.

For weeks, nay, months, before Christmas, all the stalls along the Gunch displayed Christmas cards, some of them wilder than you can imagine. We were astonished to learn from some of our Hindu friends that Christ is also a Hindu god. Over here, you see, it is the Hindus who are broad-minded, not the Christians, who are almost absurd in their narrow-mindedness. I often have the feeling of *deja vu*. This is not Lucknow, India. It is Salem, Massachusetts, and we have been through all this before.

That about brings you up-to-date for now. I hope that 1966 will be an especially auspicious year for all of you.

Love from us all,

राजर

(Hindi)

198 Faizabad Road
Lucknow, U.P., India
March 1, 1966

Dear Friends,

# SEVEN SCENES FROM LUCKNOW

## The Song of Myrtle Shukla

**W**e have just finished lunch. I am sitting in a phony cane chair (really plastic) in our living room, smoking a cigar, and thinking about my BA II class which I am to meet in exactly one hour. Today, we are taking up three essays by G. K. Chesterton, and I wonder if I will be able to make my students responsive to his urbane wit and clever writing. Probably not! William Hazlitt bombed terribly on me just two days ago.

Rudd is sitting across from me, finishing up a hand-written aerogramme to Anne Rowe in Frederickburg. The children are raising hell, chasing each other like wild cats around the dining room table. Rahat is gently clearing away dishes, carrying them on a bright red, metal tray out to the kitchen, expertly avoiding the whip-lashes afforded by Brooke and Heather as they career around him.

My eye travels beyond the immediate scene through the screen door and over the verandah to the garden, where the sunlight arrests a great swatch of red roses in an impressionistic Renoir daub against the yellow wall. Suddenly, from behind the closed door leading into the Shuklas' part of the house, comes the warm sound of piano music. I remember that the piano tuner has been there all morning, carefully tuning the piano, which needed it.

What is this song? "Hark how the breezes blow . . . San-ah-tah-ah Loo-oo-chee-yah!" I cannot see the pianist, but I know who she is. Only one person in this house would pick her way so timidly, so correctly, through a piano piece so eminently right for an Indian friend of the West—Myrtle Shukla, our landlady.

One doesn't have to see Myrtle Shukla to know she is there, sitting oh so erectly on the piano bench, glasses riding tentatively on her nose, nose held high in the air, chin straight out, thin line of red about the mouth, the diamond in each pierced ear sparkling prettily (and richly), her soft, green sari (gathered by a gold clasp at her breast) flowing about her shoulders and back ever so gracefully and lady-like.

I think of my seemingly insignificant first encounters with her. She it was who was with me when I saw my first leper in India, a boy with broken fingers held up imploringly at us as we clambered into the rickshaw we were sharing in the Gunch. I held my breath, shocked, horrified, frozen inside me, but careful not to betray overtly my feelings. I thought to gauge my reaction by her reaction. But she babbled on about the shopping at Modern Novelties as though nothing had happened. Her eyes looked right through the begging leper. There was no recognition at all. He simply did not exist. I answered her in monosyllables all the way home in the rickshaw. I remember that I was not at all well the rest of the day.

Myrtle Shukla, too, it was who first put me wise to that very pragmatic Indian advice of always doing something nice for people who are in a position to do something nice for you when you want them to. I have heard it many times since then, but, sad to relate, it is wasted on me. I could not make it work, even if I wanted it to.

I remember the pleasant upper-class times we have had with Myrtle Shukla and Julian, her husband—the privileges we have been accorded because we are guests of theirs. I recall the great Hindustani *khanna* Myrtle Shukla threw on Christmas Day to which Rudd and I were invited, I suppose, partly out of necessity, since our cook, Rahat, prepared the *Mughlai biriani* that day. And I remember that, after dinner, we all played games, like charades and magic numbers—and only one man dared to light up a cigarette, thus defying the hard eye of Myrtle's Jesus Christ staring down from his calendar on the wall.

Outside now, a rising wind ruffles the red roses, causing a petal or two to drop off and the ferns in terra cotta pots on the verandah to bend their fronds toward the ground. I take in all these meteorological signs quickly: It is the West Wind starting up now, and it will not be long before the howling hot, dry season blows in. Already the grass is turning brown and the glare is beginning. But Myrtle Shukla plays on with care and more assurance now, and *poise*. (She herself told me that "poise" was the outstanding characteristic of any I.T. College graduate like herself.)

To my back, from behind another closed door leading into the Shuklas' bedroom, lies Julian (He of the nameless servants and Kiplingesque *topee*), sick in bed with some mysterious malady. (We all break down here every two weeks or so; ill health is a way of life.) When I go out on the verandah, I will probably meet up with Myrtle Shukla, and she will whisper fears of malaria or typhoid or hepatitis. *Hypochondria perpetua!* The possibilities are endless!

But it is spring in India. Unseen planets and stars wheel in the skies over our heads. We cannot stand still here on earth. A crow screams down raucously at us from its perch on a telephone pole in Bishop Rockey Street. A catarrhal cough issues from Julian's room. Rudd finishes up her letter to Anne Rowe, and seals it, satisfied. The children burst out of the house, exploding onto the verandah in a silhouette of energy against the lapis sky. Rahat closes the glass doors of the china cabinet with a sad finality.

And Myrtle Shukla, having long forgotten her ancestral Brahmin Hindu past, plays on and on, the Italian street melody giving way now to the solider grandeur of "The Old Rugged Cross," while Myrtle luxuriates in the niceness of being (*really* and *truly* deep inside her) a Westerner and a Christian.

## Kaiserbagh Circus

"*Kee-yun op runjeedah benh?*" I ask Mahmood Hassim. "*Nuheen ganna adj?*" ("Why are you sad? No song today?") Hyderi, sitting beside me in the rickshaw, laughs and translates Mahmood Hassim's sober reply: "He says that he is sad because he does not know why."

"*Beemer?*" I ask.

"No, not sick," comes back the reply.

We ride along in silence, rounding the I.T. College corner, turning down along the many-domed and turreted Lucknow University. Hyderi and I scan the red Lucknow Union building carefully for signs of students congregating nearby. We see a group of students outside.

"Getting ready for the next strike, Hyderi?" I ask.

He smiles. Both of us think of the month-long violent strike that has just ended at the University. (Fourteen students had been thrown in jail.)

Past the Vice-Chancellor's office building now. (Police guards still stationed there to protect him.) Swinging up and over the heavily-trafficked Monkey Bridge now. Two monkeys sitting on the bridge. *"Bundurs,"* I say. Mahmood Hassim kicks out a leg at them as we go by.

Next to us, workmen hammering away on the new bridge, and then, on the other side, masons swarming over the new lingam temple being erected to Shiva.

Down the hill on the other side of the bridge now, flying at a good rate of speed, Mahmood Hassim ringing both bells, but without his usual spirit and only an occasional *"Chelly-ow!"* at the bicyclists, water buffaloes, and herds of goats in his way.

We whip past the beautiful Moghul tombs of Sadat Ali Khan and his wife, Khrshaed Zadi, tombs that are yellowed now, desolate, but perfectly proportioned and located in the center of Lucknow. (At sunset, the delicate tracery of these two great floating domes will be pointed up by an orange and pink sky.)

Soon, we pass the ruins of the Kaiserbagh Palace on the left and the Safeed Baradari on the right where Wajid Ali Shah was rumored to have held secret dance-dramas with his wives (one wife for every day of the year, as reported to me by Rahat). Then, into the traffic of Kaiserbagh Circus itself, a miniature Connaught Circus (New Delhi), with the Ashoka Pillar in the center, crowned by crouching lions, and, all around the circus, arcaded shops of white or yellow sandstone.

We aim for a shop bearing a large sign, reading,

## MUSHTAQ

Grandson of Mohammed Ishaq and Mohammed Ibrahim

### Manufacturing Opticians

There, in front of the shop, is Rahat, waving us in for a landing. Today is a significant day for Rahat because he is getting his first pair of eyeglasses. While Rudd was giving him his nightly English lesson, she suddenly realized he must be far-sighted. We sent him down to have his eyes examined, and now he is to select his glasses and frames (which I, of course, am paying for), and Rahat has requested both Hyderi and me to come and help him decide which pair he should get.

The lens part is simple. He needs bi-focals; the cheaper kind come with a line across them; the more expensive kind with just a round circle, quite invisible to anyone looking straight at one's eyes. We decide on the little round circles.

Now for the frames. Four kinds are offered, ranging widely in price: a red plastic one for 6 rupees, a brown plastic one for 18 rupees, one with thin strips of gold for 22 rupees, and another with thick strips of gold for 25 rupees. I prefer the brown plastic ones. Rahat, although he doesn't say so, prefers the most expensive one with the thick gold. He tries them all on impartially, but I notice that his fingers keep coming back to the heavy gold ones. I think to myself, "For once in his life, let him have the fun of choosing the most expensive item after the pretense of a careful game of examining and evaluating."

"Rahat," I say to him. "I think these glasses are the ones you'd really like. Consider them." He does, turning them over and over in his hands. Then Hyderi comes to his rescue. "Take those," he says with certainty. Rahat tries them on, takes a long look in the mirror, looks to the doorway where Mahmood Hassim is standing quietly watching us. Then Rahat turns back to the oculist. "These," he says.

The glasses will be ready on Friday. We agree to come back then. We turn now and head out toward the rickshaw. Hyderi laughs happily as he climbs back up to his seat. Rahat and I repeat again, "Friday at three o'clock." Mahmood Hassim manages a little smile.

One American among three Indians! I wonder about the meaning of my life to theirs, theirs to mine. To Rahat, I am the "sahib," the one to whom he daily bends his will and upon whom he is dependent for his livelihood. I pay him double what he was originally offered to me at, but he accepts all with equanimity. "Whatever you say, Sahib," he has said to me; "Whatever you do."

To Hyderi, I am obviously a prize star in his collection of foreigners-in-Lucknow. This boy, who has never been out of Lucknow in his life, satisfies his urge to visit strange places and meet new people by collecting people like Dr. Dry and Mr. Piggott, both Englishmen, and me.

To Mahmood Hassim, I am an apostle sent down by Allah to heap benefits upon him. "His eye is on the sparrow and I know he watches me."

None of the three had any initial reason to believe that there was anything special to gain from being friendly to me, however. I was the employer of Rahat, a chance acquaintance of Hyderi's, and an occasional occupant of Mahmood Hassim's rickshaw. I could have remained the aloof, impersonal traveler in India, had I so chosen. Yet from me, all three drew forth a rare kind of friendship that I don't give easily. I think this came about because of the naturalness in their personalities that somehow made me become more natural too—so that I got on well with them as just another human being and not as the self-conscious American in a goldfish bowl.

Or am I just kidding myself, reluctant to face up to the possibility of the saddest irony of them all—that their friendship has been just another one of the Great American Tourist's purchases along the way? I don't know. I hope not. But if that is the truth, then all I can say is that I got my money's worth: My friends have shown me something of the heart and mind of India that will not soon be forgotten.

Now Rahat gets on his bike. He is off to the bazaar. There will be papaya for dessert tonight, he promises. Hyderi and I, with Mahmood Hassim at the steering wheel, are off to the Gunch. A moment in time—the last that all of us will share together. Am I the only one of the four who realizes this? A wave of the hand; Rahat sets off into the crowd. Our rickshaw moves forward, and, just as in a motion picture, we vanish forever into the noisy, swirling anonymity of Kaiserbagh Circus. The camera does a slow dissolve. Fade out. The end.

## Bunny Farr Is Coming To Dinner

It has been my fate in life to be perpetually thrown into the company of spies. I have no definite proof that these people actually *are* espionage agents (after all, what identifying marks are spies likely to have handy?), but there is a particular aura, an ambiance, that hangs in the air about certain persons that makes me suspicious. Don't misunderstand me. I don't dislike spies; I am rather fond of them, in fact. It's just that I don't actively seek them out: They circumnavigate around me, so to speak, and surround me with a sense of the incredible mystery and ineluctability of the human personality.

I remember one time in Geneva, Switzerland, for instance, where Rudd and I were living for a couple of months while I was out of work and Rudd was working in a maelstrom of a typing pool (run by a French woman martinet) at the Intertelecommunications Union of the United Nations. We suddenly met one day a striking blonde young Englishwoman named Shelley Twist. Now, I ask you, what on earth is one to think of a bright-eyed young lady who suddenly pops up in front of one at lunch and says, "How d'ye do? I'm Shelley Twist." Exactly! You know right away that she is an undercover agent for Scotland Yard. And what is one to conclude when, on further acquaintance, her talk is flavored with intimate knowledge of migrations to and from Latvia, Estonia, and Lithuania, and when she conveys *sotto voce,* an undercurrent sense of urgency about the comings and goings of people to and from these countries? Wherever one went in Geneva in those days, one would be taken quite by surprise with a "Well, hello there!" and there, emerging from behind a parked car near one of the old League of Nations buildings, would always be Shelley Twist.

Imagine my surprise, then, when, upon arriving in Lucknow to teach at Isabella Thoburn College, the first person I met (even before I met the Acting Principal) was a blonde, blue-eyed Englishwoman in a sort of chemise, disheveled, in the Isabella Thoburn College yard, who offered her hand to me and said, "How d'ye do? I'm Joan Humby. Come this way through these trees. The students call it The Forest of Arden. I don't need to tell you why." Again, from Joan Humby, the mysterious background—born in Jaffna, Ceylon; educated in Germany (very suspicious in my book!); Quaker religion (You know these pacifists!); M.A. from Oxford; ten years in Australia; three years in India; mother living in London; sister married to a Hollander living in the Netherlands. And the smoke-screen interests—week end trips to Benares and Calcutta; passionate interest in Sikhs and potential prime ministers of India; night work at Literacy House; the pointed comments made against the Hindus; the friend who's visiting her who wants to start a "College of All Nations"; the guard dropped in conversation occasionally revealing a strong pro-Pakistan sympathy. Exactly! You know full well, as I told Rudd, that Joan Humby is the real power behind General Ayub Khan.

But what on earth is one to do when quite clearly an international espionage agent pops up as one of your own countrymen? Let me introduce you at this point to Bunny Farr.

Bunny Farr is a dear, sweet little woman, a cross between Helen Hayes (in *Mrs. McThing*) and Josephine Hull (in *Harvey*). She looks so much like little Helen Hayes (about twenty years ago) that all I can think of is that line in *Harriet* (in which Helen Hayes played Harriet Beecher Stowe) when Abraham Lincoln, extending his hand, said, "So this is the little lady that started the great war." One night when Bunny Farr walks in here, I am going to say the same thing to her and watch that motherly chickadee smile vanish from her lips.

You have to watch Bunny Farr carefully; among spies, she is the very trickiest of the trickiest. I don't think there is any malice in her at all, although I haven't tested her (and I don't think I will) to find out, because I have a shuddering recollection of a James Bond movie, *From Russia With Love,* I think it was, in which Lotte Lenya played a horrendous spy who cut people up by way of razor-sharp knives inserted into her shoes, and Bunny Farr might be capable of that!

The first suspicious thing about Bunny Farr is that her name isn't Bunny Farr at all; only I call her that. Her real name is Mrs. Louise Farr, and Mr. Farr being dead or out of commission somewhere (she has never volunteered information), all I know is that she is a native North Carolinian and has a married son and daughter living, respectively, in Virginia and North Carolina. She carries the pose of normalcy so far as even to bring out from her pocketbook perfectly ordinary looking snapshots of her (alleged) children and grandchildren.

She has been at Isabella Thoburn College now for two years, and, on the surface, is the Librarian there and runs an efficient library business (I think libraries are ideal for espionage centers, don't you? There is so much accumulated information there and jolly little corners in which to tuck away receiving sets and all.) Her hair is a pale cider color, worn back in a neat little bun. She wears harlequin-type glasses, giving her a slightly pixie-like, rabbity look, and she favors deceptive (for a spy) homespun calico or gingham dresses. She plays it very *Ma Perkins*.

None of this, of course, is enough to arouse one's suspicions. But there are two things she does which deserve further analysis. First of all, she pretends to be a bird watcher. Now, I know enough about bird watchers to know when their conversation is genuinely about yellow-breasted nuthatchers and great tits, and when it is not. And, I tell you, Bunny Farr's is not.

But wherever she goes, the bird watcher's typical equipment goes with her: a pair of binoculars. Why? Why, for instance, when you invite her for dinner at night, does she arrive, clomping down on your table, even before she takes off her coat, her binoculars? What birds does she hope to espy at night? Exactly!

And why, in casual conversation one day, did Bunny Farr let drop that the first thing she did as her ship neared Cherbourg was to pick up her binoculars and scan the shoreline? "You'd be surprised at what you can see," she said, framing her remark in an ostensible context of birds. But you and I know better by now, don't we? It is quite clear that Bunny Farr is a highly-regarded top-agent of the C.I.A.

She is supposed to be at Isabella Thoburn College on a missionary's status. Now, the missionaries who come to I.T. College are pretty much cut from the same cloth—fundamentalists, non-smokers, non-drinkers, non-everything. Bunny Farr happens to be hooked on cigarettes. She smokes secretly in her room, and has recently become a great campus *cause celebre,* half the faculty wanting to sack her on the spot, and the other half siding with her (rebellious ones, those!) The Acting Principal, Dr. Marie Sommerville, as Bunny Farr herself reported it to me, forced her to go see the psychiatrist down at Nur Manzil. You know Bunny. She went, had a good smoke and chat, came back to I.T., and still goes on smoking in her room.

At first, naturally, I was on Bunny's side. I invited her to dinner, and after dinner, Bunny would sit smoking cigarette after cigarette, and I would sit smoking cigar after cigar (just as her father used to, she confided to me.) But, as time went on, I fell to thinking, wasn't it just possible Bunny was using all this smoking fuss as a cover up for her secret messages to Moscow, Peking, and Washington? One thing you've got to say about Bunny: She plays it straight. There is no one on earth, I submit, who can tell whose side she is on.

We had Bunny over to dinner a few nights ago. She gave us a can of American corned beef, and so we had Rahat make a little hash out of it—all so normal and folksy that you wouldn't think this mighty little woman had the destiny of great nations in her tiny hands that night.

Shelley Twist, Joan Humby, Bunny Farr—they may not have the Greta Garbo-Mata Hari image, but you have to give them credit: They've kept the old world spinning lately!

## In Search of Wajid Ali Shah

Just before it was announced last year that I was to come to India, I received a letter from a Yale alumnus (now a professor at Tufts University) asking if I would contribute an article on some aspect of the theatre to a scholarly book of theatre pieces that he and another professor (an old friend of mine) were getting up. I replied that I would look around and see if I could find a suitable topic for research while in India.

Arriving in Lucknow, I found that Lucknow's tradition had been music (*thumri* style of singing) and dancing (*kathak*), but nothing much in the way of theatre. Lucknow, having been one of the great Muslim cities of India, was quite deficient in theatre history, largely, of course, because the Muslims frown on theatre. (Really quite puritanical, these Muslims—no drinking, inimical to music and idols in religious services, 95% of their women in purdah.) In Delhi, at the

National Academy of Dramatic Art, I carefully asked everyone if they could give me any leads on theatre in Lucknow. All gave the same answer: no theatre in Lucknow.

But two chance references in a Lucknow guidebook sent me off on a trail. The first reference indicated that "King Wajid Ali Shah, the last king of Oudh, succeeded to the throne of his father, Amjad Ali Shah. The character and habits of King Wajid Ali Shah were not such as to encourage the prospects of improvement. Singers and females, provided for his amusement, occupied all his time." And the other reference, after discussing how Wajid Ali Shah built the Kaiserbagh Palace, went on, "Now, though a great deal of Kaiserbagh has disappeared during the mutiny, yet the name is still applied to the large quadrangle where Wajid Ali Shah, wearing the dress of a dramatic performer, used to hold fairs."

Wajid Ali Shah was born in 1819 and died in 1887. I thought there must be some fairly recent material on him, and so I asked my Urdu-speaking friend, Hyderi, to find out what he could about him. Hyderi did yeoman service, seeking out novelists and professors, gleaning little bits of information here and there.

Gradually we began building up a theory. We deduced that Wajid Ali Shah performed in a drama called *Inder Sabha,* along with about 100 of his wives, sometime in 1857. Wajid himself played Indra (the god of fire) and his wives were all got up as dancing fairies. The play was performed at 4:00 a.m. at the great Safeed Baradari (which still exists), and guards were stationed at all twelve gates so that nobody could disturb the performance.

Legend has it, however, that the jealous son-in-law of Wajid told the British, who were looking for Wajid, where to find him, and they broke into the Baradari, captured him and carted him off to Calcutta where, many years later, he died in prison. At the time of the break-in, Hazrat Mahal, Wajid's favorite wife and leading lady, was reported to have been killed fighting off British soldiers.

We soon turned up other information. I gave Hyderi the names of several other plays I wanted investigated, all reported to have been written by Wajid Ali Shah—*Radha Kanahiya, Dariva Tashuq, Seemita,* and *Maha Paikar.* I thought we could get some solid research going if we obtained copies of these plays and Hyderi translated them from Urdu into English for me.

Everything pointed toward the Mazhar Alam Library, the oldest Urdu library in Lucknow. Here, surely, there would be Urdu treasures from the past.

Off we went on our first of several visits. I remember our initial confrontation with the librarian there, a thin, bright-eyed, smiling man, sitting cross-legged on a cushion and reading the Koran, bound in yellow. He nodded to me, and I stood patiently by while he and Hyderi conversed in Urdu. The first meeting lasted an hour and a half. To summarize the little man's speech (for that's what it was), he asked Hyderi what he wanted to know and said that he (the little man) knew everything there was to know in this world, because, for forty years, he had been holed up in the library. When Hyderi mentioned Wajid and drama, Little Man said "nonsense," that these were all mean lies about Waji made up by vicious Hindus and that Wahjid Ali Shah had actually been a pious Muslim who had no use for either music or dance. However, he agreed to dig out *Inder Sabha* for us, and said I could purchase it for one rupee if we would come back.

We did come back again and again, and still Little Man kept stringing us along. One time he said to Hyderi, "What are your feelings about the theory of evolution?" Hyderi, knowing what was forthcoming, replied, "Sir, I am a young man. You are an older man. I know nothing. You know everything." Little Man then did a solid hour in Urdu on Darwin and evolution!

Finally, Hyderi went back alone to see Little Man and reported to me that he had gotten him to admit that he did not have the books and could not get them. Hyderi, very angry, threatened L.M. with Muslim revenge, and told me that he had asked six of his close friends to wind up their accounts at L.M.'s bookstore—(An eye for an eye and a tooth for a tooth?)

Now it looks as though time is running out. Without Hyderi to translate, Wajid Ali Shah is a quite hopeless project for me. But, knowing the vagaries of research, I know that one day I will suddenly find in Widener Library at Harvard or Sterling Library at Yale just what the reluctant dragon of Mazhar Alam Library in Lucknow wouldn't or couldn't give me.

## Mama Chatterjee Riding on a Peacock

She comes floating down from some unseen kingdom dressed in a black silk sari trimmed with green and gold. Over her shoulders is flung a white wool Kashmiri shawl, draped with a dramatic flare, as though arranged for her by Castillo-Lanvin. She doesn't look Indian at all, but rather Italian—short, stocky, resilient, enormous black eyes which are great pools of feeling and passion—and in her shining, blue-black hair, parted in the middle (with a red line to show she's a married woman) and pulled back to form a low bun on her neck, are arranged three bright Sweet William-type flowers—yellow, blue, and pink.

Rudd calls me away from my typewriter to have tea with Mama Chatteerjee, one of India's formidable Hindu mamas. Mama Chatterjee is someone we inherited from the

Ralph Sissons, Fulbright Americans, who pulled out of Lucknow early in January saying they had had enough of disease, poverty, and the Y.W.C.A., and, besides, Ralph had finished his work and Harriet was expecting their third child. Mama Chatterjee had been cultivating them while they were here; now she has shifted her field of action to us.

Mama is a real mama. She has six children to her credit, three of whom have apparently gotten as far away from her as they possibly could—and one of whom, a daughter, broke her Hindu caste to marry a Pakistani Muslim with whom she is now living in London. But Mama doesn't mind. She is rather proud of breaking caste and loves to scandalize the orthodox Hindus in her neighborhood. Mama is "young-minded" and this means keeping up with her three younger children, Kum-Kum, Ruby, and Ranjan.

Ranjan is tall, stalwart, good-humored, working for his M.A. in English at Lucknow University. Mama has decided that he has a journalistic flair, and so she is sending him out to work on a newspaper sometime soon. Kum-Kum is chubby, inherently lazy, refuses to learn to cook and tells Mama blithely that she fully intends to marry "a man with two servants." Mama says, "Never mind. Servants get sick. Sometimes knowing how to cook comes in handy." Mama is not so modern, you see, that she is stupid.

We come now to Ruby Chatterjee. Ruby is gorgeous—there is no other way to describe her. She is a raving beauty, one of those elegant Indian women who look radiant and move beautifully, and possess an extraordinary intelligence. Ruby is the prize jewel in Mama's coffer. She is studying now for her B.A. degree at Loreto Convent College in Lucknow. (These Indian convents do turn out the most remarkable young women!) Ruby is all dark, sympathetic eyes and liquid movements, designed to arrest any man's attention irrevocably at any time and any place—and Ruby knows it. So does Mama, I think.

Today is *Basant Panchmi,* the first day of spring according to the Hindu calendar, and Mama has come to take us to a *puja* (a shrine at which one worships) which the students have made at the Lucknow Union. Mama tells us she has bathed and fasted and made her private *puja* and that we must come with her immediately—the rickshaw is waiting—and see this thing for ourselves.

Going on at great length, like Laurette Taylor as Amanda Wingfield in *The Glass Menagerie,* Mama explains the significance of this rite to us. It seems it is a spring festival, especially dedicated to young virgins (I think of Ruby), and all young virgins wear green and yellow saris (colors of spring) and come and worship at the feet of the goddess of wisdom, Saraswati, who, on this day, represents especially music, dancing, the graceful fine arts. Will we come? Of course we will. There's nothing I like better than a good fertility rite, especially when it rings in the lively arts, as well.

At the Union, we climb up to the seond floor, after I give the rickshaw driver a little more money. Mama had waved my offer aside, saying, "No, no, you are my guest. Let me pay." And so I did, but as Mama wafted up the stairs with Rudd and the children in her capacious wake, the rickshaw driver showed me that she had given him only 45 naya paise. (Mama, it seems, is tight-fisted, as well.) So I up the ante a little, and the driver is happy.

On the second floor, we meet Ranjan, Kum-Kum, and Ruby looking scrumptious in a green print sari. Then off with our shoes and over to the shrine of the goddess, before which incense is burning, lotus petals are strewn, and chalk-paste marks on the floor describe floral designs.

Mama, of course, explains the whole thing to us. Saraswati, the goddess of wisdom, who is usually depicted riding on a peacock, appears all in white today (for virginal innocence), and in her hand she is carrying a large musical instrument—a kind of sitar. Saraswati has a great peacock circle of spring colors immediately behind her, and her statue is raised higher than us because all Hindu gods must always be higher than the worshippers, whose heads should reach the level of the gods' feet.

Today, Mama proclaims, Saraswati is being prayed to by Lucknow University students, who have been told by their parents that, if they fulfill their religious obligations to the goddess—fasting and making *puja*—on this day, they will pass their university examinations (coming up in a month.) And if they don't, warns Mama, watch out!

Soon, a priest, wearing a brown wool suit and hat, appears in front of all us shoeless devotees, making the *namaste* gesture (palms of the hands together in front of one). We do the same. He is followed by a muscular young man wearing a bright orange tee-shirt who offers us little saucers made of jungle leaves in which, Mama tells us, are the fruits of the springtime. I see a gooseberry, banana slice, and little sugar-paste candy in mine. We thank the young man, and I hastily thrust all our little leaves into my jacket pocket (Amoebic dysentery to the person who takes the first bite!)

Our *puja* over, we return home with Mama in tow, talking a blue streak. Rahat pours tea for us, but sticks out his tongue at Mama behind her back, much to Heather's amusement. (Rahat does not like Hindus.) On and on talks Mama, directing most of her conversation to Rudd. Mama, it seems, knows just the place in Delhi for Rudd to buy silk saris. "Don't go to Handloom House," Mama cautions. "Stay away from the Janpath." Mama, of course, knows the S. Klein's of Delhi, "where you can pick up the most exquisite silk saris for one-third the price." Rudd is all ears; I am bored. I wish Mama would go. It's way past lunchtime now, and Rahat is looking daggers at Mama.

Finally, Mama goes, sailing out the door toward Bishop Rockey Street; but, no sooner has she disappeared, than Hyderi appears (Mama's male counterpart as a marathon talker) riding on his bike, dressed in his National Cadet Corps uniform—green beret, silver emblem, red feather. He, it turns out, has been marching today down on the Gunch, not on behalf of *Basant Panchmi,* but for Republic Day.

Suddenly, an idea occurs to me—why not Hyderi and Ruby? "Hyderi," I say. "How would you like to marry the most beautiful girl in all Lucknow, perhaps in all India?"

Hyderi looks interested.

"Don't do it, Hyderi sahib," interjects Rahat. "Sahib doesn't like her mother and the father is no good." (Rahat is scornful of any female-dominated Hindu household.)

"Ignore Rahat, Hyderi," I plead. "Her sister married a Muslim, and now, I think, Ruby should marry you."

Hyderi thinks for a moment. "My mother would kill me," he replies.

Rahat looks relieved (Muslim to Muslim for him!)

"Mrs. Indira Gandhi married a Muslim, or a Parsi," I counter.

"My mother would kill me," Hyderi repeats.

Are mothers all-powerful in Hindu India, I wonder? Do the children have nothing to say? Mrs. Chatterjee had said to Rudd, "What is the sense of discussing adolescent problems in classes? Indian children have no problems."

"That's what you think, Mummy," Ruby replied.

Well, nothing is resolved in this clash between generations and castes. Ruby and Hyderi haven't agreed to marry, haven't even met, in fact. That doesn't matter. I told Hyderi we would place an ad in the paper:

WANTED: ONE BEAUTIFUL HINDU RUBY
FOR ONE STERLING MUSLIM HYDERI

But, anyway, we have all made our *puja* and offered up our private little prayers on this first day of spring. Mine is that in the new India, may all the young people get together a little more easily and naturally. But it isn't hard to guess, is it, who is really riding on that peacock right now?

# A Tale of Two Colleges

If you enjoyed reading about Bunny Farr, I have now to give you the unhappy postlude to her story. The Acting Principal, having failed to get Bunny certified "psycho" by a psychiatrist, wrote a letter to the Methodist Mission Board in New York (under whose auspices Bunny is here) to force Bunny to a resignation. I shall paraphrase here the reply Bunny received from the Board, preserving its essential meaning and tone:

Dear Mrs. Farr:

Dr. Marie Sommerville has written us that you refuse to give up smoking. She, of course, cannot force you to resign because she does not pay your salary but you should be aware that, were you being employed by any other Indian principal, you would have been asked to leave long ago. What kind of a moral example do you think you are providing for the students of Isabella Thoburn College? The Methodist Church does not condone smoking and believes that, when it sends out its missionaries, they are perfect in every respect.

Bunny, on the verge of tears, does not know what to make of her tragi-comic role as heroine of a rusty melodrama—a little lost soul adrift on the great sea of life. Rudd and I are outraged because, in addition to being a nice person, Bunny has been a superior librarian over here and has really tried to put the I.T. College library into good shape.

I am afraid that Dr. Sommerville's attitude reveals all too clearly what I.T. College is really like. Not only are the students being cheated of a good education because of the antiquated syllabi provided for them by the parent organization, Lucknow University, but they are also being warped by the narrow religious focus insisted on by the I.T. College administration. Now, Bunny Farr, it seems, is to be officially viewed by the entire I.T. College community as some kind of abnormal freak and is to be deprived of her job as librarian. This is one measure of the kind of college I have been teaching at all year. It has been comical up to a point, but this exceeds even caricature.

In marked contrast to I.T. College is the Roman Catholic college in Lucknow. Loreto Convent College is smaller and newer than I.T. College, but already it has lured away many of the brightest female students in Lucknow. Loreto Convent is actually three schools in one—elementary, intermediate, and collegiate—numbering about 1300 students. It is run by twelve Irish nuns, who do most of the administrative work and some teaching, but leave the lion's share of teaching to regular Indian teachers.

Two of our Indian friends go to Loreto. One is Rizwana Rizvi (Muslim) and the other is Ruby Chatterjee (Hindu). Both say that the religious aspects are not emphasized so heavily as they are at I.T. College. Rizwana arranged a tour of Loreto for us, and the mother Superior took us to visit classsrooms in session and to talk with students and teachers. We were especially impressed by the elementary school which has excellent classrooms and equipment. The whole institution has a warmth and lightness about it, and a vital life force that appealed to us. Spotlessly clean, Loreto is more a little bit of

Ireland dropped down in India than an Indian institution, but one can see that the nuns understand what education really is and that they are doing a forward-looking job of teaching.

Of course, the nuns—Sister Lucy, Sister Brenda, Mother Bernadine—with their lovely Irish accents and warm personalities are "darlin' ladies, darlin'," as Sean O'Casey might have phrased it. The Irish are personable enough as ordinary Patricks and Siobhans, but put a priest's collar on them or a nun's habit, and they could easily charm psalm-singing Protestants out of their pews, if they so wished. The first thing Mother Bernadine, who runs the College, did was to sign up Rudd and me for a panel discussion on "The Impact of the West on the East," and the second thing she did was to sign me up for a lecture on "Drama in Colleges."

Talking with Mother Bernadine about the skittishness of I.T. College toward the presence of men, Mother Bernadine (who has even persuaded American Peace Corps men into teaching at Loreto and has one of them coaching the basketball team) said to me in a crisp, over-cultivated accent (reminiscent of Katharine Hepburn at her best in *The Philadelphia Story*): "If I may say so, Dr. Kenvin, (touching her wimple), please do not be deceived by our nuns' habits here. I think you would find that our attitude has a little more of what the French might call *largeur* about it—shall we say?—ironical though that very thought may be."

"I have already sensed that, Mother Bernadine," I replied.

A tale of two colleges. Sunlight and learning—that's how I see Loreto Convent. I am just thankful we are leaving here in a few weeks, otherwise I'm afraid those charming Irish nuns would have me not only converted, but also signed up to teach at Loreto for the next twenty years.

Need I add that at Loreto College I noticed that ash trays were considerately laid out on tables in the lounges for visitors who might enjoy a smoke?

# The Bishop's Wife

**I** never go out to Literacy Village in Lucknow without thinking of that planned community set up by the multi-millionaire Andrew Undershaft at the conclusion of Shaw's *Major Barbara*. Literacy Village, too, is a little set of buildings arranged in a circle with a church of all faiths (covered with a thatched pagoda roof) in the center.

The Major Barbara of Literacy Village is Mrs. Welthy Fisher, an American woman, tall, smartly-dressed, and soon to be 86 years old. I first met her about a month ago at a tea given for the Board of Governors of I.T. College. A dull occasion suddenly had life blown into it when Mrs. Fisher entered the room, very tall, dressed in silver fox furs, wearing a triple strand of pearls, earrings, and brandishing great baroque rings on her fingers. She waded through a crowd of Methodist bishops and quiet ladies in silk saris. I noticed that she used her cane rather dramatically as she walked and that she wore high heels, setting off her still-handsome pair of legs.

I went out again to see her a few days ago, this time with Eugene Schaeffer of U.S.E.F.I. who was visiting us in Lucknow and wanted to see the sights. We drove out in the U.S.I.S. jeep about seven miles to Literacy Village, and Mrs. Fisher received us in her living room where we had a wonderful conversation with her lasting over an hour and a half.

As Welthy Honsinger of Rome, New York, she originally planned a career in opera, but somehow went off to China to run a Methodist mission school and lived there for many years, until she became the second wife of Fred Fisher, Methodist Bishop of India. With him, she lived a rich, delightful life (He was a very unconventional, progressive bishop), and both of them became good friends of Mahatma Gandhi and Rabindranath Tagore.

After her husband's death, Mrs. Fisher founded Literacy House in 1953 at Allahabad, and then moved to Lucknow in 1956 where she built Literacy Village and where she has been carrying on her important work ever since—bringing literacy to the villages of India. "It is better to light one candle than to curse the darkness." You will find Mrs. Fisher's extraordinary life story in her autobiography *To Light a Candle*. She has also written seven or eight other books and has just finished a geography for Indians.

In her living room, surrounded by great brass tables, red oriental carpets, many sculptures of Gandhi, photographs of herself with Tagore, Eleanor Roosevelt, Nehru, and Gandhi, and with the odors of fragrant Indian spices emanating from her kitchen, Mrs. Fisher reminisced about her work and talked about her plans for the future. "My whole life now is public relations," she said to me. "That's all I do— raise money!"

She spoke highly of Laurie Baker, architect for Literacy Village, and laughed as she recalled her first telegram to him in which the telegraph office mistakenly put an "a" in her first name, making it "Wealthy." She received back a telegram from Baker which read:

### YES X YOU MAY COME AT ANY TIME X

### X SIGNED

### WEALTHY BAKER

"With a sense of humor like that," she said. "I knew he was just the man I wanted." She told us, also, how the name "Welthy" had originally been spelled with the "a," but her

Dutch puritan progenitors took out the "a" because they thought it gave the wrong impression.

Mrs. Fisher confided that, as a child, she had disliked missionaries because they always looked so poor-mouthed and dowdy. She resolved to be herself when she became a missionary, and that has included dressing in stylish clothes. She said the first $5,000 she ever got for her school in China came to her because the businessman she was talking with thought she wouldn't take less. Ever since, she has dressed up. The Fifth Avenue Missionary, you might call her. But she is a wonderfully warm person, human, intelligent, thoroughly delightful. You don't meet many Americans like her abroad, and you are so proud of your own country when you do.

## A Farewell to India

Quite a few of you apparently liked the story of Mahmood Hassim, the rickshaw driver. You might be interested in the happy sequal (so far) to it. I have persuaded Hyderi to teach Mahmood Hassim (who is totally illiterate, having had no schooling at all) how to read and write Hindi. They have begun their lessons in our living room under my watchful eye, and Mahmood Hassim seems to be involved in his new work. This points up what needs to be done in India and by whom it must be done—by Indians for Indians, not by Americans. India needs its own domestic Peace Corps, and a good place to begin would be with university students like Hyderi.

Good news, too, about Wajid Ali Shah. A friend of Hyderi's at Aligarh Muslim University located a copy of the plays in Urdu, complete with several illustrations. The problem now is can we get the book translated before I leave?

Several of you have asked about the aftermath of the robbery we had here. It was soon followed by a second robbery in which Mrs. Shukla's gold watch and Mr. Shukla's new electric shaver were taken. Again, the police came. Again, Mrs. Shukla felt that it was one of the sweeping daughters. Nothing was ever determined, but Mrs. Shukla banished all the sweepers, except for the sweeping mother, who is the only one who comes now.

What more remains? We've come to the end of a very rich, exciting experience in India. A few things yet to do: Brooke and Heather make their stage debuts this Saturday as Kashmiri attendants to a princess in a play at I.T. College. I have been asked to deliver my final chapel sermon (at 6:30 a.m., no less) on the morning of March 17th (St. Patrick's Day. Shall I speak to Mother Bernadine about this?) And I have also been asked to speak at I.T. College's Founder's Day on "Isabella Thoburn College in Perspective." (Do I dare?) I have also been asked by the Theatre Arts Workshop in Lucknow to direct a play for them. (They hire the Ravindralaya Theatre and do quite professional work, but I have had to turn this down for lack of time.)

We leave Lucknow on March 19th. Our plans are still being ironed out in New Delhi, so that I cannot give you our exact itinerary, but we hope to travel in Europe during the spring and expect to be back home again in June. This, then, will be the last letter I'll write to you, unless I am able to get to the typewriter in either England or France. Thanks for all the letters, clippings, packages of food, and messages you sent to us. And goodbye for now.

Love from us all,

ﺟ . ﺍﺟ

(Urdu)

# PARIS BOUND

## Letters 1953-1955

Verna Rudd Kenvin & Roger Lee Kenvin

# Preface To Paris Bound

In March 1953, when Rudd and I set sail for Europe on the *Queen Elizabeth*, Dwight Eisenhower was President of the United States. With his broad smile and pleasant manner, Eisenhower was very popular among Americans, and so was elected for a second term in 1956. Perhaps to counterbalance his niceness, the Secretary of State was a slightly inscrutable hatchet-man named John Foster Dulles, who developed the idea of diplomatic brinksmanship—a way of taking a tough stance all the way to the edge—which led the country into holding its collective breath occasionally and may have helped pave the way for the defiance and dissension of some Americans in the 1960s. The Korean War ended in 1953, though, but there was much talk about the threat of nuclear weapons like the H-bomb.

Senator Joseph McCarthy viciously set up an inquisition in Congress, especially attacking Hollywood, grilling even Lucille Ball and Humphrey Bogart about their political associations, making a name for himself by preying upon the widespread fear of Communism in the country.

The State department granted and then abruptly revoked the visa given to English comedian, Charlie Chaplin, so that he was forced to live forever after in exile in Switzerland.

Ingrid Bergman had already been banished to Italy by the Hollywood press for deserting her doctor husband for Italian director, Roberto Rossellini. She was replaced in America's affection by a gamine actress from Belgium, Audrey Hepburn, who portrayed Colette's *Gigi* on the New York stage and would later play Eliza Doolittle on screen in *My Fair Lady*.

Action Expressionism in art was all the rage in New York, allowing that city to steal some of Paris' former glory. Samuel Beckett's play of human paralysis, *Waiting for Godot,* was the English-language play of note in this period.

Joseph Stalin died in 1953, and Russia briefly eased up in a period of de-Stalinization, but the iron hand of Communism still gripped eastern Europe.

Vienna, like Berlin, was divided into four sectors with Russian, American, English, and French soldiers riding around together in jeeps, giving the city an eerie *Third Man* feeling.

Yugoslavia was also tightly controlled by Marshal Tito, who unified its disparate cultures, and was viewed by Yugoslavians as a kind of George Washington.

France and England were still recovering from the war, just realizing how much they had lost after all. France was still struggling to hold on to Algeria and wouldn't let go of it until 1962.

Israel was still a new state (since May 1948) and a controversial idea.

West Germany, bombed heavily during World War II, was slowly re-building with the help of the Marshall Plan.

London, too, still showed scars from the heavy drubbing it took, and the English were just coming off rationing.

Switzerland, which remained neutral during the war, was full of refugees, especially from the now Communist-dominated countries.

In New York City, I was working for the Crowell-Collier Publishing Company at 640 Fifth Avenue, writing copy and ads for the Direct Mail Division and the International Division, for *Colliers, The American Magazine, and Woman's Home Companion*. Rudd was working as a private secretary at the Iran Foundation in the Empire State Building. We lived in an apartment on the seventh floor in Stuyvesant Town.

Rudd had been to Europe in 1949 with her parents and sister on a deluxe grand tour. Since this was to be my first visit, I wanted to stay for a while and live and work over there. Rudd agreed, so we saved money, enough for about six months, we thought, and enjoyed the farewell celebrations in our honor.

Most of our friends, to our great surprise, praised our "courage" and "bravery" in giving up such good, secure jobs, and an apartment in New York, for who knew what?

But Rudd and I were young and confident. We felt we were flexible and could tackle any kind of job. After all, I had worked in publishing in New York for three years, had also taught at Bowdoin College in Maine, and done graduate work at Harvard. Rudd had taught in Verona, New Jersey, public schools, done graduate work in education at Bank Steet College, and been a private secretary in Manhattan. We were armed and ready for high adventure in Europe.

These letters reveal our reactions and show what happened to us in Europe. Most of the letters are to our families, who shared these letters among themselves, but others are to friends.

The most difficult thing for me in Europe was to realize that people saw me as a symbol of the United States. I was always being blamed for U.S. policy on this point or that. Nobody seemed to understand that often I didn't agree with the policy either.

The other problem I had was with students who felt the teacher was a supreme authority on any subject. I was used to presenting several points of view to students, but they always wanted only one, authoritative, point of view.

I was twenty-seven years old and Rudd twenty-five in this period. These letters cover the two years from 1953 to 1955. When we returned in 1955, I taught at Northeastern University in Boston briefly, and then we moved to New Haven, Connecticut for the next three years. We both are glad we used these early years for knocking around in Europe. It was a valuable part of our education.

R.L.K.

367, The White House,
Regents Park.
London, N.W.1, England
March 29, 1953

Dear Family,

I'm writing this on the train en route to Henley-on-Thames, so hope the handwriting won't be too illegible.

We had a great crossing on the Queen Elizabeth where both the accommodations and service were excellent. Charles Boyer, David Niven, Paul Whiteman, Bing Crosby and his son were aboard. At Cherbourg, I bumped into Crosby and his son, Lindsay, on the open deck and he posed for a photograph for me, with his trademark hat and pipe.

Susan Franks, Rudd's friend, had taken a flat for us in her Regents Park apartment house, so we have had our own little apartment, just as though we were residents. Susan has been very kind and gracious to us, helping to make our stay a memorable one. Yesterday, she took us to visit friends who kindly treated us to luncheon and a cruise on their fifty-five foot motor launch on the Thames from which we watched the Oxford-Cambridge boat race. Right now we are going to visit William and Edna Wingrove, a wonderful English couple we met on board the ship. We are passing through the soft, beautiful countryside in the Windsor-Eton area.

London is as satisfying as I expected it would be. Great stands for the coronation of Queen Elizabeth II are being erected everywhere and the grey city is revivified with window boxes filled with yellow daffodils. Prices are very inexpensive over here for Americans. Rudd, Susan, and I went to the Connaught last night for cocktails and dinner (golden plover which was too gamey for my taste) and afterward to Claridges for coffee. The whole bill came to $18.

Susan also got us fifth row center orchestra seats for N. C. Hunter's *Waters of the Moon* with Wendy Hiller, Edith Evans, and Dame Sybil Thorndike. It was superbly done. We feel right at home in London. Perhaps we'll come back later on to get jobs. It certainly is a city I like a lot, and I've found the English to be kind and courteous.

I'll close for now as I want to enjoy the beauty of the countryside outside the train window. We're traveling in one of those distinctively compartmented English trains.

Love,


Roger

En route to Paris,
March 30, 1953

Dear Harry and Family,

It is 8:35 a.m. and we are on the boat train leaving London for Paris. We had a terrific time in London, thanks to Susan's hospitality and that of the Wingroves.

Yesterday was the lying-in-state procession of Queen Mary. All London turned out for it. Rudd and I left town early in the morning to visit the Wingroves in Henley-on-Thames. It is a charming town and we enjoyed our brief time there. When we got back to London, the procession had just ended, so we joined the crowd at Buckingham Palace. Apparently the royal family had already returned because we didn't see them. We also saw the Tower of London and Tower Bridge yesterday. . . .

All London is being refurbished for the Coronation. Huge stands are going up everywhere and almost all the buildings are decked out with fresh-looking daffodils and hyacinths in window boxes. The city looks quite festive. London reminds me of a larger Boston, more refined, perhaps, more interesting architecturally, and with far friendlier people. I'm impressed with the English. They really are courteous. Tell Mother we also met a Scotsman on the Kyles' motor launch, and he claimed the two most beautiful cities in Europe were Edinburgh and Prague. Susan's mother is currently in Prague now, but can't get out because of the Communist regime.

The theaters in London are uniformly good and inexpensive. You can have the best orchestra seats for $2.80 with second balcony seats going for 35 cents. Small wonder there are three times as many theaters as in New York.

Clothing also is reasonable. Harris tweed jackets cost $18. Dinner in a prestigious restaurant costs $2.50 (minus cocktails). Last night's modest meal cost 75 cents each.

London's bus and subway systems seem superior to ours in New York. The subways are cleaner, even though people are permitted to smoke on them. The seats are also upholstered and have arm rests. Picture that in New York!

Buses are those tall, bright red double-deckers and they keep 'em coming along every minute. Taxis and autos are small and delightful. You don't go through all that haranguing you have with New York drivers.

To go back to the ship for a moment: We had a fine crossing. I won the Shakespearean competition and received a pen and pencil set as a prize. My name appeared in the day's program (British spelling: programme) which I'll send to you from Paris. They also had a daily competition on how many miles a day the ship would log, and Rudd won this once and received eight shillings. It was a relaxing, enjoyable voyage for both of us.

Will write more from Paris.

Roger

Hotel Vouillemont
15, rue Boissy d'Anglas
Paris, France


Dear Norma, Lou, and Leslie,

So this is Paris! We arrived last night after a really thrilling voyage across the Channel. It was a very rough sea and people were sick all over the ship. Rudd and I, of course, were good sailors. I almost wished the Channel had been even a little rougher to test our mettle.

Our room at the Vouillemont is very comfortable and typically French. I wish you could see the w.c. which *dames et messieurs* use jointly, plus the bidet in which you bathe just the vital parts. We have no tub. *Mais, c'est Paris et Rudd et moi sont maintenant Parisiens!*

Paris is very old and appears soft and blurred looking. I have the feeling that all the buildings were built a thousand years ago and are being left to crumble away slowly until the time comes when they will be replaced. The countryside along the way from Dieppe to Paris was pleasingly out-of-focus and lovely, just the way the French impressionists painted it.

Today we jumped on a fantastic bus and went to the Left Bank to look for pensions and rooms less expensive than the Vouillemont. It was fascinating getting a glimpse of the way Parisian families live. We finally found an inexpensive hotel near the magnificent Luxembourg Garden. We will be moving there tomorrow and stay for ten days. Our room is large, comfortable, and right out of *La Bohême*. The address is

Hotel de L'Avenir, 65 rue Madame, Paris 6, France. The pensions in the Latin Quarter are all filled for the Easter season, but we may be able to find one once we move in to our new quarters.

I went to J. Walter Thompson today and am to go back on Thursday for an extensive interview with Mr. Scott, who runs it. I hope we will not have to wait too long to find jobs.


Love,

Roger

Paris
Tuesday

Dear Tom,

We received Russ' letter yesterday and were upset to hear that you have had a bout with pneumonia. I hope you will soon be feeling better and in good health again.

Rudd and I are having a splendid time here in Paris, but have found everything alarmingly expensive. We leave tomorrow for a five-day tour through Switzerland, with job interviews in Geneva, and, if we locate jobs there or find the living less expensive, we may settle there instead.

I've contacted several American publishing companies in Paris, and, although they are interested, they have no vacancies at present. American firms have to employ 95% French and only 5% Americans. Since most are branch offices, you can imagine how difficult it is to land anything. However, I keep trying, but may have to take a job in another field. Another complicating factor is that, for the first time in French history, there is an unemployment problem. Work permits for foreigners are difficult to obtain. Plus salaries are disappointingly low. Rudd has been offered a secretarial job that pays 35,000 francs a month—$100 a month in U.S. currency. It would be all right if the cost of living were commensurate with such a salary, but it isn't. I don't understand how the French are able to manage.

In our spare time, we've been doing as much sightseeing as possible. We've climbed nearly every cathedral tower and public monument in sight. We've even had the chance to look in on Paris' fabled night life, which is fascinating. One spot, *La Caveau de la Bolée*, is located below street level in a cellar that must surely have been a dungeon in mediaeval times. The ceilings are vaulted and low, and the entertainers provide songs to match. Another spot, *Le Club de Vieux-Colombier*, reportedly an Existentialist hangout, is so crowded, one can hardly stand upright. It's a cellar also, and was jammed with jazz aficionadoes from America, England, and the U.S. Army the night we were there. Sydney Bechet, the great jazz musician, was the featured performer. He thrilled the crowd with his playing and his flashy diamond ring. The air was thick with smoke, providing a surreal nightclub scene. Drinks were $2.00 apiece. That spoiled the whole event for us.

We are living in a comfortable little hotel near the Luxembourg Garden and on the corner of the rue de Fleurus where Gertrude Stein and Alice B. Toklas lived. The Luxembourg Garden is probably the most charming park in all Paris. It's especially given over to the little pink-and-white Renoir children who frequent it. They sail boats on the pond, and watch marionette shows like *La Legende de Blanche-Neige*, which Rudd and I went to see. It was delightful, but, to our surprise, we counted only six dwarfs.

Another Parisian attraction is the Flea Market (*Marché au Puce)* on the Right Bank. All kinds of merchandise are displayed here under tents lining the sidewalks for miles. Much of it is junk, of course, but there are bargains in antiques and furniture.

Montmartre is another colorful section of Paris, also on the Right Bank, rooted around a large hill crowned by the church of Sacre-Coeur. At the base of the hill lies the rowdy night club sector and the whorehouse area. To the left of the church is the little village of Montmartre, painted so successfully by Maurice Utrillo and others. It is self-consciously quaint.

I don't think Parisians bother to paint, repair, or maintain anything until it starts to fall apart. I had expected Paris to be colorful, but, instead, it appears colorless. The shutters, doors, walls of buildings are either dirty white or a neutral color, and most buildings appear to be peeling or crumbling. It's the trees and flowers that give the city color.

In full bloom they hide the tawdriness of the buildings and give Paris that soft, impressionist appearance.

We had dinner with a French family on the Boulevard Raspail a few nights ago. They are a pleasant, hospitable family and asked many questions about the United States. The mother is a widow with two daughters and a son. The youngest daughter (19) works, the other daughter (24) is a teacher, and the son (27) studies medicine. They are a fairly typical middle-class family, I would guess. It's interesting to compare them with their American counterparts. I felt they were very independent in their thinking, but was surprised that they weren't particularly interested in traveling outside France. . . .

Please give my best to everyone at the office and to all the Grans, Macdonalds, and Stewarts. Tell Russ and Ralph that I keep my eye out for our Crowell-Collier ads in the Paris *Herald-Tribune*.

As ever,

Roger

65 rue Madame
Paris 6, France
April 5, 1953

Dear Families:

Here it is our first wedding anniversary and also Easter. Thanks for all your greetings. . . .

Since all the French are away from Paris on holiday (and all the English, Swiss, Norwegians, etc. on holiday in Paris), and most businesses closed for the three days, we have been walking our legs off sightseeing. The more we see of Paris, the more we realize there is to see and the more we want to stay here. We've also found some reasonable restaurants where we can get a good meal with wine for a dollar or less, including les escargots and chateaubriand steak, so we are much happier. The only thing that hasn't improved is the cold. April in Paris is very beautiful to look at, with the cherry trees out, tulips and May flowers blooming, and trees in bud, but the weather is cold and damp, except in the sun. And there are April showers, after a seven-weeks drought.

We are getting very adept with the autobus, as they call it. We even buy tickets the cheap way, by the booklet, and give the conductor the right number for our ride. Via the buses, we have really traveled all over Paris. So far, we have seen most of the important and beautiful churches in the city. One, Sainte Chapelle, is by far the most exquisite church in the world on the inside. Unfortunately, many people miss it since it is not well marked and is inside the Palais de Justice, but it is a veritable jewel. The whole inside is painted blue with little gold fleurs de lis. The stained glass windows are vivid—ruby red and sapphire blue colors. The delicacy of it all is unbelievable.

Another beautiful church is Sacre Coeur. I had not seen this church before, but it certainly was worth the long climb up to it. We walked through a charming park, one of the myriads of parks in Paris, and marveled at the church's white beauty from afar. The inside does not live up to the outside, though. We wandered down through the village around the church. There were numerous painters painting the various views. The walls near the church were covered with dabs of paint by which the artists sample their colors. You could buy delightful water colors for about one dollar.

Our next church was Notre Dame de Paris. However, after the other two, it was an anticlimax, except for the Rose window and the view from the top of the towers, which we climbed. The climb up is something, but descending is worse, since you have to stay to the inside and narrow part of the spiral staircase and sometimes it is pitch dark for about ten steps or so, but the view is something and much less expensive than the Eiffel Tower. A storm was gathering outside, so I wanted to get down. When we did, it was raining, and so we saw the gargoyles at work as waterspouts.

We walked through the tremendous flower market from the Ile de la Cité to the Ile St. Louis, where some of the oldest houses in Paris are found. Along the banks of the Seine were the omnipresent fishermen, who never seem to catch any fish, and we saw a boat sail under a bridge, bending back its smokestack in order to do so. The Ile St. Louis is quite crumbly, too, but many of the houses are still quite lovely, and all the buildings are of historical interest. . . .

We may be spending a little more money than we actually should be under the circumstances, but at least we are seeing Paris. . . . It is an incredible city, unfathomable, really unknowable, but always charming, crumbling, and dirty. And always the Parisians to contend with. A riddle that draws one, as a moth is drawn to the flame. Perhaps, in truth, that is what Paris is—the flame to all of us moths.

Much love,


Rudd

Hotel de L'Avenir
65 rue Madame
Paris 6, France

Dear Families,

I will write this letter now as we are about to leave for a five-day visit to Switzerland and will not take the typewriter with us.

To take first things first, we have landed one job—for Rudd—at the American Express Company. But the salary is on the French scale and is 35,000 francs a month, which means $100. We felt pretty glum until we met a woman who holds an important post at the American Chamber of Commerce in France. She is paid only 25,000 francs a month. She said it is possible to live on such a pitiful salary if one cooks one's own meals. So when we get back from Switzerland, we are going to try to find a place that will allow us to cook our own meals.

As for me, American Express has nothing right now, but may later on, they said, at Fontainebleau, an hour and a half from Paris. I've heard from some of the publishing companies, but not the most important ones yet. The New York *Times*, now located in Amsterdam, wrote a nice letter, saying that, although they had no vacancies right now, they'd like to keep my resume on file, should something turn up.

Rudd accepted the American Express offer, but we are going to see what's what in Switzerland. . . . We take the train to Geneva where we'll stay a few days, and then, on the return trip, we'll go from Geneva to Lausanne to Montreux to Chateau-d'Oex to Gstaad to Spiez to Interlaken (where we'll go up the Jungfrau to Sarnen to Lucerne to Olten to Bâle, where we'll return to France. Our tickets were very reasonable and we will see most of Switzerland, except Zurich, which we may be able to see later.

Spring in all its warmth and beauty came to Paris yesterday after a spell of scrappy, rainy weather and a truly Gallic thunderstorm. Rudd and I have been sitting in the Luxembourg Garden, following the little shafts of sunlight, and listening to the happy laughter of children, just like real Parisians. . . .

We also had dinner with the Mallets on the Boulevard Raspail. They had several other guests and conversed in fast French, leaving me, intimidated and inhibited, far behind. Topics discussed were 1) The American reaction to Stalin's death 2) Catholicism in America and in France 3) Were we Protestant or Catholic? (Rudd said she was Unitarian; I said Episcopalian.) 4) How could Boston be 75% Catholic when the city was settled by Puritans? 5) What was American cooking like? (This prompted the French to joke, jeer, and sneer at British cooking.) 6) Did we know of France's alarming tuberculosis rate? (Two of the guests were doctors.) 7) What did we think of France's tiny cars? (I told them I was astounded at the Buicks, Dodges, Chevrolets, and Fords in Paris.) And, last of all, there was a good deal of medical conversation—about hospitals, new techniques, pre-medical studies, etc.

The meal began with little patty shells of creamed mushrooms, with choice of red or white wine. Then came a jardiniere of boiled potatoes, onions, carrots, lima beans, followed by a lettuce and tomato salad and a white fish steamed in court bouillion. The fish tasted like soap to me, but Rudd thought it was very good. A curious sauterne was served with this. Mine tasted peppery and had large dregs in it. After this, orange sections in a liqueur were served, followed by strong Brie cheese on bread. Then we repaired to the living room for thimblefuls of cognac and wicked coffee. Rudd and I are in complete disagreement about the meal, but we both appreciated the hospitality of Mrs. Mallet, who is a very pleasant person. Seeing her and her family up close, we had a chance to gain an insight into a middle class Parisian family. . . .

Every evening we have our coffee at Chez DuPont, one of the grand cafes on the Boulevard Saint-Michel. Here we sit with students of all sizes and shapes from all parts of the world and watch people stroll by on the boulevard. There are many Asian students here, many other students from The United States, Algeria, and Morocco. Paris is noted for its humane touch, its kindness to the individual . . . .

Today we walked through the Tuileries, quite majestic, but not so comfortably familiar as our own Luxembourg Garden. We went to the Jeu de Paume to see the Impressionists' paintings. They have the best collection of Claude Monet's works I've seen, as well as good Pissarro and Sisley paintings. Sisley has always been a little underrated, I think. . . .

Love,

Roger

Hotel de L'Avenir
65 rue Madame
Paris 6, France
Wednesday, April 8, 1953

Dear Families,

 . . . Today we visited the Louvre and saw the Mona Lisa
and the magnificent Venus de Milo at long last. The blues and
greens in the background of the Mona Lisa were richer, more
jewel-like, than I had imagined. I feel sure this painting would
excite admiration anywhere, even if it didn't have the
formidable mythic reputation it has. As for the Venus, I
thought it was well situated at the end of the long corridor in
the Louvre. Looking at it, I thought the accidental amputation
of its arms was probably the most artistic imperfection I'd
ever see. I also liked the Veronese and Titian paintings in the
museum and was especially happy to see Franz Hals' vibrant
*La Bohemienne* at long last.

Today, also, was a good day in another respect—job
hunting. We went early to see Mr. Hill at American Express.
He was cordial and friendly and went over the cost-of-living
and financial set-ups for Americans like us. He said we would
definitely find jobs—he was certain of that—but he was afraid
practically all our money would be used for room and board.
He felt the $90 a month we were paying this hotel was
reasonable and that we should continue on here unless we
located something less expensive, no easy feat in the Paris of
today. He also said American Express would be taking on its
summer help in the next few weeks and that we would be
able to get jobs with them, although he warned that the
salaries would be small.

He also spoke about teaching positions, and when
Rudd said yes, she had an appointment with the American

Community School in Paris, he replied, "Ah, yes. I am the President of that school." He then called in the manager of American Express who said he would call us in the next few weeks about working there. Mr. Hill agreed that we should take these jobs at American Express as fill-ins until we were able to find better jobs. And he promised to help us with teaching positions, although he felt the best time for those would be next fall.

Then, this afternoon, another encouraging thing happened. The *Selections de Reader's Digest* called with the offer of an immediate job for Rudd. BUT—it required absolutely flawless French, so, of course, Rudd could not accept it. They suggested that perhaps in another month or two, her French might be greatly improved and then they would be able to use her. . . .

Rudd and I, as is typical of Americans in Paris, were both the cause of and the center of two funny incidents. The first took place this morning when I made my debut on the Parisian telephone system. Plute had told us the Stellmans lived on the Faubourg Saint-Denis, but hadn't given us their telephone number. I rang up *Renseignements* on the phone and encountered a rush of fast French from the operator. The connection was also very bad. I got the impression we were talking through two tin cans tied together by string. You can imagine the circular, convoluted conversation with me trying to explain in my halting school French that I wanted the number of the Stellmans who used to live on the Faubourg Saint-Denis, but apparently had moved, and the operator firing questions at me in shotgun French that I couldn't even hear, let alone understand. Finally, greatly embarrassed, I waited until a convenient pause occurred in her muffled monologue, and I uttered a scared "*merci*" I hoped would fool her into believing I had understood every word she said, and then I hung up, never to use the telephone again in Paris or France—ever.

At noon, Rudd and I were walking on the Boulevard des Italiens and noticed a bar-type establishment we thought might serve sandwiches for lunch. Upon entering, we saw a sign that read, *"Salle, premier étage. Lavabos. W.C."* Rudd explained that this meant the dining room was upstairs. We went up a tiny, narrow flight of stairs and found ourselves in a room with only a few tables and four or five people sitting at them. Taking off our coats and looking world-weary as travelers often do before requesting the menu to look over the *specialites de la maison,* we sat for a few minutes until a woman detached herself from the other table and came over to ask what we wanted. All in French, of course. Rudd, in English, told her we just wanted sandwiches and asked what kind she had. The woman replied, *"Jambon, fromage"* and looked even more surprised when we asked for menus. By this time, the other people at the table were watching with strange interest. One woman jumped up, smiled, and said in French, "Ah, they are English. They are looking for something to eat and they think this is a restaurant." She then explained, with great amusement, that we had invaded a private dining room and that this was not a restaurant at all. You can imagine how red our faces were as we put on our coats, hurried down the stairs and out into the street again. I guess every American is entitled to one misadventure in Paris!

Tell Harry we see branches of the Societé Generale all over Paris, along with Credit Lyonnais, Cinzano, and Dubonnet signs. When our French conversation improves, we will call on Monsieur Morel at the Societé. I don't think we'll visit him just yet because Harry said his English was rather bad, and that, combined with our French, is apt to be catastrophic at the moment.

We are enjoying our status as aliens in France very much. It is good to be on the outside looking in for once. One can understand what difficulties foreigners must have in New York City. . . .

Love to all,

Roger

6 rue Jean Jacques Pradier
Geneva, Switzerland

Dear Ivy and Bill,

We have been quite busy the past two weeks commuting between Paris and Geneva. Rudd was offered a job in Paris, but decided not to take it, as the cost of living is too high there. So we are back in Geneva where we have found a large furnished room, something almost impossible to find in Paris at present.

Did you get my postcards from our tour of Switzerland? It is a beautiful country. The high point (literally) was our trip up the Jungfrau where we had lunch at a hotel on the highest point in all Europe. We thought Lucerne the most beautiful city here. Enjoyed the mediaeval German charm of the city.

We're currently trying to find jobs in either Geneva or Paris. We've made some good friends here in Geneva, and they are helping a lot. It's difficult for Americans to find jobs with the international organizations because of the fuss raised by Senator Joseph McCarthy over loyalty checks. Rudd was offered a job with the United Nations, but it would take several months to check her loyalty. In the meantime, the job will probably go to an English, French, or Swiss person. But there are other organizations that don't require the loyalty check, so perhaps something will materialize there. . . .

Best love,

Roger

6 rue J. J. Pradier
Geneva, Switzerland
May 2, 1953

Dear Family:

. . . By the way, with regard to May Day, it is really quite a *fête* over here. Everyone buys lilies of the valley and every other one sells them. It's supposed to be good luck to give and receive them. At the Intertelecommunications typing pool, where I work now as a temporary employee, a little Russian woman in front of me brought me a little bouquet, which I thought was very nice. Madame Defarge also gave us each a few sprays, no doubt hoping our typing would miraculously improve. I wore a few of the lilies, which I had bought, in the little vase-pin which I had brought with me. The pin caused no end of comment by friends and strangers alike. I gave a few of these lilies of the valley to my Russian friend, and she was so very pleased. The night before, Roger and I had been awakened by a quartet of two men and two women singing in the little square under our window in honor of May Day. The whole occasion is really very lovely and so much nicer than our Valentine's Day. The lilies, incidentally, cost about 30 cents at a florist for a big fistful . . . .

Rudd

Le Rosey
Rolle, Switzerland
Sunday, May 3, 1953


Dear Families,

Good news, but fantastic news! Starting tomorrow, I am teaching English at this beautiful school in Switzerland.

Here is how it happened. I had written to Ecole Internationale in Geneva and had received a nice reply from them. Last night, the English master at this school was taken seriously ill and had to leave immediately for good. The Director of the school, Monsieur Louis Johannot, made a hurried trip to Geneva, talked with Dr. Roquette at Ecole Internationale, who recommended me. At 10:30 a.m. while Rudd and I were having breakfast, Monsieur Johannot knocked on our door, offered me the job. We thought it over, accepted, and at 5:30 p.m. Johannot piled us into his big American car, drove us here at breakneck speed, and here we are, ensconced in our room, and tomorrow I begin work. Sound exciting? Well, it is.

The school is a good one and is centered around an old chateau. The Duke of Kent will be one of my students, as will the two grandsons of the Aga Khan, Karim and Amyn Aga Khan.

We get our board and room free, plus 450 Swiss francs a month. Rudd may be able to get a job either here at the school or in Rolle, a sizable village. For the winter months, the whole school moves to Gstaad in the Alps where they live in chalets and ski and skate every day. We get paid for the whole year, even though we don't actually work that long.

Since we've already paid up to May 25th on our room in Geneva and since Rudd has to work a month at the International Telecommunications Union to get paid, she is going back to Geneva tomorrow and will continue there until the 25th when she will join me back here in Rolle. It's only an hour's ride from here to Geneva, so I will go in as often as possible, and on weekends. We will have to have everything sent out here, of course.

Aside from this, there is nothing else to report, but we are both amazed and delighted at this wonderful opportunity.

Love to all,

Roger

Le Rosey
Rolle,(Vaud),
Switzerland
May 6, 1953

Dear Father and Mother K, et al—

I will start this letter while on my way into Geneva by train. . .

As you know, things have been happening very quickly. It seems it is always darkest before dawn, and then it never rains, but it pours. We now seem to be at the start of a long and pleasant stay over here, provided the Directors and Roger agree. Yesterday, Mr. Johannot, the chief Director, told Roger he had very good reports from his senior English class, so it sounds promising.

Now, a little more description of the whole setup. Roger, I think, explained how we got out here, so I will take it up from there.

We have a nice size room in the new wing of the school (*Le Nouveau Batiment*). This is our bedroom *et al.* There is a little sitting room next door which is the Seniors' Room, but they never seem to use it, so we may be able to use it. The only difficulty with the whole thing is that we only have a basin in our room, which means we must share the bathroom with the boys. I'm afraid it may be a little awkward at times. But if they don't mind, I guess I won't.

The school is located halfway between Lausanne and Geneva in the rolling green countryside, about half a mile at the most from Lake Geneva. When we look out our window, we can see vineyards and snow-capped mountains in the same glance. From the front of the school, you can see the Mont Blanc chain of Jura Alps in France. On a clear evening, from the second floor, you can see the peak of Mont Blanc itself.

The chateau part of the school is made of stone and concrete. There is a tremendous wisteria vine growing up in this section. The wisteria is in full bloom now, and, needless to say, is exquisite. It perfumes the air all around. Its purple clusters are nicely set off by the grey walls of the chateau.

Mr. and Mrs. Hughes (Welsh), the Executive Director and his wife, have their apartment on the second floor of the chateau. They have a little balcony which is partially covered by the wisteria. Our first night at Rosey (pronounced "Rozay"), we had an aperitif there. It was quite a lovely introduction to the place.

We take our meals with the boys in a very attractive dining room panelled in dark wood. Roger and I sit at one end of the table and Mr. John Abbott, the other English and History teacher, sits at the opposite end, with about ten boys in between. Right now, most of the boys at our table speak French, so most of the conversation by-passes Roger and me. So far, I have only had breakfasts at the school, but Roger reports the meals are very good. Breakfast is served at 7:40 a.m. (a continental one—the only time milk is served all day); dinner at 12:30 p.m. and supper at 7:10 p.m. After dinner and supper, the faculty takes coffee in the drawing room of the chateau, a lovely room which is furnished in period furniture. Then the evening is free.

The village of Rolle has movies in French and quite a nice little shopping center, from what I saw of it, but we will have to investigate more thoroughly this weekend. (I forgot to mention that there is chocolate served between 10:15 - 10:25 a.m. and tea at 4:15 p.m.)

The Mr. Abbott I mentioned is, believe it or not, an English Mr. Peepers. Roger and I gasped when we first saw him. He is the spitting image of Wally Cox, only with an English hair-do, blinks his eyes while thinking about an answer, is very quiet, and very nice. Someday, though, I am sure I am going to call him Mr. Peepers by mistake.

I haven't met many of the faculty for any length of

time. Roger will have to tell you about them. But from the little I have seen, they all seem very nice. They are of different nationalities.

The boys are very nice, too. There are quite a few American and English boys, a lot of Italians and others from about twenty-five countries. As Roger has told you, he has the two Aga Khan boys in his class as well as the Duke of Kent (listed officially as H.R.H. the Duke of Kent). The latter is an intelligent chap, but apparently something of a trouble-maker. The Italian and French boys are the ones that Roger has trouble with, especially the little Juniors, whose knowledge of English is quite limited and who are constantly on the go. Mr. Hughes told Roger not to worry about them, though. He said if they can go home and say in English, "Please pass the butter," their parents will be satisfied.

The Anglais I class is the one Roger enjoys the most because they are Seniors who are ready for college and most are Americans. But the book situation is awful. The library is really not very good, and Geneva is no help for English textbooks. Most of the reading books are by British authors. These boys—especially the Americans—need some American authors in their background. That is why Roger needs his books and notes immediately. I hope the school will reimburse us for the mailing costs. . . .

The weather for the past week has been beautiful, sunny, clear, warm, except for an occasional stiff wind. The countryside, too, is at its best. It's the time of year when all the poster picture photographs must be taken because there are so many flowers in bloom. The fields are green, spotted with blue, yellow, and white flowers, and the distant mountains are still well snow-covered. In the center of all this, Lake Geneva, which changes from sapphire blue to blue-green, depending on the weather and time of day. . . .

As you can see, we both hope it will be possible for us to stay. It is so exactly what we had hoped to come across. Now we have a place to hang our hats, plus the vacation times to tour in. . . . Really it is all too good to be true. Just keep your fingers crossed that the contract for the fall will come through. Of course, I think they should be tickled pink to have someone like Roger on their staff. It really is marvelous how brilliant he is on all this stuff.

It will also be good background for him when we return to the United States. I do wish someone would check in the International Register of Schools, though, and find out what Le Rosey's standing is. It would seem to me that it must be good if people such as the Duke of Kent come here. Mr. Smith in New Hampton may know something about this, too.

Well, I guess that does it for now. We are just about into Geneva. Love to all and do write.

Love,

Rudd

Le Rosey
Rolle, (Vaud)
Switzerland


Lundi 11 Mai 1953

Dear Families,


. . . First of all, I hope you have air-mailed the books and notes I requested. The library is not adequate for my needs and I must have my books here as quickly as possible. After all, one needs one's notes and reference works, and this library has really very little in English or American books.

Rolle is located on the north shore of Lake Geneva thirty-three kilometers from Geneva and twenty-seven from Lausanne. The school is situated in the Chateau du Rosey, the Maison d'Horloge, and the Nouveau Batiment. It is an expensive school, but democratic in outlook, and has had many princes, dukes, counts, etc. as students from time to time. The Shah of Iran and Prince Rainier of Monaco are former Roseeans. It was founded by an American woman and her husband, Madame and Monsieur Henri Carnal. It is owned now and operated by Louis Johannot and Helen Schaub, both Swiss.

H.R.H., Edward, Duke of Kent, is one of my pupils as is Michael, Earl of Suffolk and Berkshire. Kent is tall, stooped, tweedy, resembling his father and uncles. Suffolk is blond, good-looking, very dashing—the way a young peer of the realm should look, I think. I call them "Kent" and "Suffolk." They call me "sir" and rise when I come into a room. Most of the boys call Kent "Kent," but some call him "H.R.H." Out of deference to him and Suffolk, the boys call the lavatory "the

House of Lords." Kent is an excellent student with a good mind. Suffolk less so, but the dash makes up for a lot. He pesters me with English or Latin problems. I think he is ultra-conservative, watching the British election returns, fearful of the return of the Socialists.

Prince Aly Khan's two sons, Karim and Amyn, are also in my class, both top students, nice boys, and a credit to the school and their families.

There's also a personable little Brit, all of seven years, who introduces himself as follows: "How d'you do? I'm Nicholas Clive, descendent of Robert Clive of India, y'know." He looks for all the world like a Colonel Blimp in miniature.

For vacations, we get ten weeks off in the summer, four weeks at Easter, two weeks at Christmas, and the usual holidays, Ascension, Pentecost, etc., that they celebrate here. The school has three terms: From September 15 to December 20 at Rolle. From January 5 to March 20 at Gstaad (where they have three large chalets). And from April 19 to July 4 at Rolle again. Gstaad is in the Bernese-Oberland Alps on the way to Interlaken. I believe we sent you some postcards from there.

Because of the international character of the school, the boys get an excellent education, in many ways superior to that in American schools. For instance, in some of my advanced courses I am giving them literature of a complex nature—Chaucer in the original Middle English, Shaw's *Major Barbara* and *Man and Superman,* although Kent said to me, "No member of the British royal family has ever read Shaw or seen one of his plays." In lieu of this, he is going to write up the coronation of his cousin, Elizabeth. Wasn't it Philip Barry who wrote in *The Philadelphia Story*, "With the rich and mighty, always a little patience?"

Languages such as Arabic and Russian are also taught here. I'm divided about the advantages of speaking two or three languages because some students speak, but can't write, except phonetically, but, still, the experience of teaching here is quite challenging and stimulating. . . .

At dinner last night, I got involved in an argument with Mustafa Kamil, from India, and John Abbott, from England, both faculty members, about the relative merits of London versus Paris. The argument ended abruptly when Kamil boomed out, "I'd rather starve on nothing but bread in Paris than eat like a king in London." A pretty good line, I thought.

Love,


Roger

Le Rosey
Rolle (Vaud)
Suisse
May 13, 1953

Dear Father & Mother K et al.

. . .We have discovered that in addition to Kent and Suffolk, we have an Indian prince here, plus ex-King Umberto of Italy's son, Vittorio Emmanuel di Savoia, Francesco Carracciolo, the Crown Prince of Naples, and no telling who else. Quite a few are going to the Coronation in London.

It is interesting to see the little differences between this school and its American counterparts. For example, at night, everyone puts his shoes outside his door to be polished. And there are maids and servants galore! The tuition is 7,000 Swiss francs, about $1660. For here, that is very expensive. But they certainly seem to get their money's worth. The food is exceptionally good. They always seem to have some specialty on the menu. Only thing is that they don't have enough milk. . . .

Love to all,

Rudd

Le Rosey
Rolle (Vaud)
Switzerland
May 20, 1953


Dear Families:

      . . . It has been a very interesting experience working here in the Intertelecommunications typing pool. The women are all very nice, with interesting backgrounds. One is the mother of seven children. She is thirty-five and her children's ages range from a few months to eleven years. Her husband works, but they need more than that. Another young woman is German, but now French through marriage. Her husband is studying psychology. They hope to go to Paris this summer and stay, so that he can study there. She is expecting a baby in September. Another woman who was here, and also expecting in September, left to go to Montreal where her husband hopes to find a job. Her name is Madame Bovée, in case she ever calls on you. I gave her our New Jersey address and Daddy's New York one. Another girl used to be with the United Nations in Africa, where she became very ill and tried to commit suicide, whereupon they fired her and gave her no medical help whatsoever. She is now trying to get some money from them. Another woman, as well as the Head of the pool, supports her husband, who is an artist. Two of my co-workers are White Russians. Another is a sort of Swiss Zuza. But they are all nice and certainly have made the work bearable.

      Lately, we've had very little work to do during the daytime, so we sit, write letters, read newspapers, and knit. It really is a fascinating way to work, especially after having been a private secretary in New York who never seemed to have an extra minute. But at night and on weekends, things seem to come in, and we have to work more than we should. It is arranged rather stupidly, I think. Also they have it worked out so that you can only work seven hours a day, when you are supposed to work eight. Therefore, at the end of the week, you owe them five hours, so that when you do work overtime, it doesn't count as overtime, and so you don't get paid the time and a half. Clever, eh?

But soon it will be done with, so that isn't too bad, and the 625 francs is very handy. . . .

Sharing the bath with the boys at school has already been quite amusing. One day, I was taking a shower when someone knocked on the door. I said, "*Occupé,*" and he replied, "*Qui est la?*" "*Madame Kenvin.*" Finally, one of the boys who had seen me told the other boy who I was. But I was terrified that, for some reason, the lock wouldn't hold. I feel so odd coming into a roomful of boys. . . .

Love to all,

Rudd

Le Rosey
Rolle (Vaud)
Switzerland
May 25, 1953

Dear Families:

Well, now that I am a lady of leisure, at least for a few days, I think the least I can do is get off a letter to you to tell you about our holiday.

Most of the boys are back now, their various chauffeur-driven Cadillacs having returned them. The weather was lovely, although quite hot. Mr. Johannot took about thirty boys to Germany. A group of younger boys went to the mountains, others went with their parents, and a few were left here. On Saturday I had to work in the afternoon in Geneva and finished in a blaze of fury, much too long to describe. Roger went to Lausanne in the afternoon, and then we spent a quiet evening here at the school. Sunday morning, we got on the boat at Rolle, went to Lausanne, and, from there, across Lake Geneva to Evian-les-Bains in France.

It was a lovely boat ride. All the time you can see either the Swiss side or the French side. It's amazing to observe the difference in landscape on the two sides. The Swiss side has the neat patchwork quilt appearance, with fields and vineyards. The French countryside is more informal, less defined.

We arrived in Evian at about 12:30 p.m. We walked around a bit, looking for a place to eat. We had noticed a place with umbrellas on the lakefront from the boat, so we thought we would try it. Since it was after noon and before 2:00 p.m. most of the stores were closed. But it was funny, seeing the prices marked in French francs again.

We found our restaurant, the Café de Paris, and thought the menu looked all right. We decided that, since we were on a holiday, we would enjoy a cocktail first. We asked the waiter if they had cocktails, and he said no, because they had no shaker. We told him all we needed was some gin in a glass with a little vermouth. He provided that and it wasn't too bad, especially for over here. The rest of the meal, though, was not very good. We had a nice wine with it, which helped, but we were still disappointed.

After lunch, we walked along the waterfront to see if we could find the beach. The whole atmosphere and landscaping are very Mediterranean, serene and pretty. We finally found a small public beach. Then we had to get Roger some bathing trunks. All they have in the shops are the Bikini type things. So, for $4, Roger has a beautiful pair of French bathing trunks. I was too tired from the heat and sun to go back to the beach with him, so I sat in the park on the water's edge and waited.

There really is no beach. They have little cabanas along the waterside where one can change. The only difficulty is the cabanas have no doors or curtains. You just hope no one looks! While I was waiting, I got talking to the woman next to me, and, believe it or not, I carried on a whole conversation entirely in French for nearly an hour, so you can see how my linguistic ability is improving!

After Roger's swim, we went to the Casino. It is a great big building along the waterfront. It is well kept-up and has lovely formal planting around it. They have a bar-like place where you can have drinks and dance. The entrance fee for this is 300 French francs, and the drinks are extra. We didn't bother with this because we had only an hour before the last boat would leave. Instead, we went right to the rooms for roulette, baccarat, etc. We had to show our passports and register before getting a pass, which cost 200 French francs apiece.

The game room is quite large with many tables around. They have signs by each table showing you what the minimum is that you can play for, and the maximum that can be won. Some of the tables had 10,000 French francs minimum, and we saw people calmly putting down three pieces for 10,000 each on a number. Then we watched Chemin de Fer, which neither of us knows how to play. They had a very high minimum here and money seemed to be flying. We then turned back to the roulette table with the minimum of 100 French francs. We changed two Swiss franc notes of 5 francs each into 100 French francs, and purchased our chips. It resulted in my losing my four chips and Roger doubling his, so we stopped when we were even. There were a few people around the table who had notebooks and pencils, keeping track of the numbers. And the little woman next to us kept putting 1000 French franc pieces into her bag. It was all quite entertaining and fun.

After a couple of Coca-Colas, we left on the 8:00 p.m. boat. It was jammed. I thought a couple of times that it was going to capsize, but it didn't. We got to Ouchy at 8:30 p.m. and then took the bus up to Lausanne. It is very steep in Lausanne and Ouchy. We were hoping to make the 9:00 p.m. train, but just missed it. So we walked up a very steep hill into the center of Lausanne and had a nice supper while waiting for the next train. I think Lausanne has a lot more charm and picturesqueness about it than Geneva. Its terrain reminds one very much of San Francisco. They seem to have a lot of good shops and more interesting restaurants than in Geneva. I think that, in the future, we will probably go to Lausanne, rather than Geneva, for shopping. . . .

Love to all,

Rudd

Le Rosey,
Rolle
June 8, 1953

Dear Families:

Yesterday Roger and I went on our first real excursion
with some of the boys. Le Rosey Rowing Club was
participating in a regatta in Geneva, and since Roger had
second surveillance (on duty, that is) we were invited to go
along. It was a lot of fun, especially for me, because it gave me
a chance to get to know some of the boys better. They
certainly are an awfully nice group of boys in general.

The day was quite fantastic and very long. As a result,
we are both tired today. Our crews got two firsts and two
thirds during the morning events and two firsts during the
afternoon slalom, which was really just for the fun of it. In one
of the morning races, with an out-rigger, they started off
leading by two lengths, but ended up almost completely
submerged. It really was funny, but too bad. They do most of
their rowing in yoles, which take four rowers and a coxswain.
They look very pretty when they really get going.

We were served lunch at the yacht club, but it was
mostly potatoes. The poor boys must have been starving. We
left Rolle at 8:00 a.m. and didn't return until 7:00 p.m. Roger
and John Abbott just barely made the train and they had the
collective ticket. Luckily, I had taken the tram so that there
was at least one adult aboard. We had a few uncomfortable
moments, but then Roger appeared from the other end of
the train, having run through most of Geneva to get there, so
all was well.

The boys do a great deal of rowing here because
Walter Roubik, the rowing teacher, is a former Olympic

champion from Czechoslovakia. Believe it or not, after racing all day, some of the crew, including Monsieur and Madame Roubik, rowed halfway home on Lake Geneva. Walter Roubik even got Lida Roubik into one of the races, and one of the Aga Khan boys suggested that I might row too. I'm afraid I'd scuttle the ship before we even got started.

We discovered the other day that Walter and Lida Roubik are leaving the school this summer to come to the United States to live permanently and become citizens. He has been here as hockey and rowing coach. They are Czechoslovakian refugees. Three years ago they took a small suitcase, a loaf of bread and some chocolate, and left, without even saying goodbye to their families. They set off on foot through the woods, to escape into Germany, and then into Switzerland. Madame Roubik says it was bad when the Germans occupied their country in World War II, but now, in this Communist takeover, it is their own people who are doing terrible things, which makes it harder to bear. They want to come to the United States to settle. In Czechoslovakia, Walter Roubik was a lawyer. He would like to get a job as a rowing coach and study for his law degree in the U.S. because law is his main interest. They are planning to come to New York and see what's available there. They have written to most of the colleges, but all seem to have no vacancies for coaches. The University of California said that, if they needed one, they would let him know.

What are the possibilities of having them stay in New Jersey for a bit until they can find a room or something in New York where they can live less expensively than in a hotel? I am not sure how Daddy's vacation works this year, but if there is any chance of helping these two people, I wish we could. I know how much we appreciated every little bit that was done for us over here. And we, luckily, always had something to return to, if things didn't work out over here. Since the Roubiks' visa to the U.S. allows them only four months in which to leave, they have to go right away. They do not yet know when they can get passage, perhaps in July, or it may be in August. Let me know what you can do for them, and I will relay the possibilities to them, and we will let you know when they definitely will sail. I know you will enjoy meeting them. . . .

I have been doing some typing for the Le Rosey yearbook and have made several suggestions to the Direction about doing remedial reading work and extra tutoring, but, as yet, nothing specific has been asked of me. Perhaps next fall I can do some special work with some of the boys. I think that I will at least try to do some kind of project on the boys next year on the way they pick up foreign languages. Mr. Hughes, the Assistant Headmaster, said that it was quite interesting to see what languages were easiest for what nationalities. Since this will be the last year to do my thesis for Bank Street College without having to take additional courses, I would like to get it done. You really cannot work and write a thesis too. I've also thought I might try my hand at some children's stories. It seems to me I could do a delightful series on a child visiting the various large cities of Europe. They would have to be on the six and seven year old level, though. I'll write to Miss Lewis at Bank Street and consult with her via correspondence. . . .

Love to everyone,

Rudd

Le Rosey,
Rolle
June 9, 1953

Dear Mother, Father, et al,

. . . Our vacation begins July 5th and we leave for Basle, Switzerland, then up to Strasbourg, France, over to Heidelberg, Germany, to Mainz, and up the Rhine to Cologne. From Cologne, we go to Brussels, Belgium, then down to Paris for four or five days which will include the Bastille Day festivities. After Paris, we'll head down to the Riviera to visit Plute and Phyllis Cahill in Vence for two weeks, then back here to Rolle for the second part of the summer term. At the end of that term, I have two weeks, so we'll visit Lake Constance and Zurich one week and Venice and Milan in Italy in the second week.

As Rudd told you in her letter, we spent the whole day Sunday in Geneva at the Regatta. Tomorrow we go to Lausanne for the Interscholastic Regatta. We got two firsts and two thirds at the Geneva Regatta. I took some photos and will send them on to you. Karim Aga Khan is one of the top rowers at the school. Both he and his brother, Amyn, were in Westminster Abbey for Queen Elizabeth's coronation. Their mother, Joan Yarde-Buller, is English. They live in Eaton Square.

Speaking of the coronation, we listened to it on Kent's own radio, with his permission, of course. It came through quite well and sounded wonderful. Kent arrives back Sunday. This is his last term here. He told me he may make the Army his life.

You would get a big kick out of Suffolk. He is very social and reminds me of a male Tallulah Bankhead in his breezy outlook and attitude toward life. His favorite expression is "That's dizguzting" which he pronounces that way. He told me that two years ago Karim and Amyn took him and some of the boys to Ali Khan's Chateau L'Horizon in Juan Les Pins for the Cours Rita Hayworth. He said Louis and Mimi Johannot were invited also, had too much to drink, and told dirty jokes in French all evening. "It was dizguzting," he said.

This school, as you can gather from our letters, is like an international *You Can't Take It With You*. I wish you could have attended the teachers' meeting we went to a few weeks ago. After wine and hors d'oeuvres were brought in, everybody got so convivial that the faculty meeting suddenly erupted into a food fight and one of the Swiss secretaries got up and began sexily dancing on a table. . . .

How did the coronation come over on television in the U.S? It was not good weather in London, but the British were undeterred by it. Karim told me it was the most impressive ceremony he had ever seen, and, for him, who has seen his grandfather, the Aga Khan, weighed in gold, that is something!
. . . .

Love,


Roger

Hotel Reichspost
Heidelberg, Germany
July 7, 1953

Dear Family,

Arrived here yesterday after a splendid *Fête Sportive*
at the school. Never saw so many dukes, counts, and
countesses in my life. Ali Khan was there, too, looking dashing
and animated, and the Aga Khan himself pulled up in an
enormous dark green Rolls Royce. He stayed in the back seat
and his grandson, Karim, climbed in beside him to talk, at
great length it seemed. Mrs. Oswald Lord, who took over Mrs.
Roosevelt's place at the United Nations, came, too. Her
nephew, Charles McKee, is at the school. Rudd and I think
highly of him, too.

I am disappointed in Heidelberg. It's not at all
charming, mediaeval, or *Student Prince*-like. The population is
120,000, and the city is large, noisy, and predominently 1890s
in architecture. We went to the Scheffelhaus, site of Sigmund
Romberg's *The Student Prince,* last night, but found it
unimpressive. The Neckar is a swift-flowing river, brown and
pinkish in color.

. . . There was a tremendous amount of war damage in
Karlsruhe, and almost all the railroad stations we passed
through had been thoroughly bombed out during World War
II. There apparently is a lot of coffee smuggling going on at
the moment in Germany because on the trains police come
through with dogs (*Kaffeschniffelhunden,* I think they are
called) sniffing for coffee. One man in our car was caught, but
they just made him pay the tax and didn't do anything to him.

All through Germany, I've seen the great results of the Marshall Plan—playgrounds for children, apartment buildings, etc. If you could see the extensive bomb damage, you would appreciate the importance of this plan.

The German people themselves have all been courteous and pleasant. . . .

The countryside around Heidelberg is reminiscent of the Hudson and the Catskills, and I expect the Rhine trip will be even more so. Our hotel here, the Reichspost, is one of Heidelberg's best—recommended to us by Marguerite Midas. We had an excellent meal of choice veal filets and artichoke hearts last night. In Strasbourg, France, we had one of the best Rieslings I've ever had, and we made an entire meal out of the hors d'oeuvres alone. The Strasbourg Cathedral was impressive. . . . We're off now to visit the schloss in Heidelberg. . . .

Love,

Roger

**CECIL HOTEL**
12-13 Boulevard du Jardin Botanique
Bruxelles-Nord

July 9, 1953

Dear Family,

We arrived here in Brussels this morning after a memorable trip on the Rhine River. Although cities like Mainz, Mannheim, Cologne, Wiesbaden, were horribly bombed during the war, one gets the impression now of a Germany desperately rebuilding itself, and doing a superb job of it, even when faced with steel shortages and an economic crisis.

Cologne, with its magnificent cathedral, was the most interesting city. A great many modern buildings are going up all around where the land was almost leveled to the ground. The devastation was unbelievable. It won't be the same ever, but it is being replaced.

Our trip on the Rhine was relaxing and wonderful. We saw many fascinating towns and schlosses, including the Mouse Tower at Bingen. As we passed by the Lorelei, they played the music over the loudspeaker on the boat. It was very effective.

Now we are in Brussels, staying at the same hotel where Rudd stayed with her family in 1949. Although the Belgian countryside is agreeably attractive, there is little to be said for Brussels. Picture a dirty, noisy, crowded city reminiscent of equal parts New York's 8th Avenue, 6th

Avenue, and Broadway, with a few of Paris' greasier outdoor cafes, and that's this city, complete with annoying neon signs and boisterous people. Three or four of the buildings are interesting from an architectural point of view, but, apart from that, I don't see much to recommend it.

Our dinner this evening—expensive, too—was the worst we've eaten in all Europe. The odd thing is that its inhabitants think they're living in another Paris. . . .

So long for now.

Love,

Roger

Hotel Perreyve
63 rue Madame
Paris 6, France
14 Juillet 1953

Dear Family,

 . . . It is now 4:00 a.m. and I am writing this because we slept too much this afternoon and I can't sleep now. The Bastille Day parade began at 9 this morning, but Rudd and I didn't get to the Place de la Concorde until about 11:30 a.m., so we missed most of it. The weather was cloudy all day, but, fortunately, it didn't rain.

Just read in the newspaper that the Communist parade here exploded into a riot with seven or eight people killed. We didn't go to see it. It was held in the afternoon.

This evening they had fireworks over the Seine and dancing in the streets. The illumination of Paris was very pleasant. We had dinner at Le Coq on the rue Gozelin and then went to the cafe Aux Deux Magots for coffee. Guess who was there? Clark Gable and the same blonde we saw with him in Geneva. We seem to have the same taste in cafes. Aux Deux Magots is a cafe frequented by Existentialists, students, and typical Left Bank intellectuals. It did look funny to see Clark Gable among them. He is a very big man. . . .

Our tour of Versailles was a good one. Les Grandes Eaux are turned on only nine times a year. Naturally, for us it was raining, which lessened the effect somewhat. Four thousand people lived at Versailles with Louis XIV, which should give you some idea of its grandeur and scale. It is the most ornate, gorgeous palace imaginable, the model for many others throughout Europe. . . .

Love to all,

Roger

Casa Clare,
Vence, A.M., France
July 20, 1953

Dear Families,

We have finally arrived here at Plute's after a great trip down from Paris in a luxury motor bus. The weather was clear all the way. We came through Burgundy, Savoy, and Provence, and stopped at excellent restaurants along the way. We spent the night at Aix-les-Bains, a beautiful resort in an exceptionally fine setting.

The Cote d'Azur is nice, too, but I'm surprised at all the beaches named after ones in Florida—Miami Plage, Palm Beach Plage, etc. We've been swimming in the Mediterranean for the past few days. I got a bad sunburn, so we didn't go in today, but maybe tomorrow.

Plute and Phyllis have both been very hospitable to us. We went to a musical evening with them at one of the large villas and met an assortment of Riviera luminaries, among them artist Marc Chagall and his new wife, Victoria; Countess Karolyi from Hungary; and Gordon Craig, the scene designer, whose mother was the English actress Ellen Terry. Chagall was friendly and warm, his wife, black hair, red dress, very attractive, and Gordon Craig, tall, blue-eyed, white hair, white skin. As a matter of fact, Plute, Phyllis, Rudd, and I meet him every morning at Tony's Select Bar in the center of Vence, where we sit outside, sip wine or coffee, and chat.

The interesting thing about this evening is that it marked the return to performance of a pianist named Chernayassky (or something like that) who had not played for

years because of war trauma. He played beautifully. It was an
elegant, ideal evening—the kind of setting I liked being in in
the south of France. . . .

Love,


Roger

Vence, A.M., France
July 25, 1953

Dear Family,

    . . . The Mediterranean, apart from its beautiful sapphire color, is also clean and clear, and a wonderful place in which to swim, more like a big lake than a sea. . . .
    We visited the Chapelle du Rosaire that Henri Matisse designed and decorated here in Vence. Both of us liked it very much, although it has caused great commotion among those who expect churches to be gothic, dark, and faintly mysterious. This one is light, modern, clean cut, and quite beautiful. Matisse uses white walls and his distinctive cobalt blue, and all the religious figures are depicted as stick figures, so that you can read into them what you want. This also bothers many people. . . .

Love,

Roger

Le Rosey
Rolle, Switzerland
August 3, 1953

Dear Families:

We are finally home and I have some paper and the typewriter, so that I can get off a long letter to you all and catch you up on the last two weeks of our trip.

I don't know how we could have had a more enjoyable or relaxing time than we did at Plute's and Phyl's. They were wonderful. Nothing was too planned. We slept late every morning and then had breakfast served to us on the terrace by Annette, the maid Phyl has for half a day. It was so nice sitting out there with the scent of their lemon tree perfuming the air around us. We could see all the way down to Cap d'Antibes and beyond that to the Mediterranean Sea.

But, first, I must tell you about our trip down from Paris. It was quite different from our first bus trip four years ago. We arrived at the point of departure in Paris early Thursday morning, July 16th. We found that there were five buses leaving for Nice, but only one of them had a hostess. We were assigned to a bus, and, when it started to depart, we discovered we were on the one with the hostess, a deluxe bus, which would travel by way of Aix-les-Bains. The hostess explained important sights along the way.

Our first place was Fontainebleau. The bus drove right up to the chateau, so that we could see it clearly. I was surprised that it's right in the heart of town, not set back in a park. From the outside, I'd say it was not very impressive, but, someday I will have to see the inside. At this point, Roger says he has enough of chateaux, but maybe later on he will try a few more.

We traveled through the lovely French countryside to Arnay-le-Duc, where we had lunch. We ate at a small inn. When we entered the restaurant, we noticed a patron eating snails, a specialty in this Burgundy region. One of the American women on our bus sniffed, "Oh, dear, I hope we won't have to eat those." Roger and I immediately decided we would order them. The woman's husband, noticing what we were eating, said, "Well, I certainly don't want any of them, but I don't mind sitting next to someone eating them." I refrained from telling him that I had no intention of moving, even if he had minded.

This same couple came from California where he teaches at San José. Some of their other comments: "We came over on the *Ile de France*. The food was delicious, but, you know, I don't think they ever used the Hoover vacuum cleaner that was standing in the corridor." When the woman took some bread at our lunch, she commented, "You know, I'm so surprised to find this bread is good. I'm so fond of white bread." Talking about their hotel in Paris, she said, "They served us *dejeuner* and lunch too." But the prize comment was, when the waitress in the inn asked in French if they'd like cake for dessert, the man replied in English, "No, they've already left." And, to cap it off, he tried to thrust dollar bills into her hand as payment, all the while she, in French, was telling him they couldn't accept any currency but French francs, fairly typical of small towns in the countryside.

These people always drank only bottled water, they were certain the mushrooms we had at lunch would kill us all before nightfall, etc. No wonder Americans are so deeply loved over here, when they treat the whole place as though it's a condemned slum area. Of course, sometimes you do have to be careful with the water, but in most towns of any size, you are perfectly safe. And, certainly, no bus company is willingly going to put you where you don't have good water.

After lunch, we went to Bresse, known for the quality of its chicken, famous throughout France. . . Then we climbed up some very high mountains, went through a mile-long tunnel, and descended into the valley around Lake Bourget on which Aix-les-Bains is located. We were a little late on arrival, so that it was dark when we got into the town. We stayed at the Bristol, a nice hotel in the middle-price range. (Our room, meals, etc. came to about $14 apiece.) We had a delicious dinner that night at the hotel, but we had to fight to get ordinary drinking water. Since this is a spa, they want to sell the bottled water. It took us all of dinner time to get a carafe which was under the sideboard all the time. . . .

The next morning, we were up bright and early to leave for Nice via Grenoble. Almost all the driving that day was through the Alps. We followed what is called the Route Napoleon, the path he followed on his way back from Elba to Waterloo. Since it was expected he would take the easy way, he deliberately followed this difficult passage through the mountains. At various points along the way, you can still see some of the original road, like a goat's path along the mountainsides. It was a clear day, affording us some spectacular views as we went from one peak to another.

For lunch, we went to Chateau Arnoux, where we ate at the old chateau, now an inn. Again, an excellent meal— veal, deliciously prepared. We then traveled through Digne to Grasse, Cannes, and Nice. All along the way, we saw signs saying "Napoleon stayed here," etc. What would inn-keepers do without Napoleon and George Washington? After the rolling greenery of Burgundy and Savoy, the rockiness and barrenness of the mountains in Provence was most vivid. Nearing Grasse, the perfume center, we saw fields of lavender, which added some color, although lavender is a coarse plant and doesn't really soften the rugged hills. Some mountains were covered with genet, a bushy plant with a yellow cap for a flower (called "broom" in English). Supposedly, the Plantagenets got their name from this flower, which they wore in their caps.

It was nearly 6:30 p.m. when we came into Cannes. We went right through the heart of the town, down to the Croisette, a long, lovely park along the waterfront, which runs the length of the main section of town. Cannes is more beautiful than Nice. We passed by Chateau L'Horizon, Aly Khan's home, along the Boulevard des Anglais and into Nice.

Our first morning in Vence, the sun was brilliant and the sky a bright blue. . . . We rented some bikes and headed down to Cagnes-sur-Mer, almost an eight-mile ride completely downhill. On the return trip, you take the bus up and they put the bikes on top . . . . The swimming at Cannes was very dirty, probably because of the boats there and the large numbers of people. It does have a sandy beach, though, which neither Nice nor Cagnes-sur-Mer have. These two just have rounded pebbles or stones, which one gets used to after a while, but at first it is sheer torture. The nicest swimming was at Eden Roc, where John Jones, one of the Le Rosey students took us and where we bumped into Karim Aga Khan also, visiting his father at Chateau L'Horizon. There is no real beach at Eden Roc, just a cement area built on top of the rocks. But the water is deep and has that beautiful sapphire blue color. It's a very expensive place, though, and almost entirely populated by English and Americans. We didn't hear a word of French, while there.

I think Roger wrote you about our enjoyable luncheon with the Joneses. They have a marvelous French cook, who runs the household, but who knows how to cook. She lives with them and hardly ever wants to take time off. All for less than $45 a month. I guess that is really the only thing that is inexpensive around here. We enjoyed meeting the Joneses very much. It also was nice to see Cap d'Antibes. There are many lovely villas there, giving it a different aspect from Nice and Cannes with their hotels. . . .

Our first drive with Phyllis and Plute included the Jordans, a young sculptor and his wife, who have been over here on a Fulbright and plan to stay another year. We took a local taxi to Monaco via the Moyen Corniche, Grand Corniche, and the Littorale. We saw several towns such as Eze-sur-Mer. Eze has been kept up and preserved as an artistic example of the many hill towns on the coast which cling so closely to the mountain that, from a distance, it's hard to see them. Inside the town, the streets are extremely narrow and curve a great deal. No car can go inside. You have to park outside the wall that surrounds the town. Although towns such as Eze are picturesque, they are so crowded, you might as well live in a New York City apartment.

We also saw The Trophy of the Alps in La Turbie. This was a Roman monument built to commemorate the crossing of the Alps. Although the actual monument was almost completely destroyed by local residents taking away the stones to use in building their own homes, it has been restored by an Englishman. It made one realize the rich history of this place. Everywhere there are some Roman ruins. Our guide took us as far as Menton, where Plute and Phyl had a swim . . . .

When we got to the Casino in Monte Carlo, I started out by tripling my money, but, since I had only one chance to play, I continued and eventually lost it all. Roger came through as usual, however, and made enough to cover my loss, pay the entrance fee, and still have 100 francs left over. We also looked over the gardens and saw where the ballerina in *The Red Shoes* leapt to her death. The whole place appears fairly seedy now, but one gets an idea of its former grandeur. One of the most disillusioning aspects is the visitors in shorts who swarm into the place in the afternoon. You still have the women with long black net gloves and old gentlemen with notebooks and systems around the tables, but the shorts-wearing crowd is omnipresent now. . . .

The second trip we took via taxi was not quite so beautiful. We went up the road behind Vence into the mountains. The Gorge de Loup was extremely beautiful, but it reminded us of the U.S. West . . . . On the way home, we took a boat out to the Iles des Lérins, located off Cannes. The Man in the Iron Mask was incarcerated on St. Marguerite. The islands are prettier than Catalina, but nothing too unusual. . . .

One day, Plute and Phyl gave a small party for us at their home, Casa Clare, in Vence, inviting what they called "the younger, married set." It was very enjoyable. One of the guests, an Australian member of the Labor government, not in power now, was most interesting. It's the first time, really, since we left the States, that I've had such an interesting discussion. . . . We also had some good arguments with Plute and Phyl, which were most enjoyable and stimulating. . . .

One of the biggest enjoyments of our whole stay down there, besides the pleasure of being in a private home again, was the fact that Phyl let me cook every meal I had with them, except for one or two, which she prepared. I had a field day. I had forgotten how much I miss cooking . . . .

Friday noon, we left Vence and took the bus for Geneva. We followed the sea to St. Raphael and then inland to Avignon, where we spent the night. Again, our bus was deluxe with both a hostess and a toilet. The only difficulty is that this time, most of the other passengers were French-speaking Swiss, who, apparently, have the same fear of fresh air that the French have. As a result, we nearly suffocated a couple of times. . . . The countryside along this route was not nearly as pretty nor as interesting as the route coming down. Around Avignon, we saw cypress trees planted in thick hedges to protect the crops from the fierce winds of the Mistral. These hedges are so dense and numerous that it makes the countryside very dark, even in daytime.

We saw the Pope's Palace illuminated at night. It's very striking with very simple straight lines. The next morning we saw the famous bridge, just an old arched bridge falling down, with a chapel halfway across it. A little disappointing. I was surprised to see the wall, which appears to be intact, all the way around the city. Avignon is just like Tours in that it has the fiercest, most persistent mosquitoes anywhere. We spent a most unpleasant night and had to rise at 5:00 a.m. . . . We came up the Rhone Valley—not a particularly pretty valley--and then we came through Aix-les-Bains again, through Annecy, which looks charming, nestled as it is against the foothills of the Alps, and into Geneva. We could see the city and its Jet d'Eau for miles. It was quite a lovely return.

And now we are back at the school. We had a wonderful vacation, although we spent more than we had thought and now are completely broke, although Roger's salary for July should be around somewhere. The school is very casual about such things. . . .We are freezing to death. It is very cold, raw, and rainy. . . . I got some sweaters and woolens out of the trunk today to keep us warm. It's quite a change from the Riviera. Both of us would like to take the next bus back down there.

I certainly am glad, though, that I am not living in France. It is all very lovely to visit, but the dirt and decaying dilapidated buildings, etc., depress me after a while. One wonders how it is possible to go through town after town and never see a house decently kept up on the outside. It certainly does give the appearance, at times, of one grand slum with some beautiful park areas in between.

It seems that Europe is getting more people who are able to afford at least a camping trip and who are interested in taking it. This has been going on for a long time in the States. But, whereas the States works out these things by building better highways, tremendous public parks with wonderful facilities, such as the national parks out West, I'm afraid France will be quite haphazard about it all. People are quite slovenly enough, without having campers messing up the countryside. People never hesitate a moment to throw things out of car, train, or bus windows. This might have been understandable when few people traveled, but with increasing numbers of travelers, I'm afraid France is going to be spoiled . . . . Much of it is being spoiled already with the high price of things. For example, at a good restaurant in Paris now the cover charge is 150 francs and the least expensive entree costs 500 francs. That is quite different from 1949. Our last night in Paris, we did splurge and had a marvelous dinner at the Bouteille d'Or, but it was quite expensive. On the Riviera with Plute and Phyl in Vence, we had some excellent meals for $1 apiece, but they were the exception rather than the rule.

It's a shame, too, the way tourists come in such droves. Every day at least six busloads of people descend on Vence for a few minutes. No wonder there now is a loudspeaker in the town square advertising ice cream, etc. I suppose it's just one of those things we'll have to get used to as more people are able to travel, but, frankly, I think that maybe in a few years I will be very happy to leave Europe to the travelers. At least in Rolle we are safe from them, which is a relief. . . .

Love to all,

Rudd

Le Rosey
Rolle, Switzerland
August 12, 1953

Dear Mother, Father, et al,

It looks as though I may be teaching Latin and American History this year, in addition to English, so I think I will need another shipment of books. . . . For Latin, I have two dark blue volumes entitled *Latin for Americans*, I believe. Send those, and also, a copy of Virgil's *Aeneid*, Caesar's *Gallic Wars*, and other Latin books you think might be useful. You might send my bright blue Greek books, too, and my Herodotus and other Greek books that are there. I don't think I have any really decent book of American history, so will you see if Norma or Harry has one? . . .

Our excursion today was to Geneva where we picnicked (The French word for "picnic" is "piquenique," which I think is delightful) and then we went swimming and toured the United Nations Building, where we attended a session of the Committee on Migration. It was very interesting. We had those ear phones that change it into any language you want. . . .

For the summer term here, we have had four horses, and all the students have been taking horseback riding lessons from a dashing riding master, who has all the style and attitude of a Prussian army officer. Last Sunday, they had the Grand Equitation du Rosey, complete with jumping, etc. Quite exciting. . . . The summer term finishes at the end of August. Then we are on vacation until September 14th. I hope my books will get here by then. The students this summer are predominantly Spanish and Italian, with the usual French, Swiss, Americans, English, Greeks, Iranians. One of the Iranians is Prince Chahram Pahlavi, nephew of the Shah of Iran. His mother, Princess Ashraf, is the Shah's twin sister.

Rumor has it that the Shah exiled her because she married a commoner. Chahram is one of the regular students who stayed here for the summer session. The Spanish students are here because Franco will only let people out of the country for health reasons, and so the Spaniards show up in the summer, under that pretext . . . .

Love,

Roger

Le Rosey
Rolle, Switzerland
September 6, 1953

Dear Leigh and Procter,

. . . . The two cathedrals, Strasbourg and Cologne, are indeed magnificent pieces of architecture. Both are very delicate, and the Strasbourg cathedral has such a lovely red color to it. We were amazed at the bomb damage in Germany. Did you get to Germany on your trip over here? It was the first time I had ever been there. Although they have done a wonderful job reconstructing the business areas, I don't see how there were any people left to do anything at all. I also don't see why they didn't give up sooner.

I wish more people in the United States could see the terrible destruction—whole cities almost completely flattened. They might not be so glib about pulling out of the United Nations and carrying the war outside Korea. And, yet, we found the Germans that we came in contact with to be very friendly. You would think they'd be bitter. The reconstruction done in Cologne is magnificent and very beautiful. Most of the buildings now are very modern. It will certainly be one of the cities of the future. After our trip down the Rhine, which is one lovely view after another of rolling hills, topped with majestic schlosses and picturesque villages dotting the shoreline, the view of the Cologne cathedral looming up in the distance was an inspiring finish to the trip. . . .

The new term starts on the 15th. We have changed our room so that we are now in the Maison d'Horloge where the Moyens (Boys between 12 and 15 years) live. I am a kind of house mother to them. Some of them are here already. I think it will be quite an experience. I also will be teaching a course or two. Our new room is large, and we have a separate bath down the hall, so it is more like an apartment than our other room. Still no kitchen, though. . . .

And, now to answer your questions from your previous letter. The American boys who come here are from the East or West coast usually. Many are children of people working here for the U.S. government or in businesses. All are from wealthy families and some from split families, but most come because their parents want them to learn French well or because they are residing in Europe and Le Rosey has the reputation of being the best boys' school in Europe. You asked about the Aga Khan boys. Yes, they are Aly Khan's sons. Karim will eventually become the Aga Khan when he is old enough. He is a most delightful young man, very attractive, intelligent, good at sports. He and his brother, Amyn, have been here seven years. . . .

The longer we are here, the better we get to know the faculty. They really are a nice group in general. Most are Swiss and a few are English. We are the only Americans and the first Americans in a long while. I don't know if that has been intentional, or not. Our French is improving, too, so that we can communicate with some of the non-English speaking faculty better. It's interesting, though, to see how many of them speak English to us after we tried our French on them. Whether our French was so awful, or whether they decided to meet us halfway, I don't know. . . .

Our best,


Rudd

Le Rosey,
Rolle, Switzerland
September 22, 1953

Dear Family,

.... I am teaching Latin this term. ... Rudd is also teaching two English courses this year, in addition to acting as house mother for the Moyens. Two of her young charges are General Pershing's grandson, John Pershing, and Jennifer Jones' son by Robert Walker, Michael Walker. Jennifer Jones is now married to David Selznick. She was here this summer while we were on vacation. I think she is making a film in Italy.

I was sick for several days with dysentery, no less. But the nurse, Mademoiselle Keller, fixed me up in short order, and I'm now completely recovered. I think I must have contracted it in Zurich. We had had martinis, pate de foie gras, etc. at the Hotel Bauer au Lac, and then I went swimming in Lake Zurich, which was quite cold. We also met friends of Rudd's in Zurich. He's a Czech refugee who escaped to Switzerland. He is the only person I've met over here who thinks Russia will start expanding territorially, like Germany. Even thinks Russia has designs on Switzerland ....

Love,

Roger

Le Rosey
Rolle, Switzerland
Tuesday, October 24, 1953

Dear Mother and Father K,

. . . I am really kept busy now with my three courses and the Moyens. I especially enjoy the American History class, although it means a lot of work in preparation for me. Luckily, one of the students brought the textbook he was going to use in the States with him, so I have something to go by. The only book I can get for the class is more of a literary history than a textbook, which makes it a little awkward at times.

The school has started to play football games with other schools. This game is what we call soccer. It can get very exciting, but it seems to me that it is really too strenuous. The boys play the entire game, either sixty minutes or eighty minutes, dependent upon their age, with only one time out of ten minutes. The teachers have a team, also, using some of the servants and former students to fill out, if necessary. They are always bringing the teachers into the team sports here, much more so than in the States, where sports are strictly for the students. The Swiss emphasis on winning and prizes is fantastic. There is a cup for everything! . . .

Love,

Rudd

Le Rosey
Rolle, Switzerland
October 25, 1953

Dear Janet and Cliff,

. . . You may have heard from Daddy that I am teaching
this fall. I have two English classes and one in American
history. The latter is the most fun and the most work. It is
very hard to get books on the subject over here. I have a
sneaking suspicion that Europeans don't really think
American history is important, or, that, for that matter, there
is much history to the country. I'm also a sort of house
mother to twenty-four 12 - 13 year olds. I'm not particularly
enthusiastic about that, but we do have a bigger room in this
dorm and our own bathroom. Of course, this being
Switzerland, it is just that—a room with tub and sink. But, at
least, it is a step up from taking showers in the boys'
bathroom.

We are just about at mid-term now. Over the weekend,
the boys will be going on an excursion for the Toussaint
holiday. It will be pleasant to have the quiet. And then it won't
be long before we'll be heading to Gstaad. Right now, the
leaves are beginning to fall in earnest. They all turned color the
way they do back home, but the colors aren't quite as vivid. It
was interesting to see the grape leaves change from lush green
to light yellow and russet brown and the big bunches of
purple and green grapes underneath the leaves. They have
been harvesting the grapes for the past few weeks, so that
now the whole town smells like wine. . . .

So far, I would say that our adventure has been a great
success, much greater than I really ever thought it could be. I
don't see how we could have been luckier in finding such a

set-up. Even if we had gotten business jobs, we would not have had the time to travel that we've had here at the school. Also, since we have all nationalities and religions here, we have a small world to look at. You can see all the different aspects of each nationality and philosophies from fascism right on down.

I still think the American on the same educational and economic level as a European is less provincial. At least the American is interested in seeing other parts of the world, even if he thinks he may not like it. But so many Europeans have no desire to see the United States. What is especially annoying is that they think nothing of criticizing it, without thinking of seeing it first hand. I must admit that the teachers here see a rather one-sided view of Americans. They see the wealthy debutante cotillion-goers, Princeton, Yale, and Harvard types, and, in general, the staunch materialists. No wonder they conclude Americans think only about money.

As ever,

Rudd

Le Rosey
Rolle, Switzerland
November 24, 1953

Dear Family,

. . . As you know, last September 24th, I had what seemed like a case of dysentery. It would have been all right if it had ended there—the dysentery, not me—but it didn't. Immediately after that, I had a small rupture of the left lung, in which air escaped into the pleura cavity, causing the lung to fill up with liquid at the bottom and to collapse at the top. At the same time, a collection of liquid formed around the right testicle, causing a hydrocele, or water-like tumor. This has had to be punctured several times, but it still fills up again. At any rate, several doctors from Rolle and nearby towns inspected me. Two of them made wrong diagnoses, one of them giving me maximum doses of penicillin every day for a week, causing fever, despite the fact that I told him penicillin had never had any effect on me. Both doctors suspected tuberculosis, and, as soon as space was available at L'Hopital Nestlé in Lausanne, off I went for a week of literally hellish hospitalization, in which they did all kinds of tests, some of them strongly resembling mediaeval tortures. At the hospital, I was fortunate in having a doctor who spoke English as well as French. Unfortunately, he, too, suspected TB and took various liquids from me, injecting guinea pigs, which they will later kill to see if they contracted TB.

Now I am back at school where I have resumed teaching, and where we are waiting for the results of the tests. . . .

Plans that Rudd and I have made definitely, though, are: 1) Rudd's Master's thesis on international education to be done in 1954; 2) My Italian exam for my Master's, also in 1954; 3) Writing by both of us. Rudd is planning some children's stories and has already finished one, which is quite charming. I am planning a book on the school and our adventures in Europe to be called *The Small World*, but am uncertain whether to cast it in the form of fiction or non-fiction. I would prefer non-fiction, because then I could talk freely about such interesting students as Kent and the Aga Khan boys, but how could I speak my real feelings about the school, its policies, and faculty, without, at the least, hurting someone's feelings or reputations? Which form would you prefer? I'm also planning some short stories, and, of course, will do more paintings whenever possible. . . .

. . . . We are planning to come home permanently the summer after this one. We would come home this coming summer, but the medical expenses will prevent that, I suppose. We are a little fed up with the vicious anti-Americanism found here, especially among some of the faculty members. . . . Despite the fact that Le Rosey's catalog states "no corporal punishment," there are a group of raving fascists on the faculty who slug, kick, and hit the boys on the slightest provocation. . . . I'm tired of fighting every inch of the way, having to defend even American literature in the classroom . . . . and of the teacher as supreme authority—what the teacher says is Truth. Teaching divergent points of view about a topic is not a popular idea over here. . . . The Swiss make much out of their not having been involved in World War II, and smugly pat themselves on the back for it. Any nation of real principle would and should have opposed what Germany and Italy tried to do to Europe.

Another widespread hatred is still virulent in Europe: anti-semitism. We got into a big argument with our friend Mustapha Kamil, a Shiite Muslim, the other day on the subject of Israel and Zionism. He informed me that Jews owned every big company in the United States, that every political party bowed to the wishes of Israel, that the U.S. press wouldn't print a word against the Jews, and that the whole temper and philosophy of the United States changes drastically each time a new political party comes into office. In his view, President

Eisenhower is like Louis XIV, bringing in thousands of favorites and scattering them in various cushy jobs throughout the country. He said our political system was, of necessity, corrupt . . . .

Well, I have some thoughts, too. I think Europe is really mixed-up, bogged down in foolish nationalism and local squabbles. . . . It needs a "refreshening," as Adlai Stevenson might put it, so that they can establish a basis for cooperation and a healthy exchange of goods and services. Europe has really changed very little since Bernard Shaw's play *Heartbreak House* was written about Europe after the first World War. Antiquated, fantastic notions such as the balance of power, and, yes, even the divine right of kings, are still in the air. At Le Rosey, one student said to me, "I think Kent should be king. All he has to do is kill four people." The princely son of an exiled king challenged me with "I can command, you know" when I told him to be quiet in study hall.

I don't suppose Europeans ever really liked Americans, because, of course, most of them deserted Europe and left. When Rudd and I return, it will be on another Mayflower, I'm sure.

Rudd just told me that one of the American boys (John Casey. His father was a Congressman from Massachusetts, and Casey is one of the few Democrats here) who takes American Geography from one of the Swiss professors here, was told by this great authority in class today that "Florida is a rather large peninsula. It is largely uninhabited and large bands of Indians roam its wildernesses."

Well, so much for the complaint department. Europe has its good points and its bad points, as does the United States . . . .

Neither Rudd nor I regret coming over here. We are still enjoying ourselves and finding it an enlightening experience . . . .

Roger

Le Rosey
Rolle Switzerland
November 28, 1953

Dear Family,

Some very good news came this morning. The reports are back from the hospital on the guinea pigs, and they show not a trace of TB. So that ends worrying about that. I don't know what the program will be now—we'll have to consult with the doctor—but, at least, it lifts that weight from my mind. The condition still exists, whatever it is, and I shall have to be very careful of my health and perhaps have an operation, but now I'm not at all afraid. I feel much better mentally already. It was depressing, waiting, and not knowing, all that time.

Other good news is that I've actually begun writing. I'm working on a play and have finished the first act. Rudd is quite pleased with it, so I am continuing, and, if it seems good enough, may try to do something with it. It's called *The Winds of March*, what you'd call "a thoughtful comedy.". . .

It means, too, that, as things stand, we will come home permanently the summer after this coming one. At that time, we will have been over here two and a quarter years, and I think that's sufficient for the time being. After all, we can always come back, now that we know the way. Rudd reminded me the other day how many people expressed the belief that we'd be back in six weeks once our money ran out. It never occurred to me that we would fail in our goal, and we didn't. One can do almost anything if one puts one's mind to it and takes some kind of action, instead of just talking about it.

That's all for now. Love to all.

Roger

Le Rosey
Rolle, Switzerland
November 29, 1953

Dear Family —

. . . Our reason for Thanksgiving came the next day when we received the results of all the tests on Roger and there was no TB. It is quite a relief, as you can well imagine. He will probably have to have an operation of some sort during the Christmas holidays. Then I hope he can get back on his feet. The annoying thing in a school like this is the extra duty, called "surveillance," which comes every eight days or so, and means ringing bells, keeping order in the halls, taking evening or afternoon studies, and taking students on sorties to the village on Saturday and to the movies on Sunday. It is a terrific drain on him now since he isn't really well.

Last night we went to the annual ball they hold here. They really do it up in fine style. They had decorated the Grande Salle with store windows for Hermés, Paquin, rue de Rivoli, etc. on one side and little French cafes on the other. The orchestra was excellent, although it played tunes which were popular when we were in high school. The food was, as usual, magnificent—paté, cold lobster, beef, ham, pastries, salads, all beautifully arranged. I wore my blue trousseau evening dress and my long gloves, and felt very well-dressed. We stayed only a short time, but it was a lot of fun.

Today we went to Rolle and saw the Charlie Chaplin festival, parts of his films—*The Adventurer, The Cure, Easy Street*, etc. It was delightful. Since it was silent, it made no difference whether in French or English. The theater was filled with local children and sounded exactly like the Bellevue in Montclair on Saturday afternoon. Rosey boys are very well behaved in comparison to the town children. I'm glad to know it's not just American children who are so noisy. . . .

At last I've heard from Bank Street, so will start working in earnest this week. Hope it turns out okay. I also ordered a U.S. history reference book from the Vassar Co-op Library which I hope to have for next term. In Gstaad, there is no library! Some school! Even little Alexandria, New Hampshire has a library! . . .

Love,

Rudd

Le Rosey
Rolle, Switzerland
Wednesday


Dear Family,

Received your letter today and were glad to hear that you all had a good Thanksgiving Day dinner. They served a turkey dinner to the whole school here, and Rudd and I were accorded the places of honor at the directors' table. Curiously enough, a dessert—a kind of ice-cream cake—was served, with little chocolate hearts on it. I think the chef might have confused Thanksgiving with Valentine's Day, for some reason.

I am still much the same. Better, really, because I had a cold last week, which kept me in bed for part of the week. . . .

Love,

Roger

Le Rosey
Rolle
December 19, 1953

Dear Family,

One last letter before we move out of here tomorrow. The place is gradually being cleared out. All our things have left for Gstaad, the boys are flying home to the four corners of the world, the rooms are empty, and everything is being put in order for our departure tomorrow.

I am going, first, into the hospital for the operation. Professor Decker, one of the best specialists in Switzerland, will probably do it, or else Dr. Yost, Chief Surgeon. I was to have gone there this past Monday, but I contracted a bad case of grippe and had to remain here in bed. . . .

Love,

Roger

L'Hopital Nestlé
Lausanne
December 21, 1953

Dear Family,

I am writing this from the hospital which I entered yesterday. It is located high on a hill overlooking Lausanne. I have a beautiful view of the lake and of the coast of France beyond. I am in a private room, quite a change from the ward I was in previously. A Le Rosey student, Michael Korda (nephew of Sir Alexander Korda, the filmmaker) occupied this very room last year when he broke his leg. Rita Hayworth and Aly Khan's Princess Yasmin was born at this hospital, also.

Rudd wanted me to have this room because the food is so much better. Imagine my surprise when the nurse asked me last night if I wanted white wine or red with my meals. Can you picture a hospital in the States giving wine to its patients? The room is modern and attractive. I have both a sofa and an easy chair, decorated in a dark peach color.

Rudd is subletting a small apartment in Lausanne from a Russian widow whose husband taught at Le Rosey for seventeen years. We visited her yesterday. She was charming, warm and gracious. She had that intense quality many European women have—you see it in the acting of Luise Rainer. She speaks English very well—"Vhen I vas a liddle girl, a liddle, liddle girl in Petersburg, my mather had a drawing room fool of camellias. It vas veddy lofly, veddy lofly!" Rudd has a kitchen there and will be able to cook. She is being charged only 4 francs a day, which is about $1.00. Very reasonable.

The operation is to take place tomorrow. Dr. Decker, the famed Swiss surgeon, will perform it. Mr. Hughes told me, "When you speak of Dr. Decker, you speak of God.". . .

Love,


Roger

L'Hopital Nestlé
Lausanne
Tuesday


Dear Family,

This is being written about five hours after my operation, so you can see that I'm not in bad shape. The operation went smoothly and speedily, only about half an hour. Dr. Decker said everything was benign . . .

Love,


Roger

L'Hopital Nestlé
Lausanne
December 25, 1953

Dear Family,

Rudd had Christmas dinner here with me, which was nice. I guess I am recuperating well, although there is still a lot of pain. I can get up and sort of roll into the easy chair, though. We received many cards from people here and at home, and that was cheering. I still can't believe the operation is over. It was like a hospital ballet. I began singing the theme from *Limelight* on the operating table and they told me to shut up. Then the clock on the wall appeared to be melting, and I told them so. The drugs did strange things. Another time I thought I was reading a newspaper, and, of course, I wasn't. I also sat up bolt upright once and said in French, *"Vous savez, c'est ma derniére operation."* . . .

Hope that you all had a good Christmas and that our gifts, insignificant though they were, can be put to good use. I've come to the conclusion that there's simply no substitute for Macy's.

Love,

Roger

Le Rosey,
Gstaad, O.B.
Switzerland
January 2, 1954

Dear Family,

Out of the hospital at last and here in our chalet for the winter in this charming village in the Bernese-Oberland Alps, Gstaad. We arrived on a train jammed with skiers and others on holiday. What a wonderful town Gstaad is. Lined up at the station, instead of taxis, were rows of old-fashioned cutter sledges, horse-drawn, with sleigh-bells, fur-lined rugs, and all the trimmings.

The school had sent a servant to meet us, and we were bundled into one of the brightly-painted sleighs and came jingling through the snow and this picture-postcard village to Le Rubli, our chalet, and the school. I can't tell you how wonderful it all is. It's the kind of place you see in Sonja Henie movies and don't really believe exists, but it does, and we are living in it. The air is fresh and invigorating. The snow is deep, the sun warm, and everyone goes skating and skiing and comes bundling into the chalets for meals or warm drinks. It's so festive and charming that I'm rapidly convalescing, with one eye on the slopes, when I'll be able to try some skiing again.

Our room is very nice. We have a splendid view down the valley of Saanen between the great walls of mountains on both sides. At night, we can see the illuminated Gstaad Palace Hotel, one of Europe's best-known hotels, high on the mountainside. Maurice Chevalier is performing there tonight. Prince Said Toussoun of Egypt and other leaders of Europe's smart set are staying there, along with their sons and daughters, some of them our students. . . . Today Rudd and I walked to town for a few moments and had hot chocolate at Charley's, the local hangout. I wish you could be here to see all this. It's like a Swiss Currier & Ives. The sleighs are wonderful. The air is full of jingle bells at all times. . . .

New Year's Eve I lay on my back in bed and could hear them singing "Auld Lang Syne" in the Grand Chalet below us. Then Mr. and Mrs. Hughes came up to wish me a happy New Year. They have been very kind to me, calling me when I was in the hospital, sending little messages, gifts, and all. He was operated on by Professor Decker three weeks before I was, and now he has to return for another operation in February. He is the Sous-Directeur here, the unofficial headmaster, very old-line British in teaching philosophy, but cordial and pleasant, like most of the English I've met. . . .

. . . the air here is dry and tangy. One feels very active and alert. Wish you could all transplant yourselves here for the time being. How you would enjoy it! . . .


Roger

Le Rosey,
Gstaad
January 27, 1954

Dear Family,

We have gotten an increase in our salary which improves our situation considerably. I think we will be able to go to Italy for our Spring vacation, after all. We will definitely be staying over here until the summer after this one, at least. . . . Our situation is not at all bad when you consider all our money is free and clear. Of course, the operation and medical bills, along with other bills, hit us hard, but those are unusual disturbances in our pattern of living. . . .

A few days ago I made my debut on ice here, and I've been skating every day since with the boys in the morning and afternoon and having the time of my life. The school lent me a pair of excellent hockey skates, and I've done so well that some of the boys have asked me to play on their hockey team. Masters are allowed to do so over here. But, since I'm not experienced in hockey, I've turned them down. Next week I'm going to try skiing on the slopes. This place is paradise for me.

I'm feeling completely fit again and am looking well and putting on weight. Last night, John Abbott, Rudd, and I went out to a little supper club in town, and I drank three bottles of beer, the most alcohol I've had in six months. I felt so great that, had I skis with me, I would have gone right up on the Windspillen for moonlight skiing. The air is fresh and exhilarating here. One feels active and energetic all the time!

The other night we went to the cinema in town with the two Aga Khan boys and other seniors. The picture was On the Riviera, starring Danny Kaye and Gene Tierney, who is Ali Khan's current interest. After the showing, one of the boys asked Karim what he thought of it. He replied, "Since an almost near-relative is in it, I'd rather not say." Also, Charlie Chaplin's children caused a stir in town the other day when their governess took them to dine at the Olden Hotel. The place is crowded with counts, countesses, wealthy Americans, Brits, South Americans, etc. At the school today, a countess asked Madame Johannot if she would introduce her to me. She thought I was a student! . . .

Nothing more to report for now. The avalanches were in Austria and in the Bernese-Oberland Alps, where we are, but not in our immediate vicinity.

Love,


Roger

Le Rosey
Gstaad, Switzerland
March 9, 1954

Dear Joan,

Thank you very much for your note of the other day. I am sorry to have delayed in answering it, but I've been trying to figure out just what I should write.

As far as our work is concerned, I think it is enough to say that both my husband and I are teaching at what is probably the most famous boys' school in Europe. Our students come from all the corners of the world. They are an exceptionally wonderful group of boys to work with, since they have had so many opportunities for such things as travel, which other boys their age have not had. The school is located on the shore of Lake Geneva between Geneva and Lausanne. For the three winter months, we go to Gstaad in the Bernese-Oberland Alps, where the boys have skiing and skating every day.

But the real value of our experience, to my mind, is the opportunity it gives us to look back at our own country objectively and to see its good and bad points more clearly. Since Kimberley is a girls' school, however, I'll try to stick to points which have some bearing on a young woman's education.

Living in Switzerland, where women do not have the vote and seem to have very little to do with the events of life, I've become keenly aware of the opportunities American women have. Unfortunately, there are also many who do not exercise their opportunities fully. I hope Kimberley is training its students to realize that the surest way to make democracy work is through intelligent, active citizens. Kimberley should encourage each student to participate in community life in a constructive way. Also, when studying American history, it would be a positive thing to make a thorough study of each person's town government, something I didn't have the chance to do until I was in college eighty miles away from Montclair. Women are one of the most valuable sources of energy any community has, and that energy shouldn't go to waste. Look at the good work the League of Women Voters and the College Women's Club have done.

Being an alien for the first time, more especially an American in Europe, where we continually are targets of prejudicial remarks and intolerant actions, I can see clearly how foolish it is to be prejudiced against, or intolerant of racial, national, or religious groups. Unfortunately, Kimberley has fostered prejudice and intolerance. It's about time we realized that we are all in one world together, Christian, Jew, Negro, and White, and the sooner we learn to work together and know one another, the better.

Of course, one is acutely conscious of the greatness of our country—the opportunity an individual has of improving his way of life; the availability of a good education for all, right through college; the excellent news coverage in newspapers, magazines, radio, and television; and the high standard of living which makes such things as Kleenex, refrigerators, washing machines, toasters, steam irons, etc. common household items, but which are real luxuries to some people of similar circumstances in other countries.

Because of these advantages, it is all the more alarming and disheartening to read of the increasing growth of suspicion at home. Our country was made great by people who did not look to the past and imitate the past, but who looked to the future, dared to try new things, and vowed not to follow the pack. Now it seems it is becoming a dirty word to be called a thinker, a person of ideas. It should give us pause for thought to realize that both Hitler and Mussolini came into power by trying to suppress Communism. We should not imitate the past, but look to it for guidance. We do not need Communism, because our democratic way of life is far superior, but neither do we want Fascism. Let Kimberley help students to think for themselves, to realize that progress is what made our country great, and that Democracy cannot survive in a climate of fear and suspicion.

I hope that you and your family are all well.

Sincerely yours,


Verna Rudd Kenvin

Le Rosey.
Rolle, Switzerland
May 16, 1954

Dear Leigh and Proc,

. . . We are almost halfway through the spring term now. It's nice when the time goes so quickly, because we will soon be on vacation again. Since you last wrote, we have been able to accomplish more traveling. First of all, though, I complained about the salary, and, as a result, I am now paid, not much according to our standards, but at least it is an improvement, and we are able to do more traveling because of it.

Our term in Gstaad was magnificent! It was indescribably beautiful most of the time and very gay. Now that we are back at Rolle, life seems rather drab. Neither of us did much skiing. I was not very enthusiastic after the number of broken legs kept mounting. I think there were twelve broken legs in all, one broken shoulder, and untold numbers of sprains. It takes the edge off the fun of the sport, I think. Roger went skiing a few times after he had thoroughly recuperated from his operation, but he twisted his knee badly and had to stop. It is not exactly a safe sport. But, otherwise, we enjoyed Gstaad immensely.

Incidentally, while at Gstaad, Joan Lockerty wrote me, asking for something for the Kimberley Alumni paper, and I answered with one of my usual rather scathing articles, I'm afraid. I have also written another article which I sent to the National Council of Education, or something like that. It is about this current situation in schools, i.e., the increasing vandalism and condemnation of progressive techniques. I suggested the possibility of Teachers' Aides, like Nurses' Aides. These would be people who have children in the school, or not, but who can devote at least a morning or afternoon a week to help a teacher in a definite class. The women would be given brief orientation courses and then expected to be at the school on their scheduled days. This would help the teacher to find time to give individual attention to children in classes of 30, 40, and 50 students. Since I am over here, I don't quite know how to get the idea around, so I sent it to Washington. I haven't heard from them, so they may have ruled it out, but I pass the suggestion on to you in case you ever come across a situation where you think it might be usable.

We left Gstaad at the end of March. After a day here in Rolle, Roger and I took off for a tour of Italy. We spent two wonderful weeks, with marvelous weather, seeing as much as we could. We got to Milan, Venice, Florence, Rome, Naples, and Capri, plus brief visits to Siena, Ravenna, Orvieto, Pompeii, Monte Cassino, Perugia, and Assisi. The latter places were stops of the CIAT bus, which we used for traveling. It is a marvelous way to travel. The buses are very comfortable, and they have hostesses on board. Italy has changed tremendously since my last visit. The amount of construction has been phenomenal. . . . We did see many signs saying, "Vote for the Communist Party," but we didn't see one "Go Home, Yanks" sign. France, as you may know, is covered with these and many of the French are downright hostile to Americans. There are instances where communist French truck drivers have actually forced American cars off the road.

The Italian people are a healthy-looking people, too, and the women dress with a chic the Parisians could never dream of having. No matter how poor the Italian woman is, she seems to dress tastefully. Naples, unfortunately, is an exception to all this. The poverty there is still appalling and extremely depressing. The children often beg for cigarettes, pushed out by their mothers. Northern Italy is just completely different from Southern Italy, I guess, and there is little one can do about it. Even among the Italians themselves, they realize this fact. Many northern Italians speak very deprecatingly of their southern compatriots. The tragedy is that in the United States, most of our Italian immigrants have come from Southern Italy, and that is why so many Americans have such a low opinion of Italians. It is too bad, particularly because they have a lovely country and are such warm, friendly people in general.

During our trip, one of the big thrills for me was going to the opera at the San Carlo Opera House in Naples. The opera itself, *News of the Day,* a modern opera by Paul Hindemith, was not too enjoyable, but the decor was magnificent and the singing very good. Hindemith, himself, was the conductor, since it was the premiere performance of this opera in Italy. The opera house is a treat to see, It is all white, gold, and red plush. Every seat in the house is good. It is amazing. . . .

Over a week has passed since I started this; I better finish it quickly. As far as world news goes, you can be sure you are better informed about what is happening in Geneva than we are. We did go by Molotov's house the other evening—soldiers, searchlights, machine guns, all around the place! Was pleased to hear of the Supreme Court decision, but Talmadge sure is a vicious person.

Best to all of you from us both,

Rudd

Le Rosey
Rolle, Switzerland
August 26, 1954

Dear Leigh,

. . . We have a few more days left for the summer term, then we will be able to relax for a few days until the new crop of students arrive on the 15th. The summer course isn't very strenuous, especially since I don't teach, but these past three weeks it has done nothing but rain, rain, and rain some more! It is hard when you have forty active boys and no really good indoor facilities for them. It has also been quite cold. I think I've worn my summer dresses without sweaters for only about one week this summer. Most unusual and most depressing.

Before we started on this rainy day affair, we had a wonderful trip to Scandinavia, although we had rain there too. We found the Linjebuss nowhere near comparable to the Italian CIAT buses, but, still, they are much better than the trains. Sweden, also, was a disappointment to me. The architecture was not nearly so modern as I had thought it might be, and the landscape is very much like northern New England—groves and groves of pine trees and red farmhouses with red barns by the score. It is nice for a few hours, but after three days of it, it is monotonous.

One of the things we did in Sweden, which I really enjoyed, was seeing the burial mounds of ancient Viking chiefs and drinking mead at an inn in Gamol Uppsala. We drank the mead (somewhat like a sparkling cider) from large horns. Each horn was rimmed in silver and had the signatures of the members of royalty who had previously drunk from that horn. It was great fun.

The food we had in Sweden was also wonderful. At noon, we usually had the smorgasbord for which they are justly famous. You are expected to make at least three trips—the first time for fish, the second for meats (hot and cold) and appropriate salads, and the third, for cheeses. The only really odd thing about their cuisine is their idea of having fried fish and onions for breakfast, and their habit of putting sugar into nearly everything, including fish, salads, and even drinking water. They do not eat many desserts.

We had only one full day in Stockholm. It is a very nice city with no bad sections to it, but every building seems too much like its neighbor. It made me think of one great big, bourgeois city. They do have one perfectly beautiful building in their city hall. It is a modern concept of a medieval castle, exquisitely and tastefully done.

We spent another full day visiting some charming villages, Leksand and Mora, in Dalecarlia, right in the heart of Sweden. Here you see some of the people wearing their native costumes. There is a great deal of lovely handicraft work done here. We visited a museum filled with the paintings of the Swedish artist, Anders Zorn. Our guide here, most surprisingly, was an American student, studying architecture in this area. Speaking of guides, Linjebuss supplied us with a Danish-speaking guide. Most of our fellow passengers were Danish. Our guide spoke some English, but we had to rely on our own interpretation of Danish, for the most part. It is amazing how many simple words we have in common.

From the heart of Sweden, we went south toward Denmark again, only on the west coast this time. This side is definitely more attractive, I think. The scenery is more rolling and varied. Also, the towns seem gayer. Drinking is quite heavily discouraged in Sweden. Although you can get beer, it is quite watered down, and so is their schnaps, a special liquor that accompanies the smorgasbord. If you are caught for drunken driving, you may go to jail for three years at hard labor. At any rate, there are no nightclubs at all in Stockholm, and they seem to roll up the sidewalks at 9:30 p.m. But on the west coast, they appear to be more spontaneous.

Then we came to Copenhagen. We had already learned to appreciate the fine Danish sense of humor from those Danes we had met on our tour. In Copenhagen, we saw even more of it. The tour of this city starts out by showing you the slums first. Then they showed us an old bridge, which they said one could buy for a souvenir, if one wanted to. But, on second thought, they said they thought the Swedes had already bought it. When pointing out the football stadium, our guide said she didn't know why they even had it since they never seem to win any games. And so they go jovially along. They are just overflowing with good humor and friendliness, a thing which we have sorely missed over here in many countries. One woman, who spoke no English (rather unusual since most Danes think they can speak English) actually went out of her way to take us to the proper trolley (it involved changing trolleys twice). They have a lovely city, too. Here I found wonderful modern buildings combined with lovely old ones. Nothing was very run down, but it was not uncomfortably spick and span, either. It seems to have all the good qualities of all the cities in Europe, with none of the drawbacks. I just can't rave about it strongly enough. I would like to spend a longer visit there sometime.

We traversed Germany again and went down to Ulm to stay with some army friends of ours, Larry and Barbara Putnam (she caught my wedding bouquet.) Germany is a very lovely country, as you, no doubt, remember. And the way it is rebuilding is phenomenal. They work from sunrise until after sunset, literally. Frankfurt we thought to be particularly lovely with many gorgeous new buildings going up. Munich is very nice, spread out, with a lot of green around it, but I prefer the small villages, such as Celle. Here the houses are usually red brick and half-timbered. Unlike French and Italian villages, these are all spread out, so that they get plenty of light and air.

But the gem in Germany was Berchtesgaden, where we went for a week end visit to the Army Rest and Leave Center and stayed in Martin Bormann's chalet. We went up the Kehlstein mountain to visit Hitler's Eagle's Nest. I must say he had excellent taste in this residence. The town is much like a Swiss mountain town with chalet architecture, but here the people all wear their native costumes, peasant dresses, and lederhosen. We saw where Hitler's actual home had been, and then we went up a steep, precipitous road to get to the Eagle's Nest, which is completely untouched. You get one of the most stupendous views right into Austria.

On our way back to Ulm with Larry and Barbara, we went into Austria at Salzburg. This is very nice, but not as charming as Berchtesgaden, to my mind. Another interesting visit while in Germany was our visit to Dachau. It really turned my stomach. And still there is so much anti-semitism throughout Europe. It is more than distressing. You wonder when people will ever learn.

. . . Now we've been back here for about a month. Already I am looking forward to getting back to Gstaad and then to getting back home. We will probably be back this time next year, if all goes as scheduled. I doubt now if we can get to Spain before we leave, but we hope we can at least make Vienna, and, of course, England, Scotland, and Ireland. I'm not too keen on Spain, anyhow. I did want to see Sweden and Denmark, though. . . .

As ever,

Rudd

Le Rosey,
Gstaad, Switzerland
February 14, 1955

Dear Leigh and Procter,

I am afraid that my correspondence has fallen way behind schedule. Roger and I were delighted with the news on your Christmas card of the arrival of Pamela. I'm sorry I didn't write you sooner to offer our congratulations and best wishes, but, first, we were getting ready for Mother and Daddy's visit with us, and then they were here for two weeks. It certainly was marvelous to see them after two years. They really seemed about the same. I hope that the enclosed will still be usable for Pamela.

Our Christmas holiday was a most delightful one this year, especially since both of us were in perfect health. The weather at Christmas was all that it should be. We had lots of snow and plenty of cold weather. But the day the boys started to come back, the weather changed into a spring thaw. It has been awful. For almost a month we have had March weather, lots of rain, and some really hot days. Now, at last, it seems to have changed back to winter again. Luckily, Mother and Daddy were able to see Gstaad in its full glory. It has been the worst winter in twenty-five years, according to the people here. Now, maybe we will have a late spring and make up for the lack of winter beforehand.

We are making more and more plans for our return this summer. We have our passage booked on the *Britannic,* sailing July 29th. We have made really extensive plans for our tour through the British Isles beforehand. I do hope it will be possible to do it all. Then, we hope to get to Vienna at long last this spring. We are also expecting Roger's brother sometime in April. He sails on the *Liberté* the 30th of March. Time will really start fleeting now.

We had Christmas cards from almost everyone, which helped to bring us up to date on the latest doings of various people. Josephine and Ed have bought a house in Pasadena and her family have moved into a house nearby. I also heard, at long last, from Pris and George. They have just bought a house in Wheaton, Illinois. My sister, Joan, and Rob are living at our farm in New Hampshire while Rob tries to get his thesis finished for his doctorate. Alice, our former nurse and cook, is staying with them while Mother and Daddy are over here. Joan had another miscarriage around Christmastime, so that it is a great help for her to have Alice.

In your last letter, you mentioned that Eisenhower and Dulles have lowered American prestige abroad. Eisenhower isn't usually blamed, but Dulles most certainly is, as well as McCarthy. Of course, in Switzerland, the business on tariffs with watches has had a bad effect. There was an interesting editorial from a Milanese newspaper in the Letters to the Editor section of the *Ladies Home Journal* on the subject of why Americans are disliked abroad. Most of it certainly stems from envy. It is too bad. But I don't think Americans will ever be able to understand Europeans, and vice versa. There is a great need for reform in both France and Italy still. Their whole heritage is so different. We really are lucky that our ancestors decided to say to hell with all this nobility nonsense, etc., and struck out on their own. I think, also, that some Europeans are annoyed because our ancestors chose not to live over here. It will be good to get back to good radio and newspaper coverage, though. We have to live several days behind time here, because we have no radio, and the Swiss papers don't carry much news.

That seems to be all for now. We are both fine and hope you and all your young 'uns are, too.

Best to all,

Rudd

# A VALENTINE

# FOR

# BROOKLYN

## Three Essays and a Short Story
## 1995-1999

Roger Lee Kenvin

# BROOKLYN WHEN IT WAS GIVEN TO ME

**W**hen I was born in the roaring twenties in Prospect Heights Hospital, Brooklyn, a strange phenomenon occurred. My mother and I were magically wafted up into the sky on a great cloud that flew us away from the hospital room over green trees, lush lawns, ballooning blue hydrangeas, spiky forsythias, to my grandparents' yellow and blue frame house at 1065 East 18th Street in Flatbush where my Irish grandmother, my Scottish-Canadian grandfather, and my Pennsylvania Welsh-American father were waiting to reel us in. That was the first myth I was ever part of. It was a lovely time, a prosperous time, a forward-looking time.

Brooklyn, as I remember it, centered around my grandparents Macdonalds' house. Not a huge house, it nevertheless was substantial, an enormous palace to a young being like me. I spent my first year or so there, until we moved out to East Rockaway, and, in 1931, to our permanent residence in Rockville Centre, Nassau County.

The Brooklyn house was the first house I knew. It had parquet floors and sliding pocket doors between the front parlor and living room and the living room and dining room. The dining room was wainscoted in chestnut to a height of about five feet. The kitchen was large and had three doors. One led to the outdoors and the back yard where the Macdonalds had the only detached garage on the block and a Hudson automobile. Another led to the labyrinthine cellar with its blue-black coal bin and inviting chute that led to it from a window above. The other led to a tight-fitting winding staircase designed for servants and kids on a quick escape route to the second floor. On this floor were three bedrooms, including my grandparents,' with a dressing room attached that looked out onto the roof of the large porch that embraced most of the front of the house below.

On the third floor was another bedroom, used for servants (and for grandchildren later on when they would visit). In the center of the hall was an old-fashioned, spacious bathroom with one of those little black and white tiled floors you seldom see anymore, except in ancient, respectable hotels, and an enormous clawed-foot bathtub that a small child could imagine as a lake you could swim in, and did. Down the hall an ominous door led into the attic—a mysterious troubling place of old stored furniture, pictures, clothes, and insufficient light, ideal for hiding a mean pirate or kidnapper, the kind of criminal most feared by youngsters like me in that time.

My grandparents had three beautiful Chinese rugs in their downstairs rooms. The blue one in the parlor had opalescent peacocks languidly resting in stylized trees. The red one in the living room had butterflies and moths flying to oversize blossoms on enormous plants. Nightingales sang in an enchanted forest on the green rug which was used in the dining room.

There was an enticing polished wood bannister, quite wide, just right for a kid to slide down on, leading to a landing where there was a stained-glass Tiffany window through which light was suffused, amber and violet, over a chestnut window seat, sepulchral and forbidding, underneath, a little church-like altar in my grandparents' house.

The back and side yards were wonderful places to play. I remember a mulberry tree, with its umbrella-like branches, making an ideal hut when I was in a jungle mood, weigelas, hostas, lilies, iris, and mock orange blossoms that perfumed the yard. An apple tree luxuriated in a sunny crook around a bowed living room window. This tree was my grandfather's special passion. Being Scottish, he counted the apples, until one day his young grandson took one and caught holy hell for it. Rhododendrons in the front, a long privet hedge on Mr.

Von Bergen's side, and a driveway on the Healys' side. The Healys originated in New Orleans and spent part of each year there. They had two darling little grandaughters, one with long dark hair and the other with platinum blonde corkscrew curls. Both girls appeared made of porcelain china and were frequently dressed in blue or burgundy velvet dresses with lace collars, accentuating their Dresden-like beauty. The blonde was my first real crush. I remember visiting my grandparents when I was four or five and casting shy glances at that gorgeous creature from our porch to theirs.

The Aeolian piano in my grandparents' parlor was a great attraction for me, not because it was also a player piano, but because I could get strange, strumming sounds out of it and express emotions like grief, rage, or sheer joy. My father also showed me how, if you removed the top or bottom, you could pluck the strings and create unearthly sounds and roars.

The parlor itself was the darkest room in the house, with its blue Chinese rug, and formal, mahogany chairs with claw and ball feet and elegant blue and neutral damask print on the seat covers.

Aside from the piano, an old fashioned Victor gramophone with the patient listening-dog design on it, was in the room. I first heard Enrico Caruso and Amelita Galli-Curci singing opera on this machine, and then, later, a huge Zenith radio appeared with little cathedral side doors that opened, so that when you reached in and pushed down levers, you brought in all the exciting stations and programs you wanted to hear.

This first world I ever knew was a rich one for me. On that Zenith radio, I first heard Big Ben ringing in the New Year in London and Madame Ernestine Schumann-Heink singing "*Heilige Nacht, Stilige Nacht*" in German, while my mother had tears in her eyes listening to it, because, as she explained, Madame Schumann-Heink had had two sons in World War I, one on Germany's side and the other on America's side. It was my first hint of the tragedy and irony that might be possible in any person's life and of how emotion could flow out of one person's life and into the lives of many others, connected only by radio, thousands of miles away.

My grandparents came to Flatbush in 1907, abandoning their house in Manhattan for this new one in a community that must have seemed suburban. Manhattan, with its limited space, was literally building up, and houses were disappearing daily in the wake of skyscrapers. Today, practically all Manhattanites live in apartments. In Brooklyn, there still are houses of the sort my grandparents lived in. The Macdonalds had three lively children and wanted a more spacious environment for them—more green space and fresh air. And, apparently, it worked. From what I know of my mother and father, my uncles and aunts, life in Brooklyn was dynamic, creative, and positive between World War I and 1929.

In 1931, my grandmother, Mary Flood Macdonald, died of cancer, and, by then, the country had already slid into a deep economic depression, which affected my grandfather who was the president of his company, Macdonald and Drucker, furriers, in Manhattan. He had to file for bankruptcy, leaving his son, my uncle Walter, to pick up the pieces; and then my grandfather died of heart trouble in 1934. It must have been too much to bear, losing his wife and then his business in a land where so much had been possible for a while. I felt all this and understood the loss then, but it was not something much discussed, only talked about in whispered voices by grown-ups and terminated when children entered the room.

Well, in the very early days, the house was full of life and activity. My grandfather traveled a lot in his business, to Europe, where he had offices in both Paris and Berlin, and all over the United States. My grandmother wrote wistful, lonely poems in his absence and bore him four children, of whom three survived. Her oldest daughter, Gladys Irene, was my mother. When my brother, Harry, was born on a February 22nd, my father burst through the front door, announcing,

"George Washington has been born." "Whisht now," said my grandmother, thinking my father had a snootfull in the Irish manner. "Get up to bed now; nobody will ever notice." Since both my grandparents were immigrants, relatives and friends popped in from all over—Ireland, Canada, Scotland, England. In 1930, my uncle Walter married into the Stewart clan and soon we had a grand alliance of Stewarts and Macdonalds, which meant parties, scotch, pinochle, and laughter echoing up to the third floor where children were supposed to be sleeping, but weren't, not with that kind of ruckus going on.

The Stewarts were based at that time in Sheepshead Bay, and I particularly remember one huge New Year's Eve party with everyone linking arms, walking in the new year, and kisses and hugs all around, and the three of us children being bounced up and down on the beds upstairs by Walter and other wild Scots. When Calvinistic Presbyterians celebrate, the roof really comes off the place. It's a little-known fact.

People: There were lots of interesting ones on my grandparents' block. The Purvises, for instance, catty-cornered across the way. They went to Europe one summer, and, after they had been gone for a few weeks, a moving van pulled up and took away all their furniture. The neighbors stood around and gaped. No one knew it was to be a permanent move. It wasn't. It turned out that it was the biggest wholesale robbery of the year. The Purvises must have boasted too much to the wrong people about their forthcoming lengthy sojourn abroad.

Mr. Von Bergen, called "Vonnie," was a quiet man, grey hair, light blue eyes, very gentlemanly, always puttering about in his garden, watering his lawn. His home bordered the Macdonalds' on one side. The Tenneys: They lived next to the Healys. A dashing, energetic family. Elzita, a beautiful doe-eyed brunette, was my aunt Ivy's close friend. Ivy, Elzita, and my mother all went to Erasmus Hall High School, the most beautiful school campus I had ever seen, with impressive historical buildings, the original one built in 1787, and a statue of the great Dutch writer, Desiderius Erasmus on the grounds. I wonder what it's like today.

Across the street from the Macdonalds, there was a house with two ferocious stone lions guarding the door. King, an orange chow-chow lived there. He was known to bite. I was scared to death of him. If he came out for his walk, I would run into the house and hide. My grandparents had their own dog, Louie, a black and tan terrier, who was my friend and protector. I learned early that dogs differed greatly in their personalities.

Down the block was Avenue J. If you turned to the left, you could walk down to where some stores were, like Pifco's Bakery and Woolworth's Five-and-Ten. I went with my father and mother to see the first movies I ever saw at the Midwood Theatre—*Night Flight* in 1932 with Clark Gable and Myrna Loy and then in 1934 with my father to see *Treasure Island*. When the rotten pirates came after Jackie Cooper, I picked up and ran clear out of the theatre, I was so scared. My father had a hard time convincing me to return, that it was not real.

If you turned to the right at the corner, you could walk up Avenue J to Ocean Avenue, the Champs Elysees of Flatbush, lined with trees, lawn, and benches full of children, parents, grandparents, friends, all on the capacious center strip that ran all the way from Prospect Park down to Sheepshead Bay and that magical place, Coney Island, site of the vanished Dreamland, burnt-out Luna Park, but still flourishing Steeplechase with its dazzling Cyclone roller coaster and the nearby Nathan's hot dog stand, and its assortment of boardwalk attractions, fortune tellers, gypsies, toss-and-win-stuffed-animals joints, and its wide beach jammed with striped beach umbrellas, athletes, and human beings of all sizes and shapes, coy and flirtatious in their bathing costumes. Coney Island was a legend, fading, flashy, provocative, but still with a charm about it, not yet deadly, not yet down and out. It began as a poetic vision when Dreamland was conceived as a place for beautiful people; it was still a raffish poem when I was a boy, and, in my mind, it came alive again in the New York World's Fair of 1939, but when the fair was over, so was the world into which I was born.

It slid away gradually. After my grandfather died, the house was sold, in 1937, I think. I remember the division of possessions. The rugs went their separate ways, but still exist in family residences: the blue one in New Hampshire, the green rug in Connecticut, and the red one in California. But no one wanted the Aeolian piano and I remember my horror at seeing it being chopped up and set out as garbage on the street to be collected in the morning. And I remember my mother turning the key in the front door lock for the last time, tears in her eyes, saying goodbye to her youth, her childhood for the last time. I felt her pain and have held it in my heart always.

I haven't been to Brooklyn in years. The last time I was there, a horrendous blizzard fell on the city as we were driving up from Virginia and aiming for Rockville Centre via Brooklyn. Our first child, then an infant, was asleep in the back seat, we were out of formula for her, and hopelessly lost somewhere in Brooklyn, now totally unrecognizable because of the way snow changes everything. Somehow we forged our way through, got directions and thanked God we got through Brooklyn. But the Brooklyn of my youth is something sacred and precious to me, shared with others that I loved in a time that was inviolate, and that is not gotten through so easily, nor ever forsaken.

# CONNECTING THE BROKEN LAND

**B**rooklyn—the name is Dutch in origin, from "Breukelen," after a town of the same name in Holland. It means "Broken Land" Why? Probably because of all the inlets, canals, and little bays in and around this land which lies on the western end of Long Island, itself surrounded by the Atlantic Ocean, the Long Island Sound, and the East River. Long Island, one hundred and twenty-five miles long, stretches out like a giant fish in a mighty sea. Brooklyn and Queens, two boroughs of New York City, occupy what might be the head of the big fish.

Because of Long Island's great length, people pushed out east from New York City, stopping off in Brooklyn or Queens only long enough for intense urban *angst* to chase them out farther east to Long Island's Nassau or Suffolk counties. Those who didn't choose that path could go west to New Jersey or north to Connecticut or New York's Rockland, Dutchess, and Westchester Counties, which is why Metropolitan New York is so vast and diverse and all New Yorkers want to know exactly where you're from. Change has always been a central dynamic of New York culture. New Yorkers are far more accepting of it than most Americans, and so a changing landscape and culture are well understood in this part of the world, and not only understood, but often welcomed.

Consider the diverse, talented celebrities that originated in the cauldron of the Broken Land of Brooklyn—the composers Aaron Copland and George Gershwin; opera singers Beverly Sills and Robert Merrill;

actors Mickey Rooney, Mary Tyler Moore, Danny Kaye, James Farentino; singers Barbra Streisand, Neil Diamond, and Lena Horne; movie stars Mae West, Richard Dreyfuss, Rita Hayworth, Susan Hayward, and Barbara Stanwyck; theatre writers and humorists Woody Allen, S. J. Perelman, and Betty Comden; authors Joseph Heller and Frank McCourt; comedians Jackie Gleason, Eddie Murphy, Chris Rock, and Buddy Hackett; plus poet Marianne Moore, playwright Arthur Miller, novelist Norman Mailer, preacher Henry Ward Beecher, and poet Walt Whitman all lived much of their lives in that fertile corner of New York City. Opera singer Dame Joan Sutherland chooses it for her American home.

Places, some of them quite beautiful: The Soldiers and Sailors memorial arch at the entrance to Prospect Park in the Grand Army of the Republic Plaza, the arch based on the Arc de Carrousel in Paris; Prospect Park itself, five hundred and twenty-six acres beautifully landscaped by Frederick Law Olmsted and Calvert Vaux, consisting of hills, gardens, a lake for ice-skating and boating, a zoo, bridle paths and walkways for visitors; the glorious Brooklyn Botanic Gardens; the art deco public library; the Brooklyn Museum in the elegant Beaux Artes style designed by McKim, Mead, and White, boasting superlative collections of Pre-Columbian, Egyptian, and American art; the Brooklyn Academy of Music; the quaint streets of Brooklyn Heights with its esplanade and spectacular view of downtown Manhattan; the Brooklyn Bridge, John A. Roebling's great cathedral of bridge architecture, completed in 1883, its twin towers the tallest structures around, which probably gave neighboring Manhattan the idea that they should build up, hence, skyscrapers; the crescent sweep of land called Shore Road, winding around the Narrows, where you could stand and watch the U.S. Navy fleet arrive in the old days before World War II; Ebbets Field, where the Dodgers played baseball from 1890 to 1957 and where I first saw the Barnum & Bailey circus as a boy; Bay Ridge with its prosperous middle-class houses looking like the suburbs of London; Bensonhurst, about which Thomas Wolfe wrote and tried to give readers a sense of how the people talk there by imitating their colorful lingo; the Williamsburgh Bank Building, once the tallest building in town; Brighton Beach with its Russian and Jewish populations, later immortalized in Neil Simon's play *Brighton Beach Memoirs*. It was a big world, an expanding world, a variorum when I was growing up.

Other things I learned along the way: Did you know that Brooklyn has the largest contingent of Norwegians in the world outside Norway? I learned this when we sailed on the *Bergensfjord* for Oslo in the 1970s. Most of the more than one thousand passengers aboard lived in Bay Ridge and were heading home to Norway for their vacations.

Modern Brooklyn is an area somewhat over seventy square miles. The Canarsie Indians were the original inhabitants. Then the Dutch came and named it Breukelen after a town in Holland, which it probably resembled in its flatness and waterways. There were four other Dutch towns nearby: Boswyck (Bushwick), Midwout (Flatbush), New Utrecht, and New Amersfoort (Flatlands) and one English community, Gravesend. These were settled around 1636. Then in 1642 a ferry sailed over the East River to New Amsterdam. In 1654, the first church was erected in Midwout and the first school appeared in 1662 in Boswyck. After the English conquered New Amsterdam in 1664 and changed its name to New York, the community in Brooklyn was called Kings County, and the assimilation process continued until 1898 when Brooklyn no longer was a separate city, but became one of the five boroughs of New York City.

To any Brooklynite, the individual localities are still important, and some even have their own particular flavors and cultures. To the north on the East River and Newtown Creek lies Greenpoint which contains a Polish community, then, inland, behind it, is the Bedford-Stuyvesant area, two long avenues with Tomkins Park in the middle, constituting the largest black section in New York City. Behind Bed-Sty on the inland side is Bushwick, at one time famous for its

breweries, but now, along with Williamsburg, a volatile
mixture of blacks, Hispanics, and Hassidic Jews. Downtown
Brooklyn is where Atlantic Avenue, Flatbush Avenue, and
Fulton Street converge and the business center is found,
although Brooklyn remains largely a residential area. Crown
Heights has many West Indians as residents. Brooklyn
Heights on the East River still attracts artists, writers, and
affluent executives, as do Carroll Gardens, and Cobble Hill.
Red Hook, a piece of land shaped like a hook slicing into
Upper New York Bay, is separated from prosperous Park
Slope by the Gowanus Canal. Flatbush, in about the
geographical center of Brooklyn, is the largest
neighborhood. Borough Park and Bensonhurst lie between
Bay Ridge and Flatbush. Bay Ridge has the magnificent Shore
Road girdling it as it sits astride the Narrows with Staten Island
across from it.

The southernmost part of Brooklyn used to be an island
full of rabbits, hence its name, Coney Island, but the land was
filled in to make a peninsula which has four distinct areas, Sea
Gate on the west, Coney Island, Brighton Beach now called
"Little Odessa," and Manhattan Beach. Sheepshead Bay, the
old Flatlands, Bergen Beach, Canarsie Beach on Jamaica Bay,
all stretch along Belt Parkway which parallels the old Shore
Road around Brooklyn's coast toward eastern Long Island.
Above them, in the interior, are Brownsville and East New
York, largely tenement areas. A rich variety, an urban mural,
worked on by many artists, never completely finished.

What is now called Gateway National Recreation Area is
where Floyd Bennett Field used to be when I was a kid.
Amelia Earhart took off from this field, as did Wiley Post and
other early aviators. So did my father. I remember going
there as a small boy and watching him sail aloft in a small
plane for a short ride—harbinger of the future.

When I was in college, a female friend invited me to a
graduation party and dance in Flatbush when she graduated
from St. Joseph's College. What a nice group of kids were
there, laughing, singing, celebrating, telling nun, priest, and

pope jokes, and then we went on to the Roosevelt Hotel in Manhattan to dance to Guy Lombardo's music. Brooklyn seemed secure, wholesome, winsome to me still.

Another odd thing happened to me later on. My Brooklyn blood still boils when I think about it. When I was in my forties, a large university in the Midwest invited me to an interview for a position as professor of drama in its theatre department. The Dean interviewed me, obviously impressed that I was a Phi Beta Kappa graduate of Bowdoin College in Maine, with an M.A, in English literature from Harvard University, plus a Master of Fine Arts degree and Doctorate of Fine Arts degree in drama from Yale University. What he wanted to know, it turned out, and why he had invited me, is that he wanted to know how anyone from Brooklyn could ever get into Harvard. He, in his singular insularity, thought Brooklyn was some kind of hellish ghetto from which there was no escape. How I fought my way out of the nightmare ghetto and got into America's poshest university is what he wanted to know. Unfortunately, his view typifies the way Brooklyn often appears to uninformed people. Brooklyn is just another victim of bad press in America, I suppose. The label somebody hangs on you rides with you forever.

Brooklyn accents: Why don't people get it straight? The "youse guys, dese, dem, and dose" comes direct from County Cork, Ireland. Go there and listen. They say "doime" instead of "dime," "Toime" instead of "time." That's the way they talk in County Cork. The Irish also say "tirty-tird Street" for "thirty-third Street." That's how these sounds got into what was called Brooklynese. "Why are you aggravating me? This is something I'm not liking," comes right out of the German language. "You should ask how I'm doing?" "This is the way I'm supposed to look?" Answering questions with questions. Check the German or Yiddish. But, notice, in Manhattan, New Jersey, Connecticut, Milwaukee, or Miami, with the same mix of people, you're likely to get the same linguistic results.

Churches: I went to my mother's old Sunday school at the Congregational Church on Ocean Avenue when I was a boy. They always welcomed me warmly, a guest from Long Island whom they incorporated into their activities and projects. I remember we made Mother's Day cards in a group project one year. Appropriately, I always thought my mother appreciated Brooklyn more than others in the family. She must have. She made the long trip back from Rockville Centre each time to have all three of her children born there.

Although Brooklyn is technically a part of New York City, all of it is in fact on the western half of Long Island, which it shares with the Borough of Queens. Long Island is one hundred and twenty-five miles long and only about twelve or thirteen miles across at its widest point. It has the placid, but cold, Long Island Sound on its northern shore, and the wild Atlantic Ocean on the southern shore. The terminal morain from the Ice Age stopped right in the center of the island, so that the north shore has hills and rocks, while the south shore is flat and sandy. With urban Brooklyn and Queens on its western boundary and charming old villages like East Hampton and Southampton on its eastern south shore, Long Island boasts towns with big executive estates on its north shore like Sands Point, Oyster Bay, and Cold Spring Harbor, and suburban towns like Freeport, Bay Shore, and Patchogue on the south, with relatively new suburban communities filling out its middle. So, actually this island is a whole world unto itself as islands go, quite big and prosperous, including the urban, suburban, and rural in an arm of New York City that keeps stretching out farther east each time, blurring whatever distinctions the old Long Island communities once had. Long Island was all I really knew of the geography of America in my early days, but it was substantial.

However, I was aware that there was more to geography than Long Island. I had already started collecting stamps in the manner inspired by President Franklin D. Roosevelt, and, with magnifying glass in hand, I carefully inspected and studied every fascinating stamp given to me by accommodating relatives. I remember the tall, artistic figures of Dahomey, the regal, reserved stamps from England, the colorful birds and butterflies of Switzerland, the brilliant stamps of Brazil, among others. They made Brooklyn and the rest of Long Island seem pretty mundane.

Another odd fact about Brooklyn: It was once known as a city of churches. Even though huge percentages of people aren't using them these days doesn't mean the church buildings themselves aren't a significant part of the landscape. At St. John's Church in Bay Ridge, Generals Robert E. Lee and Stonewall Jackson worshipped there when they were stationed at Ft. Hamilton. Henry Ward Beecher did most of his effective preaching at the Plymouth Church of the Pilgrims from 1847 to 1887 in Brooklyn. A Unitarian minister in Brooklyn, the Reverend Cornelius Greenway, inspired me to undertake an extensive autograph collection when I was a teenager. I read an article he wrote for a newspaper in which he told of the fascinating people he had encountered and whose autographs he had collected. I wrote to him and he replied with advice and encouragement. I followed up on it, receiving letters and signatures from General Douglas MacArthur, King Carol of Romania, naturalist William Beebe, Mayor Fiorello LaGuardia, actors Katharine Hepburn, Bette Davis, Paul Muni, among others. Stamps and autographs, constructive hobbies, born in Brooklyn.

For me, Brooklyn was an exciting, vast land, sometimes overwhelming and frightening, especially when the Lindbergh baby was kidnapped and the fear that this could happen again, perhaps to you, a sibling, or a friend, became the news of the day. The fact that my grandfather's house was burglarized five times in the depression years also scared me when in Brooklyn. But the museums, avenues, parks, people somehow all attracted my attention, connecting all the pieces of the Broken Land, so that it became a known, loved, and permanent part of my personal geography and cultural landscape. And there it remains, the original port from which I sailed, my own personal, not-so-mysterious Shanghai.

# TODAY I'M CARIBBEAN

**S**eptember 2nd, 1996; it looks as though we will go after all. The hurricane zooming up the coast from the Caribbean is passing by at the very eastern end of Long Island, and so will not threaten metropolitan New York. Our trip is on. I feel excited just thinking about it.

It is years since I've been in Brooklyn. I've heard it has changed and slid into becoming a huge slum. Will none of the color and vivacity it had be left? I was born there and remember it as a place where various Scottish and Irish relatives lived, where I first saw the Barnum and Bailey Circus, where I went to the Midwood Theater with my father to see *Treasure Island* and raced out of there fast when the mean pirates began beating the hell out of Jackie Cooper, where we went to see fishermen displaying their catch on the pier at Sheepshead Bay, and risked life and death on the thrilling Cyclone roller coaster at Coney Island. It was also the place where my mother took me to see Erasmus Hall High School (We both approached it reverentially), where we went on excursions to the Brooklyn Museum, Library, and Botanic Gardens, and where we stood on the esplanade at Brooklyn Heights to wonder at the skyline of Manhattan and the Brooklyn and Manhattan bridges arching over to it. But it also was the place where my grandparent Macdonalds' home on East 18th Street had been robbed five times by burglars in my youth, so that I was aware of the evil that comes in the night and sometimes in mid-morning.

What would this return to Brooklyn mean to me? It began in a jaunty enough style. A 1970 Volkswagen minibus, in less than mint condition, pulled up to our Manhattan hotel to pick up my wife and me. The hearty driver and guide introduced himself as Hermann Pichler, a former editor from Austria, with an American wife, a son now at Dartmouth, and a resident of Brooklyn since 1977. We went to two other hotels and picked up a father, mother and daughter visiting from Austria, and a single woman from California en route to Israel. Herman laughed and joked in both German and English. "I love America," he said. "You will see. Perhaps I will sing. You won't object?" The man from Austria said he hoped Hermann would sing because he had heard about Hermann on a television show in Vienna. Hermann promised to show us "*das andere New York*," the "other New York." There is nothing like it in Europe," he averred.

We went down the length of Manhattan, crossed over the East River to Brooklyn on the Williamsburg Bridge, Hermann pointing out the Brooklyn Navy Yard on the right and Peter Luger's expensive steak house right in the middle of a sinister-looking warehouse district, and the Williamsburgh Savings Bank, tallest skyscraper in all Brooklyn. He took us into a neighborhood in Crown Heights where we were suddenly plunged back into 1912 because this was the home of Hassidic Jews, dressed in black, with spit locks trickling down the sides of their heads on which they wore black ill-fitting hats. Hermann explained that they clung obsessively to their traditions, still waiting for the messiah, refusing to acknowledge the existence of the country of Israel, and, surprisingly, having the highest birthrate of any group in Brooklyn. They looked so peaceful and sweet, fathers walking along holding their daughters' hands in a protective manner. Hermann alluded to a sensational case from 1991 in which a car carrying a rabbi ran a red light and collided with another car, accidentally killing a black boy from Guyana. This caused a group of black youths to stab an innocent bystander, a Jewish student from Australia. The acquittal of these youths precipitated summer riots in the area. Mayor Edward Koch, Hermann said, was not held in high esteem in this neighborhood because of his equivocating remarks about the case.

We lingered for a while, I thinking of the continuing problems of assimilation and the struggle early immigrants in New York City had, as seen in movies like *Hester Street* and *Crossing Delancey*. Then Hermann jolted us into action again. We were aiming, Hermann said, for the Caribbean parade annually held every Labor Day on Eastern Parkway, where all the West Indians, majority inhabitants of Crown Heights, would wear colorful costumes and sing and dance their way along the route. But the crowds were a problem this time, and the police had cordoned off roads that made direct access impossible, so Hermann had to change his plans somewhat, driving east through Bedford Stuyvesant and Crown Heights on Atlantic Avenue until he was able to turn on Utica Avenue and find a parking place on East New York Avenue near Lincoln Terrace Park from which we walked through a sea of people up to Eastern Parkway where the parade participants were gathering.

"Today I'm Caribbean," Hermann sang out cheerfully. "Tomorrow I'll be Russian. That's Brooklyn for you. I love America." We were engulfed now by people obviously in a holiday mood, anticipating a gala parade. I noticed band members in their shiny satin outfits, lugging instruments, former residents of Trinidad resplendent in feathery plumes and wings, people bringing up aluminum and plastic chairs onto their front porches or stoops or inside their tiny green yards to get a better view.

A sturdy man with a gold shield covering his torso, a gold crown on his head, and sneakers painted gold, passed in front of me, looking like the Ulysses of Crown Heights about to board his ship. A battalion of women dressed in bottle green and tomato red, all carrying what looked like sheaves on sticks, followed. Two young women in two-piece lavender outfits struggled to float aloft a huge purple and white wing with flower designs on it that looked like a Leonardo da Vinci drawing for a primitive airplane. An older woman, wearing sunglasses, had managed to attach the same semi-circular wing to her shoulders. She stood there preening, turning around proudly in the bright sunlight for all the world to see and admire, Queen Butterfly for a day.

I looked around at the edges, at a grocery and candy store at 280 Utica Avenue; a group of adolescent boys dressed in baseball caps, tee-shirts hanging out over blue jeans, watched silently. A young father with a red bandanna on his head, a handsome print shirt, long white shorts, and new Nike sneakers, carried a young baby in a sling on his front. His free hand grasped a bottle in a brown paper bag. The Utica Grocery & Deli across the way took advantage of this festive day to bring out wares on the street. All kinds of plastic, cotton, housewares were piled up, an open-air market that would go on all night. "OPEN 24 HOURS," the sign proclaimed. Hermann said the celebration would go on for three days. Everywhere there was animated conversation, the sounds of tuning up, an air of anticipation and happiness.

Suddenly, the crowd achieved a focus. Straining, one could see Mayor Rudy Giuliani of Manhattan and other dignitaries shaking hands and talking into microphones. There was a great increase in the number of policemen around us. We watched briefly, and then we returned to our minibus because this was as close as we were going to get. Later, that night, the parade was shown in all its splendor on television. I was impressed with this insight into a part of Brooklyn I had not experienced before.

Hermann decided that the day was hotter than he had expected, and since the minibus was not air-conditioned, we would have to go to his house to pick up his other minibus, which had air-conditioning but less character than his good luck bus. We drove through Brownsville down Rockaway Parkway into Canarsie, where Hermann lived. He explained that the Canarsie Indians were the original inhabitants and that there was Old Canarsie, still with a neighborhood aspect, and new Canarsie which was mostly post-World War II buildings. We drove down a tree-lined middle-class street to Hermann's house, a duplex with an American flag proudly flying from a staff near his door. We met Hermann's wife and saw his neighbor across the street, busily raking up a pile of leaves in his driveway. The neighborhood looked clean and well-tended. Hermann was proud of where he lived.

From Canarsie, we zapped onto Shore Parkway, Hermann pointing out Gateway National Recreational Area, Bergen Beach, and Floyd Bennett Field, until we came to Sheepshead Bay and eased off onto Emmons Avenue, with its long pier and fishermen and their boats lined up along it, most of them for rent by the hour or for the day. I remembered this from my youth, and, essentially, it hadn't changed a bit—still fresh and crisp looking, many white frame houses, boats bobbing up and down in the sunshine, invitation to the sea.

A short hop away is Brighton Beach, where we parked and had lunch, at Mrs. Stahl's, a place famous for its knishes. Hermann ordered for all of us—the meal consisting of a knish and a coke, which Hermann assured us, was the standard lunch in this part of the world. The knish, a heavy lump of potato dough, was heavily saturated with mustard. We ate at the counter in this rather tacky, unimpressive store, right on the corner of Coney Island Avenue and Brighton Beach Avenue, a junction where an elevated subway train goes flying by, making a constant clickety-clack over one's head that is not entirely unappealing, giving the aura of great vitality to the place. And, as we walked around this area, it did indeed seem very colorful and lively to me, with its profusion of open air fruit and vegetable markets, store fronts and signs in Russian as well as English. This area has been called "Little Odessa" because of the great number of Ukrainians and other Russian emigrés who have settled here. We walked out to the splendid broad boardwalk which flanks the sea over the sand. Tall apartment houses, cafes with red-and-white striped umbrellas, tables, and chairs extending out onto the boardwalk, groups of men playing quiet games of chess, women strolling with friends, people in bathing suits flicking the sand off their feet—an endlessly fascinating, diverse passing parade. And always out there the grey-green Atlantic with Mother Europe at its farthest reach.

In the car once again, we entered neighboring Coney Island, a dim memory of its former glory when it was Dreamland, Luna Park, and Steeplechase. Hermann said it was safe by day, but by night the place has now become a rendezvous for drug dealers of all types. The Cyclone roller coaster is still there, the original Nathan's on Surf Avenue, the broad beach and boardwalk still exist, but it would take a miracle and a lot of work to resurrect it now— a great shame, since it once was one of the shining attractions of Brooklyn and the nation.

We drove northward now to Bensonhurst which Hermann said had not suffered deterioration as severe as other parts of Brooklyn. "Many Italians live here," said Hermann. "You can see how nice their homes are kept because they have family values. They have pride in their neighborhoods." I saw row upon rows of neat middle-class homes in what I would call congested areas. I thought of a Thomas Wolfe story in which he awkwardly attempted to write out the dialogue in a Bensonhurst accent.

Next, we went up to Borough Park, another Hassidic neighborhood. More black hats, coats, and old world behavior. Then, with barely a mention of Park Slope, Bay Ridge, and Flatbush, we were plunged into the yuppie neighborhood of Brooklyn Heights, watching the teeming East River below and the impressive skyscrapers of Manhattan across it. On the Esplanade in this elegant neighborhood, we saw people walking dogs, young lovers sitting on benches gazing longingly across the river, and well-dressed people out for their daily constitutionals. All the old houses and apartment houses looked prosperous and well-tended, a mixture of the old and the new. "Norman Mailer lives there," said Hermann proudly, pointing to Columbia Street. Lots of brick and wrought iron here.

Our trip ended here. We did not see Prospect Park, Flatbush, the areas I knew best, but the Caribbean Parade, Hassidic neighborhoods, and Hermann's own home in Canarsie were new experiences for me, invaluable facets to my personal portrait of Brooklyn.

We crossed back into Manhattan via the Brooklyn Bridge, that great cathedral of a bridge that one can travel over by car or foot, and which never disappoints as either engineering or artistic marvel, or justly rich symbol of the borough of Brooklyn.

"I hope you have not been disappointed," said Hermann apologetically in parting, searching my eyes to find an answer. Not at all, Hermann. My feelings about what I saw are not as pessimistic as I thought they would be. I expected change, and, of course, one always hopes it's positive change, even though it isn't always. Brooklyn began quite simply as Indian, Dutch, English settlements, then the Irish and Germans migrated there, and it went through a long period of being a bedroom for Manhattan, until, reflecting stress particularly in Europe, many immigrants began settling there, forcing housing to build up into apartment houses, as in Manhattan, and causing those seeking peace and quiet in single-family homes to flee farther east to Nassau and Suffolk counties on Long Island. Then, World War II brought in new residents, seeking escape from Hitler's holocaust, and, after the war, Hispanics and Blacks from Central America and the Caribbean looking for better lives and situations for themselves and families.

Brooklyn, like some other American cities, is a kind of stew, still simmering, always fascinating, quite dangerous in places. If it is to survive, the citizens must manage their affairs and their differences harmoniously with sensible governance and the certain pride and assurance that any urban area neighborhood needs. With such a dramatic heterogeneous population as Brooklyn has—Russians,

African-Americans, Hassidic Jews, Europeans, Hispanics—the common good becomes more important than ever. And Hermann Pichler, the happy new Brooklynite, is exactly the kind of citizen the area needs, intelligent, caring, hard-working, expecting better things to come. *"Kein problem,"* as he might put it.

# MEASURING MARIGOLDS

**T**he most beautiful girl in the world loomed spectrally through the morning mist on the front porch of the house next door to my grandfather's when I first saw her. The place was Flatbush, Brooklyn and the time was the relative antiquity of the 1930s. She was quite simply a china doll, long blonde hair, sky-blue eyes, a white porcelain face. She wore a dark green velvet dress, white stockings up to her knees, black patent leather shoes. Perfection. The radio in my grandfather's parlor, just behind his wrap-around porch, was playing the popular song "Did you ever see a dream walking? Well, I did. Did you ever hear a dream talking? Well, I did." The man who wrote that song was a clairvoyant genius. He clearly saw what I saw. I smiled at this gorgeous vision shyly and then withdrew. Why press my luck?

I was an impressionable seven years old when this happened. A genuine angel dropped into my life by some thoughtful God above. I could hardly breathe. I peeked out again. What was this delectable apparition doing? Had she seen me? Was she smiling back? To my amazement, she was soon joined by another young beauty, only brunette this time. Long hair, red velvet dress, darker eyes, but easier in her demeanor, more of a flirt. I could see it coursing around her mouth. "Hello," she floated in my direction.

"Hello," I said. "This is my grandfather's house." I opted for directness, as I always do when confronted by stunning supernatural events I can't explain.

"We know that," the brunette replied. "This is our uncle's house." The two girls giggled, as though that or the dumb bunny they were addressing was funny.

"What's your name?" The blonde angel actually asked me that.

"Tom," I lied. My name was Edgar. Unacceptable to a celestial being, I was sure.

"I'm Angela," the blonde Venus replied. "She's Olivia. We're sisters."

"Twins," said Olivia.

"Fraternal, not identical," said Angela.

"Can't you tell?" said Olivia. Giggles and wiggles again.

They leaned over the side of the porch. I did the same on my porch. We were now only ten feet apart. A motherly voice from inside their house called, "Girrls, Girrrls."

"We've got to go," said Olivia.

"We live in New Orleans," said Angela, throwing a tiny Mona Lisa smile my way.

"Oh," I replied, with brilliant wit, retreating to my grandfather's dark brown wicker rocker to think things over. I was suffocating in the unexpected luxury of glamor and the happy avalanche of the opposite sex right next door.

Of course I was ready for this. In my own mind at least, I was a certified knight of the Round Table, skilled in all the mediaeval arts, like jousting with pampas grass spears at shiny, hard-bodied automobiles.

In fact, I really was King Arthur himself, in disguise as a seven year old boy. Few people knew this about me. I didn't tell anyone, even my parents. They wouldn't have understood. They thought they had a regular boy in me, but they didn't. I came from hidden realms and I was always on one quest or the other. Adventure was my middle name. Lancelot was my right arm and Galahad was my left.

Suddenly, to have had a palpable fair lady to lay down my life for was a boon few other modern knights had been given. I would have to think this whole matter out carefully. My horse would have to be groomed and decked out in my livery. I would have to ride taller in the Broken Land now. I would have to look to my castle in the umbrella tree and maybe lay claim to new lands for my lady fair.

The Knight of the Green Bower. That's who I was unofficially. I dwelled quite simply in the umbrella tree on my grandfather's front lawn in front of the sticky red rhododendrons that flanked the front porch of the dark blue and yellow wooden palace with fine dust from busy, nearby Emerald City covering its surface.

But my true city was the mysterious Camelot, far away, hidden now under a great body of water from which the fabled city would emerge once again some day when I gave the signal. But not yet. Not yet, please. There was work to be done.

As a knight I had to reclaim the Broken Land of my grandfather and secure it for my brother and sister and future generations. That was my calling, my task. And now that I had a fair lady, I had to make a special effort to make it safe for her and her twin sister, the sloe-eyed Olivia, while they sojourned here before making their way back to New Orleans, that tangled jungle of dangerous bayous populated by reckless pirates, alligators and boa constrictors, demons I had not yet encountered in my travels. How to fend them off?

I could call on Cerberus, the huge, orange, imperial chow that lived across the street from my grandfather, guarding the gates of a solid brick home with stone steps, white stone lions, and human beings inside to match.

But Cerberus, like his owners, was no friend of mine. He would sit out on the top step in the mornings looking longingly toward my umbrella home. His look was definitely not friendly. It was more Attila the Hun and it spoke of territorial aggrandisement with a few human beings, me included, as midday snacks along the way. I was scared to death of this orange menace of my youth, so he was out. Days had to be planned around Cerberus. Mornings were his. I ventured out at that time only with the greatest of caution.

"Edgar, come in now. Lunch is ready." The grating call of my mother's voice.

"Please don't shout." How ignominious and crass to call a knight summoning him to lunch. Have parents no sense of what's right and wrong?

"Coming, mother." God, am I really some dumbo Henry Aldrich and not King Arthur at all?

Angela, angelica, angel-heart, angel-face, the vision of my dreams, fallen to earth at last and next door at that. I thought about her all through the unwelcome night, and the next morning I repeated my humble lurking bit once more on the front porch, hungrily searching the gaping maw of the Healy's house across the abyss for a clue.

At nine o'clock, the door suddenly opened and a procession came out. First, Mrs. Healy, dressed for church with a hat and long overcoat, chattering away and laughing. Then another woman whom I didn't know, followed by Mr. Healy with his huge mustache and big stomach, then Angela and Olivia, wearing cartwheel hats with streamers on them. They spotted me, I just know it. Then Philippa, their maid, who always smiled and waved at me and asked if I believed in God. She was also dressed to the nines and carried their sniveling, spoiled-rotten, orange pomeranium, Sunny.

Their chauffeur had pulled up the elegant, slim, blue Packard to the curb and they all piled in, off to their Catholic church somewhere.

Why couldn't we have been Catholic, too? Why did I have to be what's called a Protestant. I'm not protesting anything. I want to join the angels and be a Catholic, I say. But my Scottish grandfather wouldn't hear of it, I'm sure. I've heard him rail against Catholics before. He's something called a Presbyterian. That's a grim, serious Scottish business, no fun at all.

Well, maybe I'm, wrong about that. Sometimes it is. Once it was, I know that for a fact. But just once. It happened at New Year's. We had come into the Broken Land for the holidays from our English Tudor manor house out in the hinterlands, as my grandfather called Long Island. It was determined that the children, meaning me, Alice, and Bert, were to stay by ourselves in our grandfather's palace for just a few hours while the adults went to Uncle Tippie and Aunt Jean's sandcastle on the shore at Sheepshead Bay for a Scottish New Year's celebration. That's what I didn't like—not the Scottish celebration which I wanted to see—but the "determined" part. I never liked it when something larger than I, especially something mysterious and ill-defined that you couldn't see, determined that I had to go along with it. Fate, I guess you'd call it. I hated it. I fought it. What was it? Some kind of strange fog? Why should it envelop me and my life? No way.

So I bitched. Threw a huge fit and let my parents know I thought it was really cruel to leave kids alone like that. Didn't they care if we got kidnapped or robbed, or worse? Why should we be deprived of a Scottish new year anyway?

They seemed to agree with me, but other adults who shall be nameless—grandfather and Aunt Elizabeth, take a bow—and the mean hosts, Tippie and Jean, who made it clear to my parents that they should "park the menagerie"—I heard it myself over the phone—stood their Scottish ground and made my parents feel like over-protective fools with three wretched, ungrateful brats.

I was put in charge—Athos, Porthos, and I as d'Artagnan, standing our ground against murderers, burglars, and kidnappers, who we knew abounded in the Broken Land.

The only consolation was at the last minute, I heard from the fair maiden Angela next door that the Healys would be having a shindig at their house and that Angela and Olivia would be allowed to stay up. Angela conveyed that message to me and I could see the secret delight in her eye that meant things might get very interesting for all kids who were up for it that evening. When adults will play, kids make hay, I say. Zowie.

But it didn't turn out that way. Fear and Trembling via Imagination suddenly leaked into the ominous palace. Every cracking noise, every rattling window, each darkened room took on sinister overtones. Bert sniffled and began to cry softly. I got annoyed because I felt he didn't trust me, although he said it was just because he missed Mom and was afraid he'd never see her again. Alice refused to go two feet from the phone. She kept repeating Tippie and Jean's phone number until finally her panic got to me, too, and I called Dad, but got some drunk who kept yelling, "We're havin' fun, babe. Happeeee new year."

Finally, I got Aunt Jean and she went to find Dad who said he would be driving back to bring us to the party after all. This made Alice and Bert blubber even more, so that I too was awash with tears when the headlights of our father's car criss-crossed the front window with jazzy, welcoming streaks of light. It took us fifteen minutes to gain our composure, during which all three of us hugged Dad repeatedly and asked him if he was having a happy new year.

When we calmed down, he drove us to Aunt Jean's house of boozy mirth, loaded with assorted Scots now, some in full kilt, some weaving, many smiling and singing, all in a convivial holiday mood.

A cousin from Canada bounced us up and down on an upstairs bed in a pink and green floral bedroom where we were stationed, until finally the slats broke, people rushed up stairs to see what the commotion was, and, at Aunt Jean's urging, no more bouncing was permitted. But, the good news was that we could go downstairs now and watch the New Year come in.

What happens is everyone holds hands and walks in the New Year singing Auld Lang Syne full tilt. The crowd forms a huge circle that takes up the whole living room, siphoning off into the big hall and into the dining room across from it, and then the circle begins undulating toward some indefinite center, backs up, repeating the advancing step again, and finishes Auld Lang Syne, tears streaming down some people's face.

Then everybody kisses whoever's available, even the dog. Alice and Bert got picked up and passed around like footballs. I got hugged, thrown up in the air, smothered with powdery smooches from ladies which made me sneeze. And then, Tippie, in the dress Stewart kilt, bright red, jumped out into the center and danced a fling while a tall, rangy man in a dark green kilt accompanied him on a bagpipe. God, what a screeching racket that made.

Next, we all ran to the front door, grabbing pots and pans from Jeannie, and out into the night we staggered, banging the hell out of the pans to welcome in the New Year. The Broken Land really rang out that night, I can tell you. And there were little echoes of all the same kind of slam-bang noise throughout the whole neighborhood.

I can't tell you what happened next because the three of us fell asleep in the back seat of the car on the way home. It was very late, that I know. I think it was four o'clock in the morning, or something. It was the latest I'd ever stayed up. I remember thinking, *Well, it does feel different this new year we're in*, but maybe it's just because I was so tired and excited. After all, my first grown-up party. Boy, do they drink a lot.

Around noon, I finally woke up and had to have something called brunch which was not breakfast or lunch but a little of each, so they said, but it looked like leftovers to me. Then I slipped out on the front porch and saw the golden girl and princess Olivia sitting on the glider on their porch and shooting glances my way.

"Hello, Tom," said Angela.

"Hi." I hated the stupid shyness in my timid soul.

"Happy new year," giggled Olivia.

"Did you have fun last night?" asked Angela.

"Yeah," I said. "We got to go to the Scottish new year at our aunt's house."

"No wonder we didn't see you," said Olivia.

"We had a party here," said Angela. "We looked to see if you were out there."

"No. We got invited, after all. It was really fun. I think we got home about dawn."

"Oh," said Angela. "We stayed up until midnight. We had fun too."

"We have to leave tomorrow," said Olivia.

"Will you come back again?" I asked.

"Maybe in a year or so," said Angela. "We don't know."

"How far is it?" I asked. "New Orleans?"

"Thousands of miles away," said Angela.

"Too bad," I said, and I meant it.

"Angela and Olivia, come in now," called their mother from the inner recesses of their house.

"We've got to go now," said Olivia.

"Goodbye," I said. And to myself, *Farewell, twin goddesses of the new year and the old.*

Tippie is dying. That's all I know. It's the news of the day around here. He's in the hospital and he's fighting mad. He won't cooperate with the nurses or doctors. He threw a bedpan at the nurse. He pulled out all the wires they stuck into him. He pissed on the floor and aimed it at an orderly. Nobody can deal with him. If he doesn't shut up, he's going to die. That's the report from the front. The whole family is spinning. They don't know what to do.

Uncle Rupert has been sent in to take charge, but Tippie won't see him. He refuses to talk to him because they had an argument over a pinochle game a year ago. Rupert has stationed himself in the hall outside Tippie's room. He sits there in a chair, fixed, a stony look on his mug, a stoic Scotsman who won't take no for an answer. "Tippie canna' die," he announces in an angry voice as though he can do something about it. "He owes me two hundred dollars."

My mother says Rupert's will is stronger than Tippie's. "Tippie would not dare do anything unusual," she claims.

What are we supposed to do about it? "Nothing," Mom says. "Nobody can make a difference in such a situation. It's a battle of wills. We'll just have to wait and see."

I get it now. Tippie is the old King dying in the castle. Rupert is the heir apparent. The old king will not give in. I have this sudden idea that if I were to see Tippie, I could give him sound advice—ship out, old king. It's time. Surrender your territories gracefully. Quit this Scottish raging. You've son-of-a-bitched your way too long. Your relatives are concerned, very disturbed.

I'd be ideal at this, I think. I know how to deal with tyrants. I have ties to Merlin and Morgan Le Fay. It's Rupert's turn to be King of the Stewarts and claim all Scotland and all Scottish people as his own, even as I claim Camelot and all true English folk as mine.

Just when I get up enough courage to ask Mom if we children can go to the hospital to see Tippie, Mom announces that Tippie has miraculously gotten better, has popped up out of bed and stormed out of that hospital on his own. Jeannie was delighted, picked up the fugitive in her getaway car and sneaked him back home.

Rupert gave up his siege and went back to his cliff-dweller castle in Manhattan, but Tippie still wouldn't speak to him and said he had no intention of ever doing so, even when he was told that Rupert had kept vigil outside his hospital room to ward off evil spirits and to will Tippie into getting better, which he did, didn't he? Tippie refused to accept this as proof of anything and just continued his mean, petty ways.

"But Jeannie loves him. That's what's important," says Mom.

Isn't love an odd sort of thing? I well understand it because of Angela. One of my quests will definitely be to journey to New Orleans, but it will have to wait until I'm eleven or twelve, I guess. God, I'll be ancient by then. Do you think she'll wait for me?

Something unexpected happened. King Tippie got better, but my grandfather died quite suddenly of a heart attack. "Ironies abound," says my father about the strange lives we all live.

My grandfather apparently just sat down in his mohair chair after dinner, turned on the radio to a ranting Father Coughlin and keeled over. Now the whole kingdom is in parlous turmoil. Possessions are to be divided three ways; the house itself is to be sold. We are clearing out of the Broken Land forever. Nothing will ever be the same again.

People were sad for a while. There was a funeral and those long, black limousines that command respect in the streets. We three children sat in the back of a longo limo, as Bert refers to them, and went along through slowing traffic to a cemetery on a hill where my grandfather was buried in a crypt in a marble mausoleum.

Very eerie this huge museum of dead people behind slabs of marble. Why he wanted that, I don't know. Maybe so no worms could ever get at him. But what about dust? And what if an earthquake came? Then you'd be knocked out of your crypt, and arms and legs, as well as parts you wouldn't want anyone to see, would be exposed for all the world to see. Not for me, thanks.

Slowly the house was dismantled. Huge vans drove up and powerful workmen with big arms and tattoos came and carefully threw blankets over the furniture, carrying the entire living room, then the parlor, then the bedrooms out into their elephantine trucks.

Then, cleaning people came in, washed everything down until all the dust went away and the house smiled again in its bright blue and yellow colors.

Philippa, the maid from the Healys came out and stood on the porch with a broom, watching. My father went ahead to get into the driver's seat of the car. Alice and Bert followed him.

My mother and I were the last to leave the house. Out on the curb by the gutter lay the wreckage of a piano they had to chop up because nobody wanted it—the bare ruined choir of a piano with no music to play anymore and no one to listen to it.

My mother turned the key in the lock. I saw history in her eyes. I could guess what she was thinking. In a rush, she pushed me out into the waiting car and we sped away, my mother looking straight ahead now.

I looked to the right, just to catch a glimpse, and saw Philippa lift her hand in a puzzled goodbye gesture, as though why were we doing this. I waved back to her because she was a nice, considerate person, but I also waved to the dream walking that I once saw and loved, and wondered if I would ever encounter such a vision again or if Camelot would really rise from the sea.

Rudd and Roger Kenvin, Gstaad, Switzerland, 1954

## About the Authors

**Roger Lee Kenvin** has taught at Mary Washington College, Fredericksburg, Virginia; Bowdoin College, Brunswick, Maine; Northeastern University, Boston, Massachusetts; University of Notre Dame and St. Mary's College, South Bend, Indiana; Isabella Thoburn College, Lucknow, India; and California Polytechnic State University, San Luis Obispo, California. **Verna Rudd Kenvin** has taught at The Foote School, New Haven, Connecticut; St. Agnes Episcopal School, Alexandria, Virginia; and University of Virginia Extension Division, Fredericksburg, Virginia. Both Kenvins taught at Le Rosey School, Switzerland.